Psychotherapy With Deaf and Hard of Hearing Persons

A Systemic Model

Second Edition

Psychotherapy With Deaf and Hard of Hearing Persons

A Systemic Model

Second Edition

Michael A. Harvey
Boston University

Routledge
Taylor & Francis Group
NEW YORK AND LONDON

First published by:

Lawrence Erlbaum Associates, Inc., Publishers in 2003
10 Industrial Avenue
Mahwah, NJ 07430

This edition published 2011 by Routledge:

Routledge
Taylor & Francis Group
711 Third Avenue
New York, NY 10017

Routledge
Taylor & Francis Group
2 Park Square,
Milton Park, Abingdon,
Oxfordshire OX14 4RN

First issued in paperback 2016

Routledge is an imprint of the Taylor and Francis Group, an informa business

Cover design by Kathryn Houghtaling Lacey

Library of Congress Cataloging-in-Publication Data

Harvey, Michael A.
Psychotherapy with deaf and hard of hearing persons : a systemic model / Michael A. Harvey.—2nd ed.
p. cm.
Includes bibliographical references and index.
ISBN 0-8058-4375-2 (cloth : alk. paper)
1. Deaf—Mental health. 2. Psychotherapy. I. Title.

TC451.4.D4H37 2003
616.89'14'0872 —dc21 2002192792
CIP

ISBN 13: 978-1-138-99694-6 (pbk)
ISBN 13: 978-0-8058-4375-0 (hbk)

To
Janet, Allison, and Emily

Contents

Preface to the Second Edition

It is a pleasure and honor to author the second edition of *Psychotherapy With Deaf and Hard-of-Hearing Persons: A Systemic Model.* This edition reflects the feedback I have received since the text was initially published in 1989. For example, although I was thrilled to learn that the text is used in many university counseling courses, I also learned that many professors advise students to read chapter 1, A Systemic Model, either last or not at all. "It has a lot of information in it, but it's laborious reading," they warn. Accordingly, this chapter received a major face lift. Chapter 1 begins with my recollection of receiving a telephone call from a hearing mother who was anxious about her deaf adolescent getting her license. The story quickly unfolds to encompass covert and overt conflicts among family members, school personnel, professional systems, and so forth. At various points in the story, a systemic framework is introduced to makes sense out of the overlapping scenarios and to elucidate the rationale for interventions. Rather than overwhelm the reader who has minimal familiarity with systems theory, some of the technical terminology was taken out from this chapter and from the entire text. This more "user-friendly" presentation makes for easier reading.

Many readers suggested that a spiritual level be added to the biopsychosocial hierarchical analysis. Admittedly, now at age 50, I am more aware of spiritual issues than I was 15 years ago, on a personal level as well as how they affect the lives of my clients. Typically, people who have experienced any major loss strive to articulate what influence spirituality does or does not play in their lives. There are many possible answers to the "God-question," and what answer one chooses strongly influences the way one interprets an experience, including hearing loss. Accordingly, this spiritual level is addressed and clinical examples are provided.

Chapter 11, Coping with Ordinary Evil, is new to this edition. It specifically addresses the cultural level of the ecology and how this larger context affects the daily functioning of deaf and hard-of-hearing persons. By "ordinary evil," I mean those behaviors that seem evil to the observer, but not evil enough to make the news. In chapter 11, we learn about a deaf adolescent's feelings of betrayal and victimization by his hearing friend and how these feelings resonate with pervasive "ordinary evil" of the oppressive culture. It becomes more complicated for this family and for me as their therapist, as our context unexpectedly expanded to include extraordinary, newsworthy evil.

Finally, new clinical material was added, including elements from my question and answer column, "What's on Your Mind?", which appears regularly in the journal *Hearing Loss, of Self Help for the Hard-of-Hearing.* The questions and comments sent in by readers provide a rich source of insights into the process of adjustment to hearing loss. In addition, updated references are noted throughout this edition that reflect the many important publications in the mental health and deafness field in the past 15 years.

ACKNOWLEDGMENTS

Many have contributed to the thinking that is represented in this book. A special, yet anonymous, thanks is due to the several deaf and hard-of-hearing clients, their families, and their larger networks from whom I have learned so much. All the names and details of the case studies have been modified to preserve confidentiality, but not so much as to change the spirit of the cases.

My wife, Janet, has been a constant source of emotional support and has provided invaluable feedback for my writings, particularly the last chapter on ordinary evil. For her love and help, I am truly appreciative.

I would like to express my deep appreciation to Jean Brennan, Janey Greenwald, Karen Harvey, Robert Hoffmeister, Gillian Kerr, and Hilde Schlesinger for their painstaking and thorough reviews of the first edition of this book. Their support and perspectives made the process of writing this book stimulating and enjoyable. I am also grateful to Barry Dym, Neil Glickman, and Kimberly Grebert for reviewing particular chapters and offering their contributions.

There are several colleagues and friends who have been particularly influential in teaching me about the subject matter and in helping me shape my ideas. Many of the systemic principles and techniques in this book are a product of many years of consultation from Barry Dym, to whom I am greatly indebted. I have profited tremendously from formal collaborations and many informal discussions with Ruth Coppersmith, Frances Demiany, Roger Freeman, Neil Glickman, Warren Hanna, Bob Hoffmeister, Stephen Nover, Marie Jean Philip, Susan Philip, Bob Pollard, Richard E. Thompson, and Barbara (BJ) Wood.

For prompting me to write this book, thanks are due to Jean Brennan. The encouragement I received along the way from Jerome Schein is also very much appreciated.

I am indebted to Susan Milmoe, Judith Suben, and the staff of Lawrence Erlbaum Associates for agreeing to publish this book and for their consistent guidance.

—Michael A. Harvey
Framingham, MA
March, 2002

Introduction

Since the 1990s, I have taken to jotting down clinical observations, ideas, successes, failures, and reactions on scrap pieces of paper and then stuffing them in a folder marked "miscellaneous." Although, initially this was an efficient method of warehousing information, the contents of that folder soon accumulated to become a disarray of scribbled notes that made no contextual sense and that had begun to overflow in the file cabinet. What began as a simple clean-up intervention to organize and synthesize the contents of the "miscellaneous" file eventually culminated with my writing this volume. This was the clerical reason for writing the book.

More officially, the goal of this book is to present a systemic model for understanding and treating deaf and hard-of-hearing persons in the context of their families and larger ecology. Its objectives are to describe and illustrate a systemic framework for understanding functional and dysfunctional relationships that often occur within families and among therapists, counselors, and other professionals who may be involved with deaf or hard-of-hearing persons; and formulating and implementing clinical interventions to modify dysfunctional individual, family, and larger-than-family dynamics.

The intended readership includes clinicians who provide psychological treatment to individuals, couples, families, and groups of this population—not only family therapists. Also the innumerable professionals who inevitably find themselves in counseling or therapeutic relationships with deaf or hard-of-hearing persons, as exemplified by vocational rehabilitation counselors, independent living skills trainers, case workers, early intervention workers, pastoral counselors, teachers, tutors, audiologists, speech and language therapists, dormitory counselors, otolaryngologists, and the like.

Chapter 1, A Systemic Model, begins with the story of a telephone call from a hearing mother who was anxious about her deaf adolescent getting her driver's license. The complexity of the story quickly unfolds. It is a "jumping off point" to introduce the systemic conceptual framework for diagnosis and intervention that is used throughout the book. Symptomatology in a client is viewed as related to, and as a metaphor for, dysfunctional relationships within the multiple biopsychosocial levels of the ecology; that often include such diverse persons as family members, audiologists, physicians, teachers of the hearing impaired, interpreters, rehabilitation counselors, independent living specialists, a variety of clinicians and counselors, and several other members. It is illustrated that hearing loss per se need not be a handicapping deficit; rather, this disability may be molded to become such a deficit in the context of the ecology.

The evolution of "relevant systems" across time is the subject of the next two chapters. Chapter 2, Life-span Development of the Deaf Ecosystem, outlines how functional and dysfunctional interactions may develop within an ecosystem that includes a deaf person. The longitudinal sketch highlights the family stages of pregnancy, birth of a child, suspicion of deafness, diagnosis, entrance into school, postsecondary placement, marriage, having children, and the death of a parent.

This developmental analysis is continued in chapter 3, Life-span Development of the Hard-of-Hearing Ecosystem, with particular emphasis on those unique characteristics of the hard-of-hearing ecology. A longitudinal sketch of one prototypical family–ecological system and transcripts of interviews with hard-of-hearing persons demonstrate that the psychological effects of a moderate hearing loss should be considered as qualitatively distinct from the effects of deafness, and as distinct from the hearing population. Alternately, this chapter specifies how hard-of-hearing persons may be similar but unique in relation to profoundly deaf persons.

Chapters 4, 5, and 6 describe methods of conducting systemic interventions within the individual level of the ecology. Chapter 4, Treating the Hard-of-Hearing Individual in Context, presents theoretical and pragmatic guidelines for treating hard-of-hearing clients, particularly as distinguished from working with the deaf population. Case examples with therapy transcripts are presented that illustrate the therapeutic process of untangling and modifying common dysfunctional cognitive beliefs, assumptions, and images that characterize the internal experiences of many hard-of-hearing clients.

Similarly, chapter 5, Treating the Deafened Individual in Context, describes the psychological effects of traumatic or progressive deafness and presents appropriate therapeutic interventions for this underserved and largely ignored population. The concept of loss is examined and illustrated with several therapy transcripts. Finally, chapter 6, On Joining the Deaf Client, discusses common characteristics of the prelingually, profoundly deaf client; identifies bilingualism and crosscultural therapy variables; and describes the process of establishing a therapeutic relationship.

In chapters 7, 8, and 9, the context is broadened to examine the family level of the ecology. Chapter 7, Communication Logistics of Family Treatment, analyzes how spoken English and many forms of manual communication affect the treatment of a family where there is a deaf member, both from linguistic and systemic perspectives. Chapter 8, The Use of an Interpreter for the Deaf in Family Therapy, continues this analysis by describing the psychological influences and modes of including interpreters in family therapy, including the "nuts and bolts" of the evolving relationship between the interpreter and therapist. The unique strengths and problems associated with deaf parents and hearing children families are illustrated in chapter 9, Hearing Children of Deaf Parents. Chapter 9 presents systemic intervention strategies toward ameliorating inappropriately disengaged boundaries that may characterize the relationship between hearing children and their deaf parents who are seen in treatment. In one case, outside-of-family professionals appear to usurp parental authority from the deaf parents; in another case, presented with verbatim therapy transcripts, hearing grandparents "parent" a deaf single mother and her hearing children and support disengagement and an inverted power hierarchy within the nuclear family.

The professional level of ecology is again examined in chapter 10, Treatment of the Individual–Family–Vocational Rehabilitation Systems. Clinical interventions are described for treating a deaf or hard-of-hearing individual's presenting problems when the ecological context of those problems includes a Rehabilitation Counselor for the Deaf (RCD) from the state Vocational Rehabilitation Agency. Given that the clinician and RCD—to be maximally helpful to a given client—must often modify the surrounding context, which includes the other, it would therefore make sense that they work together. This chapter documents in detail one such case.

Finally, in chapter 11, Coping With Ordinary Evil, our lens widens to include the effects of cultural oppression, including interactions between deaf and hearing persons that are fraught with conflict, misunderstandings, and power dynamics. We learn about a deaf adolescent's feelings of victimization by his hearing friend, how it affects his family, and how such victimization is inorexibily bound up in culturally based ordinary and extraordinary evil.

Throughout this book, I have attempted to balance theoretical descriptions and intervention guidelines with actual case studies and verbatim therapy transcripts. In this manner, the concepts were made more clear and vivid to the reader. However, this emphasis has consistently been tempered by confidentiality considerations. It is important to emphasize that all of the case studies and therapy transcripts presented in this book are disguised sufficiently to protect the identities of the participants, but not so much as to change the spirit of the cases.

It is also important to note the cultural context in which this volume was written: Namely, from the perspective of a hearing clinician from the dominant hearing culture. As much as possible, and as much as my own insight permitted, I have taken great pains to avoid stereotyping, stigmatizing, and at the extreme, oppressing the minority Deaf and hard-of-hearing cultures. However, I must humbly admit that, as with any perceiver, my own epistemology—what I choose to focus and elaborate on and therefore how I understand the populations—inevitably is constrained by my own context. The Deaf and hard-of-hearing readers need to be the final judge of the ethnocentric fairness of this volume.

Finally, feedback is most welcome and can be addressed to me at 14 Vernon Street, Suite 304, Framingham, MA 01701; or e-mail: mharvey2000@earthlink.net

—*Michael A. Harvey*

1

A Systemic Model

One day, I received a frantic phone call from a hearing mother. She told me that her 19-year-old deaf daughter insisted on taking driver's education classes in preparation for her license. The mother requested that I "talk her out of it." I explicitly noted her distress, and strongly recommended that both of them come to my office in 2 hr, emphasizing that "this is obviously quite serious." (In terms of indicating potential family dysfunction, this news was serious.) They appeared in my waiting room 30 min early. After listening to both sides of the parent–adolescent conflict, I questioned the daughter, Susan, on her motivation for wanting to drive and asked her if she had considered all of the disadvantages of driving, such as paying for gas, upkeep, insurance, parking tickets, excise tax, depreciation, and so on. She emphatically replied affirmatively to all of my inquiries. I sensed that she had only a vague idea of what was being asked, and that her affirmative answers were designed to mollify her mother and me. However, in the process of my questioning, she was getting educated as to how one goes about getting a license, about the logistics of increasing her independence from her parents, and was clearly becoming more animated and motivated. That was, in part, my intent.

In addition, I was also establishing rapport with her mother, Ann. It was important to support and reframe her intent as being "thoughtful and concerned" as opposed to being "a dork," as Susan so eloquently put it. I commented to Ann that she obviously was quite concerned about her daughter, not like other parents who are neglectful. It was vital to join with Ann who appeared to be gatekeeper, the most powerful and influential of the family system, which included two younger siblings. If I had simply quoted insurance statistics to her about deaf drivers having safer driving records than do hearing drivers, rather than responding to her underlying fear, she probably would have politely thanked me for my time and hung up.

The impromptu session lasted 2½ hr. To join Susan, I summarized my earlier "mother is concerned" reframe in American Sign Language (therefore without voice) which she could understand quite easily but Ann could not. (As the rest of her family—including a 17-year-old sister, Marsha, and 12-year-old brother, John—was hearing and did not sign, Susan could not understand most of the informal discussion in the household. Important discussions were equally difficult unless directed at her, and then she often understood only a small amount). I then voiced my reframe to Ann. Following this brief exchange, I requested that Ann and Susan continue their dialogue through an interpreter who happened to be available at the time. Because Susan could more easily articulate what she wanted to say to Ann through the interpreter, she appeared to appreciate this suggestion. The session culminated with Susan simultaneously signing and clearly articulating "fuck you" to her mother, smiling at me as if to say "thank you," and walking out of the office.

"Is this progress?" I thought to myself. The answer came soon enough. In reaction to Susan's abrupt exit, Ann began to discuss her own fears of letting go and seeing Susan grow up. And she verbalized her wrath at her husband for "not being there to help in raising Susan." However, she countered my suggestion for a series of joint meetings with her husband by requesting individual meetings on the condition that he not be included. After some hesitancy and thought about the pitfalls of this arrangement, it seemed important to honor her request "at least for now." In retrospect, perhaps it might have been helpful to initially insist that Bill or the whole family attend the session; however, that might have been too premature a move because Ann probably would not have accepted it.

During these individual meetings, Ann discussed her fears of letting go of her daughter, her attitudes toward deafness, and the inevitable logistic stresses, such as attending numerous school meetings, evaluations, and medical appointments. Ann reported that Susan had a profound, bilateral, sensorineural hearing loss of congenital origin as a result of maternal rubella. She also had a mild cardiac abnormality and "soft neurological dysfunction," both secondary to the rubella syndrome. Consequently, in addition to regular audiological check-ups, Ann stated that she brought Susan on occasional visits to cardiologists and neurologists for monitoring.

The topic of marital discord became particularly relevant when Ann announced that Susan had convinced her father, Bill, to help her register in driver's education classes. Bill had historically spent most of his days and evenings at work and had left Ann alone to worry about the children, particularly Susan. Ann exclaimed, "how dare he interfere now!" As I have seen this pattern many times before, I made a tentative systemic hypothesis: that the more Ann becomes overtly angry at Bill, the less he productively deals with the confrontation by retreating at work and at home, and the more Ann misses Bill and resorts to overprotecting Susan. Feeling the sole burden for taking care of Susan triggers Ann to feel overwhelmed and thus to become angry at Bill. The sequence of family interactions which contains the symptom is referred to as the recursive cycle—an important systemic diagnostic tool, that is enumerated in detail later in this chapter.

After three meetings with Ann, it was time to include Bill. Continuing to meet and ally with her would have exacerbated the marital–parental split and would likely have resulted forming a coalition with Ann and myself against Bill. Moreover, I would have implicitly communicated blame to Ann. It is tempting but fallacious to attribute the blame or sole responsibility for the enmeshment on the mother. In North American culture, and particularly with families in which there are disabled children, the mother is often the one who is with the child the most and is a central attachment figure (Combrinck-Graham & Higley, 1984; Lederberg & Prezbindowski, 2000; Schlesinger & Meadow, 1972; Walker, 1983). However, from a systems perspective, we learn that it is difficult for an enmeshed mother–deaf child dyad to function without a disengaged father–mother dyad. Systemic case descriptions of deaf–hard-of-hearing-member families indicate a common pattern of an enmeshed mother–child relationship that is supported by a disengaged father. A clinician, for example, can ask a father: "How do you participate in mother holding on too tightly to your child?"

A Complicated but Familiar History. Bill and Ann began by sharing their perspectives of how the family strife began. The following scenario became evident. Two years before, Ann noticed that Susan was "withdrawing too much," that she seemed to be losing her fluency with speech and was not doing her homework. Ann believed that these changes were due to depression: "Susan can't accept her deafness." Ann tried to discuss this observation with Bill, who was impatient with the idea of depression, because of his own history with denying episodes of depression and sadness. He critically dismissed Ann's observation and lectured her about being overprotective. According to Bill, Susan was "simply lazy" and Ann's concern was making the laziness worse. The argument that ensued was to repeat itself again and again, becoming a ritual in their marriage.

Feeling abandoned by her husband, Ann sought consolation and support from her daughter, Marsha, who was 2 years younger than Susan and was vying for more attention. Together, Ann and Marsha approached Susan, half compassionately and half scoldingly, to say that she "should stop moping around." Susan felt infantilized by this strategy and believed that they were ganging up on her. As a result she became sullen and more withdrawn.

At the same time, Susan's grades were in decline. Ann called her school, which was a specialized day program for deaf children within a regular high school. Ann and the program director were already in an ongoing struggle, with Ann insisting that the school should mandate more speech therapy for Susan and the director finding Ann's concerns unreasonable. The director supported "total communication," which he erroneously understood to mean using a signed language predominately as a communication methodology. As a matter of fact, through my conversations with the school, I learned that the director had tacitly agreed with Susan's teacher to "forget" to remind Susan to attend extra speech therapy; for the teacher, too, felt threatened by Ann's involvement. Susan complied because of her own sense of futility with speech.

During the several meetings with the program director, the teacher, and a school counselor, Ann accused the school of being incompetent: "Why is Susan reading at a fourth-grade level?" she asked. The director sparred with Ann by disregarding her attention to academic concerns by describing in detail how Susan was "acting out" in school. He recommended family therapy with a therapist who understands and uses Sign Language, thus trading accusation for accusation with Ann in an ongoing struggle for power.

Within the school system, the mainstream teacher, who did not fully understand the implications of deafness or about appropriate support services and the role of personnel, repeatedly requested the interpreter–tutor to discipline Susan when she misbehaved in class. This, the tutor reasoned, was a demeaning request and was not within her job description or area of expertise, so she covertly refused to comply. Instead, she discussed with Susan "how it feels to be Deaf in a hearing world." As Susan continued to disrupt the class, the interpreter–tutor complained to the director of the deaf program about the mainstream teacher. The director and the mainstream teacher argued. As with Ann and the director, but in reverse, sides were drawn. With conflict raging around her, Susan continued to act out at school and at home.

As complicated as this situation became, it went further. Ann, already angry with the director of the deaf program, refused to join him in a team effort to discipline Susan, and instead called the director of special education for that city. She complained about the program and inquired about other programs. Furthermore, this time she was angry enough to call other parents. Seeing trouble brewing, the director of special education called the program director to suggest programmatic modifications and to "offer some constructive criticism of the curriculum and the faculty." The program director expressed his frustration with Ann and with the lack of administrative support he received by yelling at Susan directly. Susan's behavior worsened.

Susan's behavioral and emotional problems were now undeniable, and Ann did initiate psychotherapy for her, but with a clinician of her choice and with an individual format. The therapist neither signed nor had much experience with deafness. He met with Susan with all good intentions, was careful to talk loudly and with exaggerated lip movements, which unbeknownst to him, made speech reading more difficult (Liben, 1978). He diagnosed Susan as depressed and elaborated that "she has not yet come to terms with her deafness." He went on to say that "she is impulsive, egocentric, and has difficulty introspecting since she is unable to understand abstract concepts," such as those he had tried to explain to her. Thus, he strongly recommended long-term individual psychotherapy to begin prior to post-high school placement. This, he advised, "would improve her self-esteem as a deaf person. She is not yet ready to function in a *hearing environment*" (italics added). In addition, he suggested psychotropic medication and a psychiatrist. The psychiatrist prescribed an antidepressant. Ann and Susan complied with the recommendations.

All of these proceedings were upsetting to Bill, Susan's father. He had been depressed since Susan was first diagnosed as deaf, but his sense of manhood, an "I need to be strong" mentality, made it difficult for him to express these and other feelings and to work through grieving issues. He felt helpless as he witnessed Ann and others making important decisions regarding Susan, and did not sufficiently realize his own role in perpetuating the situation. Thus, he viewed the therapist's assessment as colluding with Ann against him. He was also much more concerned with Susan's ability to get a job in the future, as his job was the focus of his own life. "That's what we should focus on," he insisted. "A job will make her independent."

Accordingly, Bill contacted the vocational rehabilitation counselor for the deaf (RCD) with whom Susan had been meeting since she turned 17. The RCD had referred her to be evaluated at a specialized vocational evaluation center for deaf people. Based on their evaluation, the RCD advised that "Susan would benefit from vocational training in a *Deaf environment*, with Deaf peers and role models who use Sign Language. This placement should be away from her parents in order to encourage independence" (italics added). Bill approved of these suggestions and viewed them as bolstering his opinion against Ann. Accordingly, Ann viewed the RCD as colluding with her husband against her. The pitched battles continued, augmented with increasing numbers of experts, and placing Susan in the middle.

Susan's escalating depression and identity confusion, fueled by so many people speaking for her, soon alarmed the individual therapist who sought the help of a family therapist fluent in sign language, experienced in working with deaf people, and capable of meeting with the whole family. The individual therapist indicated in his referral that Susan had made no progress, partly because her parents provided little support. The family therapist accepted the referral and commenced meetings. However, family therapy rapidly reached a similar impasse. The family seemed immovable and soon began to miss appointments because of "car trouble" and other such rationalizations.

Both the individual and family therapist conceived the scope of the problem too narrowly. Each failed to place the problems in the broad ecological system that had developed around efforts to help Susan. As a result, each therapist soon felt without adequate resources and, after trying interventions suited primarily to smaller treatment units, each encountered control struggle with the clients. It was approximately 6 months after the family terminated treatment that I received the original phone call from Ann, following the altercation between her and Susan concerning driver's education class.

A SYSTEMIC EPISTEMOLOGY

The threads of this story are initially overwhelming. (A supervisor once told me, "The challenge is seldom not enough data, but too much data.") A systemic "lens" is a useful way to make sense out of these interactional threads, as it is of sufficient breadth and flexibility to encompass both the generic family dynamics and deafness–hard-of-hearing perspectives (Clark, 1998). As I will elucidate shortly, the *systemic perspective* views behavior as the product of reciprocal, circular interplays between different hierarchical systems of the biopsychosocial field—between environmental conditions and intrapsychic processes. This is referred to as the *circular nature of causation* (Hoffman, 1981). This is in contrast to a *linear idea of causation*, the theoretical basis for psychodynamic approaches, which focuses on one direction of change; either the environment causing individual change, or individual change causing environmental change. For a more complete description refer to Fig. 1.1, and the myriad of general descriptions of systems theory as exemplified by Keeny (1983) and Hoffman (1981).

Systems theory teaches us that natural systems or groups of persons, such as an individual, family, or a larger social network, are always part of larger systems. Thus, any system containing an individual or group of individuals is simultaneously a whole and a part of a larger whole. For example, depending on our frame of reference, an individual can be viewed as a complete entity, as the sole object in our perceptual field, or as one part of a family; a family

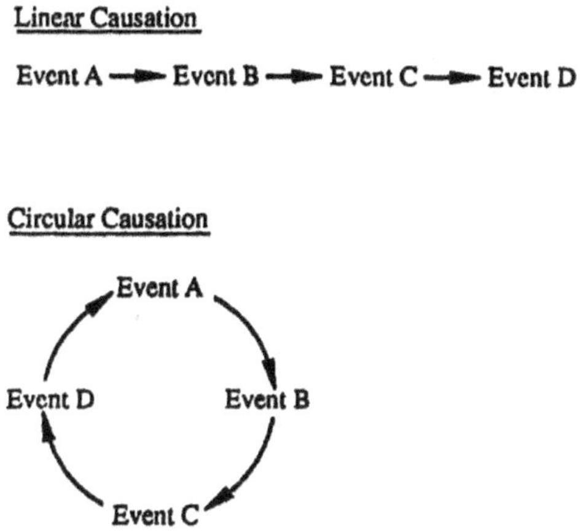

FIG. 1.1

can be viewed as a complete entity, as part of a neighborhood, or of an informal network system. We speak of a *hierarchy of biopsychosocial systems* to refer to systems that are both a "whole" and a "part." As clinicians, we gain a humbled appreciation of the complex series of biological, psychological, and interpersonal interactions within the spatial systems hierarchy—the biopsychosocial field—in which individual symptomatic behavior is embedded. This ecological perspective as it related to deaf persons was also described by Clark (1998).

We can now be more specific about the spatial characteristics, or hierarchy, of the biopsychosocial field. There are many levels of organization in human experience, from subatomic particle and living cell, to complex organs and organ systems, to whole persons, to families, to communities, to cultures and to larger societies (Bronfenbrenner, 1979; Engel, 1977). These differing systems levels appear to be arranged hierarchically, with each level more complex than the one before and encompassing all those that come

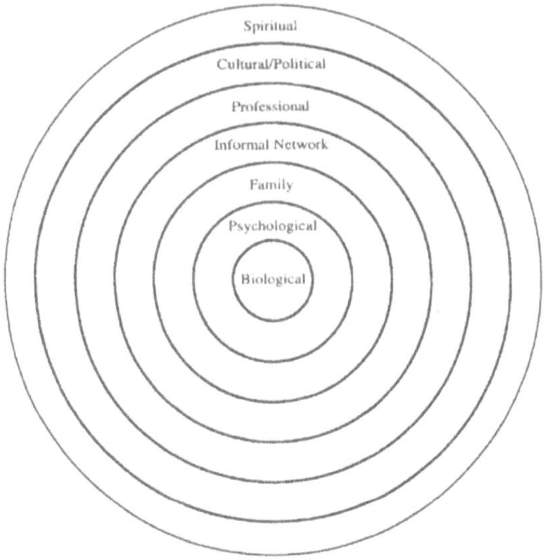

FIG. 1.2 Nested systems levels.

ate (40–65 db), severe (65–95 db), and profound (95 db or more; Boyd & Young, 1981). There may be related medical conditions in addition to hearing loss, depending on etiologic factors. For example, maternal rubella contracted during the first trimester of pregnancy is often associated with hearing loss, heart defects, cataracts, chorioretinitus, cerebral palsy, mental retardation, autism, delayed growth, diabetes mellitus, thyroid problems, and panencephalitis (Shaver, 1987).

A variety of assistive listening devices, including hearing aids, are biological–technological interventions. Certainly, there are a wide variety of analogue and digital hearing aids on the market. Since the first edition of this book has been published, cochlear implants has been both exalted as a biomedical breakthrough (Cochlear Corp.) and disparaged as an instrument of cultural ethnocide (Christiansen & Leigh, 2002; Lane, Hoffmeister, & Bahan, 1996).

Psychological. The particular characteristics of an individual have a great influence on how he or she adapts to being deaf–hard of hearing and on how the hearing loss is treated by his or her family, school, and greater society. Although such children may well pass through some common and identifiable stages of development, each will do so in a unique way that is determined by his or her personality. This idea of personality can be further refined by discussing cognitive, behavioral, and emotional elements. For example, an individual with a hearing loss who is taught that being deaf or hard of hearing is severely limiting will develop differently than a child who is not. Psychological factors associated with hearing loss have been extensively reviewed (see Chess & Fernandez, 1980; Levine, 1960, 1981; Marschark & Clark, 1998; Pollard, 1998a; Schirmer, 2001; Schlesinger & Meadow, 1972; Vernon & Andrews, 1990).

Family. The family is the main environment for the developing child, particularly the young child. Its behavioral patterns, concepts about hearing loss, emotional responses to the loss, interactions with the child, and so on, all exert powerful influences on development. Furthermore, family development is powerfully influenced by the child and by the demands of raising a deaf or hard-of-hearing child. In this sense, the child influences everything from the use of time and space to financial arrangements, travel patterns, patterns of communication among all family members, and even the family's image of itself as well or not well, competent or incompetent, nurturing or nonnurturing. The deaf or hard-of-hearing child influences, and is influenced by, hearing siblings, grandparents, and extended family members. Family factors have been reviewed by Scott and Dooley (1985), Featherstone (1980), Harris (1978), Harvey (2001a, 1998, 1994), Mendelsohn and Rozek (1983), Murphy (1979), Pollard and Rendon (1999), Robinson and Weathers (1974), and Shapiro and & Harris (1976).

Professional. As with virtually all disabled or chronically ill people, many deaf or hard-of-hearing clients have extensive and often intense relationships with a number of professional systems, including school, medical, audiological and other service agencies (Harvey & Dym, 1987, 1988). In this regard, it is important to note that for each ramification of hearing loss, there is often a corresponding professional. Professional systems can be more or less relevant at different stages of one's life. For example, as will be illustrated later in this chapter, physicians tend to be important early on, with school systems later becoming the most influential.

Professional systems and their relationships with family members may become patterned and rigidified over time and thereby exert an ongoing influence on the family. For example, parents often differ in their attitudes toward plans for their deaf or hard-of-hearing child, and a particular professional's advice can tip the scales. Continued support for one parent's position can exacerbate the split between the parents. Alternately, continued support and guidance toward the child can undermine parental authority, as when a professional exclusively meets with the child, the identified patient, although covertly assuming that he or she does a better job at parenting than do the child's actual parents. The undermining of parental authority also may emerge in the relationship among schools, parents, and children when the school and parents compete about who is in charge of the child (Bodner-Johnson, 1986; Pollard & Rinker, 2001).

The interpersonal patterns that emerge between parents and professionals may become so powerful that the boundary between these two systems virtually disappears. Therapeutic efforts to help the deaf or hard-of-hearing child and their family are frequently impossible unless the ways that professional systems reinforce family patterns, and vice versa, are also addressed. The "oral–manual debate" among professionals—that is, whether deaf students should exclusively use speech and speech reading or a signed language to communicate—is a well-known example of how the professional level influences families and the child. For example, Moores (1987) stated that "the centuries-old 'oral–manual controversy' has accounted for more confusion than any other question in the field, and it is not surprising that professionals on the periphery are not clear about the issues." A decade later, this theme was echoed by Stokoe (1998): "to people who hear and speak and, against all evidence, believe that speech and language are the same thing, deafness is a calamity, a disease. However, when it becomes more widely recognized that arbitrary (i.e., spoken) signs could have become language only a surrogates for gestural signs with their meanings, deafness will have to be viewed in an entirely new light."

The bilingual–bicultural controversy also predominates in current professional circles and generates intense hostility. Supporters of bilingual–bicultural education assert that deaf children's native language (ASL) is the primary language of Deaf persons and that appropriately trained teachers should use ASL to teach English as a second language. Opponents assert that teaching in ASL tend to support separatism and absorb time, energy and resources that should be used focused on the essential task of learning English (Lane, Hoffmeister, & Bahan, 1996).

The interrelationships of professional systems and agencies and their relationships to families has been documented by Imber-Black (1987, 1986), Imber-Coppersmith (1983), Carl and Jurkovic (1983), and Harvey and Dym (1988, 1987).

Informal Networks. Informal networks made up of friends and acquaintances of both the child and parents can exert strong influences on family development and thereby on the development of the individual child. The simple amount of support parents receive may determine how well they cope with the extra demands a deaf or hard-of-hearing child may place on them. But networks may play more complex functions in much the same way that professionals do (i.e., support or opposition of one kind of educational programming over another, or support of one parent over another). Networks, like professionals, reinforce functional and dysfunctional family patterns. Informal networks play an increasingly major role in the development of such individuals, particularly during adolescence. Informal network factors have been addressed by Attneave (1984), Erickson (1984), Harvey (1985b), Luey (1980), and Speck and Speck (1979).

Cultural–Political. The way that a particular culture or subculture views being deaf and hard of hearing and, through its political process, the way that a culture provides for such persons, exerts a major influence on the development of each child (Glickman & Harvey, 1996; Lane, 1987; Lane, et al., 1996). With reference to deafness, Moores (1987) reported that "most of [deaf peoples'] problems are caused by the dominant society. Deaf people have survived and endured in the face of an indifferent world that must be dealt with daily". Culturally-based oppression—not just indifference—exerts a powerful influence on deaf people, a phenomenon which in chapter 11, I have referred to as "ordinary evil." Glickman and Gulati (in press) listed several examples, including control of Deaf schools by hearing people; forbidding of sign language in schools; obsessive focus upon speech and speech reading to the exclusion of other academic subjects; imposing hearing aids on students who do not want them. Lane (1984) coined the term, *audism*, to describe the oppressive hearing bias within the cultural level of the biopsychosocial ecology.

In contrast, the Deaf community is a minority group with its own hierarchical social structure, culture, and language (Baker & Cokely, 1980; Jacobs, 1974; Padden, 1980; Woodward, 1982). It provides a vital supportive network for diverse human needs, such as the exchange of information, social–emotional support, and political action. With reference to cultural issues of deaf children in hearing families, Schlesinger (1986) stated,

> Many of the parallels drawn between deaf children and other minority children are accurate and helpful in conceptualizing developmental, psychological, linguistic, and academic issues. Deaf children are like minority children in that there is a deaf culture and a deaf language different from the majority culture and language. However, deaf children are different from other minority children in that they *do not* share that minority status with their hearing parents (Champie, 1984), which is true in 90% to 95% of the class. (Schein & Delk, 1974; p. 109)

Spiritual. Unlike the previous levels that are clearly defined, the definition of spiritual is anything but clear. One client, for example, defined her spirituality as "feeling like everything's connected; like I'm part of a larger whole." Others define it as "a power beyond us, an organizing principle." In the popular movie *Star Wars*, Obi-Wan Kenobi blessed Luke Skywalker with "May the force be with you." And 12-step programs teach about "the higher power." Some people hold a belief in "some kind of God" and may participate in sacred rituals and prayer. Others—such as atheists, agnostics, or secular humanists—do not hold a belief in God.

Perhaps because, as human beings, we are able to acknowledge our mortality, we are "wired" to at least consider the question whether there is some indefinable powers or energies beyond us, (Armstrong, 1993). In fact, it is often beginning in elementary school that we first wonder whether there is a

God; and if so, what is "it" (Coles, 1991). In addition, as adults, we often continue to ask ourselves that question, particularly surrounding a crisis or major loss. There are many possible answers to the "God-question." However, what answer we choose strongly influences the way we interpret our experience, including experiences of hearing loss, as described in chapter five. Therefore, although spirituality is difficult to define, it deserves separate category status. In this regard, I happen to come across an article in the local Boston newspaper entitled "Spirituality Makes Rounds." It described "new areas of inquiry" for physicians doing medical rounds at Massachusetts General Hospital: "We need to go to patients and see what they see as spirituality. Often that takes away the conflict between spirituality and medicine; they don't have to be in opposition." (Tye, 1997, p. 1).

In summary, all of these systems levels comprise the context in which symptomatic behavior may be embedded. It is not enough to say that "it is a family problem" or "it is an individual problem"; because, as was described earlier, a whole is simultaneously a part. Consequently, it is necessary to thoroughly understand the interactional patterns within and between each systems level to provide effective treatment. As Bateson (1971) stated, "if you want to understand some phenomenon or appearance, you must consider that phenomenon within the context of all *completed* circuits which are relevant to it" (p. 244).

Systemic Diagnosis of Susan's Symptomatology

Let us examine the "completed circuits" in which Susan's symptoms re-embedded. First, we must summarize the rough formulation of the structure of interactions within and between systems levels. Beginning at the biological systems level, we note that Susan had a profound, bilateral, sensorineural hearing loss of congenital origin, resulting from maternal rubella during the first trimester of pregnancy. At the psychological level, testing described Susan as depressed, angry, and filled with denial about the short- and long-term meaning of her disability. She was experiencing identity confusion: She did not identify with her deaf peers, yet she felt alienated from her hearing peers.

At the family level, concern for Susan's deafness and her multiple needs tended to "detour" or modulate the fighting between her parents in favor of maintaining harmony between them. Focusing on Susan stopped her parents from dealing directly with, and perhaps resolving, their own issues of intimacy, autonomy, and power. Boundaries within and surrounding the family appeared to be porous (e.g., Susan's younger sister, Marsha, was encouraged to comment on her psychological state). In terms of the informal network level, each parent found support in groups outside the family—for Ann, it was a formal support group, for Bill, it was his cronies.

The boundary between professionals and the family served to shape and to reinforce family splits and alliances, as did the informal support groups. Educational and vocational rehabilitation professionals entered the family or were brought into it by Ann and Bill to bolster various opinions and alliances. The professionals themselves were frequently in conflict with each other or were disengaged, as suggested by the minimal interaction between school personnel and clinicians. Finally, Susan's psychological functioning and her relationships with parents, teachers, and school administrators was greatly impacted by the unresolved cultural conflicts about Deaf people and the role of the Deaf Community. These conflicts center around the issues of sign language, Deaf and hearing cultures, and mainstreaming versus residential schools. In this case, there were no dominant spiritual themes.

Although this description begins to simplify the wealth of data, we need a heuristic tool that we help us tract the relevant completed circuits. The *recursive cycle* refers to the sequence of seemingly repetitive interactions in which the symptom is embedded. Tracking the recursive cycle provides a specific map of the changes within and between the systems levels, which includes the symptom of Susan's depression. Of course, in describing this cycle, we can arbitrarily start at any point. Ann and Bill argue about Susan. Bill pulls in his friends and the rehabilitation counselor against Ann. Ann, in turn, pulls in her support group and the individual therapist against Bill. Similarly, the professionals argue or do not talk with each other.

Susan acts out more. Her behavior exacerbates the conflict between Ann and Bill. They then attend Susan, often pulling in her younger sister Marsha, to assist them. Marsha feels validated as "the parental child," now feeling responsible for Susan's well-being. Susan becomes more depressed. After a dormant period, Bill and Ann again begin to argue about Susan. This cycle then repeats.

Intervention

The pragmatics of systemic intervention can be conceptualized as the pragmatics of disrupting the recursive cycle in which symptoms are embedded, so that the cycle no longer provides a context for symptoms to occur. It is important to note that the recursive cycle encompasses space and time. The spatial dimension is organized by the biopsychosocial field; symptoms are entrenched within dysfunctional recursive transactions among the hierarchical systems levels. Changes in these levels serve as a catalyst for one another to amplify change or may impede change. As is illustrated throughout this book, attention to the multilevels of the biopsychosocial field is particularly important when working with deaf or hard-of-hearing clients because of a myriad number of systems that are involved in the lives of these clients, such as school personnel, physicians, and other professionals who may support the presenting problem.

We must also account for the temporal dimension of the recursive cycle when planning intervention strategies. Changes in systems levels contained in a given recursive cycle may be separated by only moments, hours, days, weeks, months, or even years. Furthermore, and most importantly, any single system level contained in the recursive cycle is more or less stable as a function of temporal factors and therefore may only respond to interventions that are implemented at a certain time (Dym, 1985). As an example, intervening in the moment to moment sequences within a therapy session may prove effective if, and only if, that temporal unit is responsive to change and if that change significantly impacts the cycle in which the symptom is embedded. In some cases, modifying the interactions that transpire during the therapy session does not generalize to modifying interactions that transpire over longer periods of time or in different environments, such as at home. On the other hand, an intervention, no matter how well formulated and implemented, may need to be implemented simultaneously with a shift in one or more spatial levels of the system, such as at the time when the "symptom bearer" or another family member experiences a crisis, or when a member who serves to stabilize the system is absent (Dym, 1987). Whether an intervention is effective is a function of the interrelationships of systems levels at any given time.

To clarify these rather abstract concepts, let us return to describing the series of meetings with Ann and Bill. It quickly became clear that Ann and Bill, at least as a parental unit, needed to cooperate more in order for Susan's symptoms to remit. Thus, the treatment with Bill and Ann focused on elucidating and ameliorating unresolved issues of grieving about the original diagnosis of deafness, as well as more generic issues of intimacy, autonomy, and power that had made it difficult, if not impossible, for them to serve as effective parents and marital partners. Instead of engaging in conflict with each other by pulling in nonfamily persons or their own children, it was more helpful to work with them to fight more directly with each other.

Bill and Ann came to realize that their feelings of mutual betrayal were, in part, fueled by their difference in punctuating blame. *Punctuation* refers to the "who started it" controversy. Two partners, for example, may perceive and organize their ongoing interaction into different patterns of cause and effect. For example, Ann accused Bill of withdrawing, whereas Bill accused Ann of "always being angry." Ann punctuated the sequence as "I am angry because you withdraw," whereas Bill punctuated it in reverse as "I withdraw because you are angry." Consequently, their heated conflict could be reframed, not as whether one is right while the other is wrong, but as differences in punctuating (creating) reality.

The meetings also focused on unresolved grieving reactions having to do with the original diagnostic trauma of Susan's deafness. Bill and Ann's alternating withdrawal and expressions of anger were reframed as manifestations of grieving and I prescribed several "homework" tasks to encourage them to grieve more directly and openly with each other. They were requested not to try to "make each other feel better," as they had been doing; instead, it was preferable for them to list and discuss disappointments, fears, anger, sadness; and, in short, all of the emotions that heretofore they had avoided sharing with each other. These discussions were, in turn, brought into therapy. Having begun to affectively reconnect Bill and Ann paved the way for them to work with each other "as a team to make more effective parenting decisions."

Both Ann and Bill made significant progress. At home, they had "late night intimate talks" more often. Their relationship changed so that Ann and Bill slowly came to accept Susan as ready to achieve more independence, both in regard to driving an automobile, opening up a checking account, and going on job interviews alone. Bill also became less disengaged and more active in decision-making responsibilities with respect to the children. Both Ann and Bill discontinued pulling in other professionals as weapons for their own marital or parental struggles.

After 20 conjoint sessions with Ann and Bill, a meeting with the nuclear family of Ann, Bill, Susan (age 19), Marsha (age 17), and John (age 12) was requested. Because no hearing person in the family signed, an interpreter who interpreted voice-to-sign for Susan, and sign-to-voice for the hearing family members was included. I communicated with Susan directly via ASL while the interpreter interpreted sign-to-voice. This procedure is described in chapters 7 and 8.

During that meeting, it became apparent that the previously stabilized recursive cycle had changed. Ann and Bill had begun to frequently go out by themselves and, at home, became actively involved in investigating college for Susan. Susan, herself ambivalent about either attending a school for Deaf students, a mainstreamed hearing college, or training program, became increasingly anxious and depressed. Unlike before, she discussed these feelings with her parents, who, in turn, were more uniformly supportive. However, Marsha, in reaction to the increased amount of attention Susan was receiving and to her dethronement as parental child (i.e., as when she had joined Ann in worrying about Susan), found herself daydreaming in school and achieving declining grades. At home, she did not eat well. John was always out with friends and was relatively unscathed by the systemic changes around him, perhaps because he had consistently obtained gratification from playing sports with his peers and with Bill. Ann and Bill, partially in reaction to the combined turmoil that both Susan and Marsha were experiencing and to their new found marital closeness, became increasingly overwhelmed with "child problems" and more often left the house to "get away by ourselves." And the cycle would repeat itself.

The change with Susan, triggered by a change in the marital–parental system, was noteworthy. In light of her behavioral changes within the family and recent anxiety concerning school, it became clear that Susan's intrapsychic functioning had destabilized and that she therefore would benefit from more treatment. Moreover, it became apparent that the family system around Susan would support individual change. Consequently, a series of individual sessions of psychotherapy with Susan was set up to help her begin resolving self-concept issues, identity issues, and formulating future plans.

Treatment went well. Susan appeared eager to gain new insights about her attitudes, feelings, and behavior, and used these insights quite productively. We terminated our individual sessions after approximately 15 to 20 meetings. Susan was no longer depressed, as evidenced by, in her mother's words, "increasing stubbornness about telling us when she doesn't understand something we say and her increased enthusiasm about applying to a college for Deaf students." She became more animated about achieving more independence and, after a few weeks' time, began to reestablish an alliance with her father, and began driver's education. Furthermore, as Ann and Bill now enjoyed a more supportive marital–parental relationship, Ann talked about Susan's stubbornness with mock dread and much humor. During a final meeting with the entire family, we reviewed progress and agreed to terminate treatment. A 1-year follow-up visit indicated the progress was sustained. Susan was attending a "Deaf" college; Marsha and John were "hanging out with friends and complaining about school"; and Bill and Ann were eagerly but anxiously preparing for Marsha to soon leave home for college.

Let us review where we began in this chapter. In some ways, the study of human behavior begins with a story. Then one steps back and attempts to make sense out of it. We began with a case study of Susan and her relevant system. Then I introduced a systemic framework and some basic concepts to be used throughout this book: linear verses circular nature of causation, biopsycho–social hierarchy, recursive cycles, and punctuation, to name a few. The next case study further illustrates these tools.

Case Study: Jill

Jill was an adolescent with a moderate bilateral hearing loss of congenital origin and of unknown etiology. Her 50–decibal hearing loss had been diagnosed at age 2 and was nonprogressive and flat across all frequencies. She had a history of middle ear infections and gastrointestinal (GI) distress. She was also quite overweight. Physicians had debated for years over whether her GI symptoms were caused by physical or psychological factors; the etiology of her symptoms have always been somewhat vague.

Jill is an intelligent, insightful, and articulate young woman, frequently astounding her teachers with her perceptiveness and somewhat precocious ability to express herself. She took great pride in her oral–aural skills, which were excellent, and in her beginning sign language skills. When we met, she had only signed for 1 year. Although Jill, on first glance, exuded a persona of confidence and stability, projective testing indicated depression and a significant level of inner turmoil. Her responses to pictures presented during testing included several themes relating to death and accidents happening to people (e.g., "a woman thinking to herself that she was about to die"). She frequently complained of "emptiness and not knowing who I am." In addition, behaviorally, she was somewhat impulsive and displayed frequent outbursts of temper, both with peers and adults. Jill appeared to be exhibiting borderline personality traits, as defined by the DSM-IV (American Psychiatric Association, 1994).

Jill was the oldest of two siblings in a family whose other members had normal hearing. Her biological parents, unable to cope with long-standing marital problems, which has been exacerbated by dealing with Jill's hearing loss, divorced when she was approximately 3 years old. Her mother, Alyce, was awarded physical custody of both children. For 3 years subsequent to the divorce, Jill's father "Bob" did not visit her at all, and for several years thereafter only visited sporadically. During this time, Alyce remarried. Bob also remarried, had more children, and then, perhaps out of obligation or a need to catch up on lost time, increased the frequency of contact with Jill. She, however, did not know exactly what to make of her father's change of interest, and did not feel comfortable with him: "He is like a stranger," Jill said of her father. Jill also recalled frequent episodes of intense conflict with both sets of parents—her biological father–stepmother and biological mother–stepfather—largely related to "blended family" issues, such as tenuous bonding with her parents' second spouses (Visher & Visher, 1979). Jill alternated between "loving mother and hating father" and vice versa, frequently fighting with her sister about the reasons for their parents' divorce.

Amidst this family turmoil, Jill began experiencing academic and social problems in elementary school, where she was enrolled in a mainstream program of hearing students. Her problems were, in part, due to linguistic inaccessibility in the classroom; she could not always understand the teacher and could not keep up with the hearing kids, particularly because the school did not have acoustic tiles or rugs in the classroom to minimize excessive background noise. Moreover, the school did not provide specialized support services, such as counseling or another person to take notes while Jill focused on lip-reading the teachers. Although she had a couple of acquaintances, Jill had no real friends; she often went home right after school while her peers played sports or participated in after-school music and dance lessons.

This situation persisted unnoticed until junior high school when an in-school audiologist recommended that Jill begin to use an auditory trainer, a system to amplify the teacher's voice and to transmit this signal to her hearing aid. "This," she said, "would help Jill keep up in the classroom." Jill, her mother, and stepfather agreed with the audiologist's recommendation, hoping that it would lessen her academic frustrations. However, the auditory trainer only seemed to make her feel like more of a social outcast: "Everyone looks at me weird, and I feel like a freak."

As Jill's grades continued to decline, she began to exhibit behavioral problems in school, such as frequent episodes of anger, walking out of classrooms, and fighting with peers. As these problems escalated, Jill's mother and stepfather had more frequent conferences "behind closed doors," eventually deciding that her mother would be the advocate with respect to the school, as she was viewed by both of them as having better assertiveness skills. (Moreover, the stepfather was secretly a bit shy & embarrassed.) Alyce and school personnel then began to enact what would become the first of a series of conflicts. Alyce felt that Jill should repeat a grade in school, but the school administrators vetoed her idea. Both sides then accumulated evidence to support their positions, much like two opposing attorneys in a courtroom. As within her blended family, Jill keenly sensed this conflict and felt caught in the middle, frequently vacillating between feeling loyalty to her teacher's point of view or to her mother. She withdrew further and soon became clinically depressed.

At home, her mother and stepfather disagreed on how to best handle Jill's depression, which she manifested as increasingly recalcitrant behavior. Her mother had been the primary disciplinarian but eventually relinquished this role, explaining that "I am not strict, so I let her stepfather set more of the limits." Her stepfather at first enthusiastically acquiesced to his new role, viewing it as a golden opportunity to "set Jill straight" and perhaps elevate his status with her. However, as they fought more over rules, Jill acted out more by beginning to stay out until dawn. As the tension between them escalated, he felt increasingly ineffective and soon began to withdraw and sulk. This, in turn, precipitated strife between him and Alyce. Witnessing this chain of events, Jill felt what would become familiar feelings of responsibility and guilt.

Jill and her mother now began fighting almost daily about "almost anything," but most often about getting up on time for school. Alyce herself vacillated between reprimanding Jill, and feeling compassion and pity for her because of her hearing loss and whatever effects the divorce had on her. As the conflict between Jill and her mother and the conflict between mother and father escalated, so did the conflicts between mother and school. Jill herself added fuel to the tension by frequently being truant from school. She was now in Grade 9.

The school counselor, feeling alarmed by Jill's frequent absences and "daydreaming in class" strongly suggested to Alyce that the family go to a private clinician. Alyce complied and made an appointment for herself, her husband, Jill, and Jill's sister. They attended family therapy for approximately 2 months. During this time, the therapist attempted to facilitate more cooperation within the parental unit in disciplining Jill and also to provide a forum for Jill to vent her feelings about hard-of-hearing and divorce issues. However, the more Jill vented, the more ineffectual the parents felt, and the frequency of fighting dramatically increased, now with Jill's sister supporting her parents against "Jill being so spoiled." The family terminated treatment.

As the general level of tension around Jill mounted, she decided to live with her biological father, hoping to reconnect with him and to "find peace" from the turmoil at home. However, in this new family consisting of Bob, his second wife, and their two children, she felt like a stranger. In addition, even though her parents had divorced well over 15 years previously, she suddenly found herself more entangled in their ongoing post marital conflicts. Jill complained that "my mother gets pissed at me because I am more like my father, and I do look like my father, but my father says I do things like my mother." To further compound her confusion, she was frequently told that "mother blames my father, but my father blames my mother, but my father's family blames my father, but my mother's family blames my mother." And similar to many children of divorced parents, Jill felt "caught in the middle between mom and dad," in regard to loyalty: "Who was right, my mother or my father?" (Wallerstein & Kelly, 1980). As she had done several times in her past, Jill cognitively attempted to minimize her own confusion by attributing the cause of the strife to herself, a stance that provided some clarity but that caused her extreme guilt. She reported, for example, that "sometimes I wonder if my parents' divorce was my fault." She took this self-attribution of blame one step further by also stating that "I have always thought that it was my fault that I was hard of hearing, and I think my hearing loss caused my parents' divorce."

After only a few weeks of living with Bob and his family, she began experiencing acute nausea, headaches, and stomach distress. Logistic transportation problems with regulating visits to the myriad of physicians with each biological parent blaming the other for Jill's somatic complaints, served to intensify their conflicts, which now included threats of legal action to discontinue the other's custody rights. Bob responded to this stress by becoming more irritable with Jill. As tension escalated, Jill snuck out one night and moved back with her mother, stepfather, and sister. Soon afterward, she became more depressed and began running away from home, again because she felt, "I did not feel I belonged or that my mother cared about me."

Meanwhile, the conflict between Alyce and the school system also continued to escalate. Alyce was beginning to feel increasingly helpless against the system. In addition, it became evident that Jill was struggling to fit in with her hearing or deaf peers. She very much wished to affiliate more with hearing people, and in fact used the ability to hear as her standard for maturity. Much of her fantasy life was devoted to how she would someday function comfortably "in the hearing world." She stated that hearing persons are "more mature, they know more. Deaf people are stupid and immature." However, she had already experienced many of her previous hearing teachers and hearing peers avoiding her and labeling her as deficient, apparently because of her hearing loss: "I have no hearing friends, they avoid me because they think I am deaf and make fun of my speech."

Jill, feeling helpless and increasingly stuck, briefly attended a spiritual cult group and meditated regularly. However, this did not alleviate her pain and she attempted suicide in her junior year of high school. This led to a referral for a psychological evaluation. The psychologists, considering Jill's significant degree of hearing loss to be the primary reason for her difficulties, immediately recommended a change of educational placement from the mainstream high school in her neighborhood to a 5-day specialized residential program for deaf students, located several hours from her home. Jill and her parents welcomed this recommendation, for it offered respite from dealing with the family turmoil and a new sense of hope. During the week she lived at school, and during weekends she continued to live with her mother, stepfather, and sister. Bob had moved to a different state, now seeing Jill only a few times per year.

However, as with her earlier move to live with her biological father, the change of educational placement was not the answer to her problems. Once her classes began, Jill emphatically felt that she did not belong in the "deaf school." Although she enjoyed signing with the deaf students and felt a certain kinship with them because they were also hearing impaired, she complained that "they talk about boring things." Moreover, some of the deaf peers ostracized her because of her use of signed English[1] as contrasted to their own futility with American Sign Language,[2] and for her "snobbish hearing attitude." Thus, Jill felt ostracized from both peer groups of her informal network: "Sometimes I don't know who I am, what I'm doing, and why I'm here. It seems like there is no middle in the world; with either world, there are problems." Furthermore, Jill added that "I feel like I'm the only one with this kind of problem."

Jill became more disillusioned and depressed, reported more physical complaints, and more frequently considered the option of suicide. As before, this precipitated a psychological evaluation. The new psychologist recommended a medical consult, more intensive individual treatment, a

---

[1]Signed English is an invented, artificial sign code system that details the structure and grammar of spoken English, as opposed to a language that has naturally evolved, such as American Sign Language (Freeman, Carbin, & Boese, 1981).

[2]American Sign Language (ASL) is a visual–gestural language that makes use of the signer's eyes, face, head, and body posture as well as his or her hands and arms. It is a naturally evolved language used among many Deaf persons (Baker & Cokely, 1980).

hard-of-hearing support group, temporary respite from residing at the school, and a social meeting between Jill and a prominent hard-of-hearing adult role model. But these interventions were neither sufficient nor practical. Jill's behavior and psychological functioning continued to worsen. During an emergency scheduled Individualized Education Plan (IEP)[3] meeting, the deaf school personnel and Alyce decided that Jill would be transferred to another school for emotionally disturbed hearing students. The meeting ended with the educational liaison from her town warning Jill that she must "behave" next time (i.e., not become depressed or suicidal), for he had spent an inordinate amount of time (& the town's money) for the unsuccessful placement. The liaison was reacting to pressure from his boss to document more successful placements.

Discussion of Case Study

Although this broad case presentation is complex and perhaps at first overwhelming, it is important to note it is not uncommon; in fact, it should be quite familiar to professionals who work with deaf or hard-of-hearing persons. Let us first turn to the nested structures, or the biopsychosocial hierarchical systems, in Jill's world. At the biological level, Jill has a congenital, moderate, bilateral, sensorineural hearing loss of unknown etiology, and experiences other physical and psychosomatic symptoms.

At the psychological level, her oral–aural skills are excellent and signing skills are average. Jill exhibits borderline personality traits. Furthermore, psychological testing describes her as depressed, filled with inner turmoil, and suicidal.

The interactional transactions within Jill's family are noteworthy. Jill's difficulties provide fuel for the intense bitterness and feuds between her divorced parents and their respective families, and in turn, her parents' discord provides fuel for Jill's difficulties. She feels like a child without a home, and her attempts to "see the forest through the trees" are unsuccessful. Boundaries between the marital and sibling subsystems of both families appear to be quite porous, as are the boundaries between the two family systems. Conflict between Jill and any parent causes intramarital conflict and also causes interfamily conflict; that is, between the dyads of mother–stepfather and father–stepmother. Moreover, conflicts within the biological parent subsystem get deflected onto Jill who, in turn, reports increased somatic distress. Jill's alliances with both sets of biological and stepparents are tenuous. Finally, the hierarchical structure in the biological mother–stepfather–Jill subsystem is frequently in flux. This is the family level.

[3]The Individualized Educational Plan (IEP) is a year-long plan required for every handicapped child between the ages of 3 and 21, as mandated by Public Law 94–142 (Freeman et al., 1981).

At the informal network level, the phenomenon of feeling stuck between deaf and hearing worlds is vividly illustrated. She feels rejected by both groups, and indeed ambivalently rejects both groups herself, thereby providing her with no respite from family conflict.

At the professional level, professionals are consistent and profound actors in the drama, alternating between viewing Jill's hearing loss as the essential reason for her distress, and viewing Jill as primarily emotionally disturbed; as exemplified by the transfer to a school for emotionally disturbed adolescents. Furthermore, the relationship between many of the professionals and Jill are tinged with much of the same anger, frustrations and resentments that characterize Jill's relationships within her family.

At the cultural level, Jill's and the professionals' ambivalence about "who she is" is a microcosm of our culture's ambivalence about how to properly view the issues and effects of being hard of hearing (Schein & Stone, 1986). Finally, at the spiritual level, it is important to note that Jill had attempted to get solace from a spiritual cult group.

Consider the ecology that includes Jill. We can list several patterns.

1. Jill's tenuous and ambivalent relationships with deaf and hearing peers (informal network level) is related to her identity confusion (psychological level).
2. The more Jill exhibits symptoms of depression (psychological level), the more mother and stepfather argue (family level), and the more the biological parents argue (family level).
3. The more intense the conflict between Jill and her mother (family level), the more intense the conflict between mother and school (professional level) and between Jill and school (the professional level).
4. Professionals being uncertain about the clinical importance of Jill's hearing loss (professional level) is related to physicians being uncertain about the causes of her physical symptoms (professional level); both are related to Jill experiencing a plethora of somatic complaints (biological level).

Analysis of these several relationships reveals the following "threads" that pervades Jill's ecology: The cultural vagueness and ambiguity about the characteristics and effects of a moderate hearing loss (cultural level) is related to the vagueness and ambiguity among professionals about how critically important the hearing loss is (professional level), which is related to Jill's vague and ambiguous relationships with deaf and hearing peers (informal network level), which is related to the vague, ambiguous, and triangulated relationship with respect to Jill's parents (family level), which is related to her internal vague, ambiguous sense of self (psychological level), which is related to the medical vagueness and ambiguity in regard to the origins of her somatic complaints (biological level).

We can track a recursive cycle, which presently appears to be largely stable and that moves through the complex ecological field previously described. We begin with Jill feeling depressed, as if she does not belong anywhere. Mother is the first to notice her depression and discusses it with her husband. Both attribute the cause of Jill's dysphoria to school and agree that mother will be the primary spokesperson for the school whereas stepfather will take on more of a disciplinary role with Jill. However, both parents quickly feel overwhelmed with their tasks and, in their frustration, begin to yell more at Jill and blame each other. Jill attributes herself to be the cause of this turmoil and feels that she can get support neither from her parents nor from her peers. She alternately looks toward either set of opposing parents for stability and support. However, she feels guilty and confused, becomes overtly suicidal, or develops somatic symptoms. Although her response temporarily unites all of the factions within the ecosystem, it leaves Jill feeling culpable and unstable. The cycle repeats.

This recursive cycle contains eight discrete steps that transmit and process information (i.e., information about Jill). It is important to note that Jill's borderline psychiatric symptoms are quite entrenched in this interplay of ecological relationships, and, in fact, are metaphors for the vague and ambiguous loyalties that occur throughout the field. As noted before, although the steps and events in the cycle constantly change, these changes may be imperceptible, as they are in the case of Jill and her family.

RAMIFICATIONS OF A SYSTEMIC APPROACH

The systemic model, as presented in this book, offers the clinician several choices about how, when, and where to intervene in the context of the biopsychosocial field. The clinical vignettes of Susan and Jill illustrate that phenomena at different levels of the ecology may involve biological, psychological, familial, informal network, professional, cultural, and spiritual influences. A modification in one level will frequently influence, and be influenced by, all other levels to varying degrees. Intervention at one particular level may well exert a "ripple effect" across several other levels, and therefore may be the optimal point of intervention. Alternately, as in Jill's case, all the systems levels may reinforce each other like glue to preclude effective intervention at any one level, and therefore may require simultaneous or sequential interventions at several levels.

The systemic model disputes what has been the erroneous and unfortunate interpretation of the psychology of deafness and psychology of being hard of hearing—as if deaf or hard-of-hearing individuals exhibit certain characteristics that can be predicted a priori, based on the simple existence of the disability. In contrast, the systemic model posits that the behavioral and emotional characteristics that may be presented by many deaf and hard-of-hearing clients have come about, are supported, and are reified as a function of the interaction within and between systems levels across time; they are context based (Chess & Fernandez, 1980; Lane, 1987; & Marschark & Clark, 1998). Both Susan and Jill clearly exhibited depressive symptoms; however, we can now easily understand their symptoms as intimately "woven into the fabric" of the ecology. The following chapters take a closer look at systemic diagnosis and intervention.

ACKNOWLEDGMENT

I am indebted to Barry Dym for much of the theoretical descriptions in this chapter.

2

Life-Span Development of the Deaf Ecosystem[1]

This chapter illustrates the systemic interplays of developing ecological relationships across time that support a presenting problem(s) of a deaf individual. It uses a case vignette as an example of the longitudinal patterns of ecological relationships that may occur during the development of a deaf individual who exhibits psychological difficulties within a hearing family. It is important to emphasize that this presentation is both pessimistic and limiting: It depicts one example of an ecosystem that is dysfunctional, and that therefore becomes a context for supporting presenting problem(s) within a particular deaf person. This attempt is not intended to describe the general course of development of a typical psychologically healthy deaf person or of a typical deaf person who is in need of psychological treatment. Rather, this mode of analysis, the longitudinal sketch from a systemic perspective, can be used by clinicians as a backdrop to guide their understanding of the particular system that they are treating.

The longitudinal sketch is organized into periods of ecological transition; those times when a person's position in the environment is altered as a result of a change in role, setting, or both. At each ecological transition, individu-

[1]A portion of this chapter has been adapted from an unpublished manuscript by Harvey and Dym.

als are required to accommodate to new roles and behavioral expectations created by a revised systemic organization. Periods of ecological transition often represent optimal opportunities for clinical intervention because, by definition, the system is destabilized. The following junctures are described: pregnancy, birth of a child, suspicion of hearing loss, diagnosis, entrance into school, postsecondary placement, marriage, having children, and death of one's parents. For each transition, with the exception of pregnancy, theoretical considerations are described and a clinical vignette is presented.

JUNCTURE 1: PREGNANCY

Vera and Jake, a young hearing couple, have been married for 4 years prior to conceiving their first child. The effects of Vera's announced pregnancy ripples through all levels of her ecology. Her biological makeup markedly changes as her endocrine system releases increased levels of hormones. This affects her psychological functioning—her moods fluctuate wildly, and her thoughts, feelings, and actions become more oriented to the future. Vera and her husband Jake feel more permanently connected to each other in light of their unborn baby. They also sense that their respective parents and other extended family members have come to legitimize them more as a couple because they will soon be parents. With regard to their informal network, they begin to associate with other expectant friends. Vera's pregnancy also affect the couple's other networks. Both Vera and Jake enroll in a Lamaze class at a nearby college, and Vera looks through her old child psychology notes. In terms of vocational changes, Jake requests a promotion at work and Vera inquires about maternity leave from her job. They immediately access the professional levels of their ecology by joining a pregnancy support group and by finding an obstetrician. As Vera becomes more visibly pregnant, she begins to sense compassion and approval from her church and from strangers on the street—representatives of the society–culture ecological level.

JUNCTURE 2: BIRTH OF A CHILD

This initial sequence of ecological changes culminates with the birth of their son, Timothy. Timothy, being a full-term, seemingly healthy infant and a product of a normal delivery, gives Vera and Jake no cause to suspect any disability or impairment and certainly no reason to suspect congenital deafness. Timothy seems to develop on schedule and according to the predicted developmental milestones. This scenario is certainly common for parents of deaf infants, for deaf infants display the same kind of sensorimotor and babbling behavior during the first 9 months as hearing infants (Mindel & Vernon, 1971, 1987a). It is during the period from the infant's birth to approximately 18 months that issues of basic trust versus mistrust take on primary importance (Erikson, 1968).

Naturally, all parents go through normal developmental crises attendant on the birth of a new child. There are suddenly three people in the family, not two. Parents must demonstrate their abilities to nurture and supervise a child. The distribution of time, energy, and space in the family is altered. For the first year or so, parents can be said to be in crisis; that is coping with major changes, not the least of which is a change in sexual life and in the redistribution of family roles. Because this juncture is extensively described elsewhere (i.e., Walsh, 1983), it is not elaborated here. However, it is important for the clinician to understand later crises that the parents will face and the many adjustments they must make in the context of these normal developmental crises. The clinician must know in what type of soil the diagnostic seed was planted.

JUNCTURE 3: SUSPICION

Freeman et al. (1981) noted that, prior to 1955, parents, on the average, first became suspicious that there was something wrong with their profoundly deaf infant when the infant reached the age of 10 months: The diagnosis was finally confirmed, on the average, approximately 10 months later when the infant was 20 months old. Currently, with the advent of more sophisticated medical technology to assist in the diagnosis of deafness in newborn infants and the increased education of pediatricians about congenital deafness, the situation is somewhat improved. However, even with current biomedical advances and increased awareness, there frequently appears to be a significant lag time, often 6 months, between the time parents first become suspicious that there is something wrong and the time deafness is finally diagnosed (Mertens, Suss-Lehrer, & Scott-Olson, 2000). Newborn audiological screening will undoubtedly improve this situation.

It is often the mother who first acknowledges that there is something wrong (Freeman et al., 1981). She may notice that the child is not responsive to her. Partly, her reaction will depend on her own imagery of how a mother should be and on her general degree of competence (the psychological level). For example, she may take her infant's lack of auditory responsiveness as a sign of her own inadequacy. However, her reaction will also depend on the responses that those close to her—chiefly her husband, her parents, and close female friends—have to the child and to her description of the problem. For example, the husband can join his wife in her concern and they can rationally figure out what to do. He can be very anxious about his child if, for example, that was the mode of reacting to unexplainable behavior in his family of origin and escalate both his wife's concern and her fear about her own inadequacy. He may blame her for using incorrect child-rearing techniques and therefore causing the problem. Or he may accuse her of overreacting and "making a mountain out of a molehill."

It is during this juncture that the boundaries between the nuclear and extended families may begin to blur. If the reactions of both mother and father in the nuclear family serve to escalate the level of tension between them, and if the nuclear family system cannot tolerate this high level of tension, then one parent may gravitate toward his or her own parents. In our culture, it is usually the mother who will gravitate toward her parents, as there remains an implicit cultural proscription regarding males expressing dependency needs (Gilligan, 1982). The mother may look to her parents, particularly her mother, for the support and assistance she feels her husband cannot or will not give her. If the mother was viewed by her parents as competent while growing up, for example, the type who took care of others and performed well in the world, then the mother's parents might simply take what she says at face value. They might join her in reasonable problem-solving activity and be sympathetic toward her anxieties. If, however, the mother was a dramatic child, one who expressed many of the family's anxieties, whom the family thought reacted too strongly or hysterically to situations, then they might discount her concern and invalidate her. Or her parents might be split, with the mother taking her daughter more at face value and the father discounting his daughter's concern. In the latter case, the mother's concern about her baby simply triggers the normal organization of alliances in the family, leaving mother with some resources and not others. There are many possibilities.

Let us return to Vera, Jake, and Timothy. Vera notices Timothy's lack of responsiveness when he is 8 months old. She initially feels as if she is doing something wrong, begins to feel quite inadequate, and then reasonably but anxiously wonders about how well her son can hear. She expresses her concern to her husband, who is tired and a little disinterested in his wife's constant monitoring of their child. His irritability also relates to increased work pressures "It costs money to have a baby!" At first, he tries to reassure her: "Oh, things are fine; they'll all work out." When she does not respond to his reassurances, he feels helpless and slightly incompetent to console his wife, and expresses these feelings to her by becoming a bit angry and by discounting her concern. After this sequence repeats itself several times within a few weeks, Vera becomes more focused and obsessed with Timothy, whereas Jake becomes more focused and obsessed with his work. In this manner, Vera and Jake escalate their conflict in symmetry with each withdrawing and taking turns trying to outdo each other, much like a game of ping-pong.

Jake, in a desperate, last ditch effort to mollify Vera, and because he is secretly a bit concerned himself, proposes an experiment. He proposes that they sneak up behind the baby and yell or bang pots. Both agree to this experiment, and to their relief, Timothy responds. However, in actuality he responds, not to the auditory stimulus, but to a fleeting image of the pots and pans that he catches via his peripheral vision and to the vibrations he feels from pot banging. The parents, not knowing this, are reassured.

Timothy, however, still seems unresponsive and Vera's sense of inadequacy grows. Moreover, it is important to note that Vera has not yet returned to work, and therefore finds herself cut off from the invaluable support of work friends, and she has not taken any coursework at school. She feels increasingly isolated and frazzled. Consequently, she begins to turn to her mother for comfort. Jake becomes more anxious, shows growing impatience with her worries and tends to stay away from her. He becomes more involved with his work and begins a ritual of "Friday night poker with the guys." As this sequence continues, Vera becomes more and more involved in a vigilant, close, upsetting, often angry relationship with Timothy, and increasingly allies herself with her mother and with a few close female friends. Hence, a schism grows between the parents; they begin to become more different than alike. Thus, at this time we see the emergence of a family organization around the deaf child who is not yet labeled deaf.

A few months later, Vera, no longer reassured by the homemade tests for deafness, perhaps spurred on by friends or simply provided the opportunity by a long-planned well-baby visit, raises the question urgently to the pediatrician. After Vera shares her concerns with the pediatrician, he proceeds to ring a bell on both sides of Timothy who indeed appears to respond. Having heard similar concerns from many "overanxious mothers," he then reassures her and recommends that she join a mother's support group.

The pediatrician's discounting of Vera's concerns is best understood as an inadvertent intervention into the ecosystem, much like someone accidentally kicking an anthill and disrupting its internal organization. The impact of the pediatrician's intervention in this system serves to exacerbate the growing split between Vera and Jake. Jake feels angry and vindicated, "See, I wasn't being an uncaring father and husband. And you were being an alarmist." Vera reacts by feeling confused and less self-confident than ever. Although she too is aware of feeling angry, she does not feel justified in expressing her anger to anyone. After all, everyone seems to be acting in good faith. The doctor did say that there is nothing to worry about.

There is one other important aspect at this juncture. Vera's visit to the doctor can be understood as her aligning with the professional level of her ecosystem (pediatrician) whereas disengaging from her husband within the family ecosystemic level. This is the first time that the doctor or any health professional has been consulted about the deafness. Although the pediatrician's advice has exacerbated the split between Jake and Vera and has served to promote an alliance between Vera and her mother, in no way can one say that at this time, the physician is an integral part of the ecological system around Timothy's deafness. This will happen later on. Doctors, school systems, and others will become integral to the ecology of deafness for Timothy. At this juncture, however, the physician's involvement is minimal.

As Vera's level of anxiety rises, Vera sees her friends significantly less because she feels a little embarrassed in front of them; they had admonished her to stop worrying so much about Timothy. She finds herself feeling embarrassed even in front of Jake. In general, Vera is afraid that she is using up her welcome with many significant persons within her family and informal network levels of her ecosystem. Vera does not return phone calls from her friends; the informal "let's compare our children" routine has been quite painful for her.

However, Vera can find solace with Audrey, her own mother. As is often the case, Timothy's grandmother is not bound by what Jackson (1965) referred to as "family rules," in this case, the implicit family rule to "avoid mentioning concern about Timothy." Audrey is freer to bring up what has become a taboo topic. Thus, at this time, Vera's vigilance and concern for Timothy, temporarily squelched by the pediatrician and her husband, now gets resurrected by Audrey. Audrey is quite concerned and now moves to a closer position to Vera. (Vera's marriage to Jake had temporarily estranged mother and daughter.)

It is important to note that Vera and Audrey were becoming more the parental pair than were Jake and Vera. Vera and Audrey decide that "their child," now 18 months old, is developmentally delayed or retarded. From observational evidence, this appears to be the case; after all, there is so much restriction of information that Timothy receives from the environment, especially because no one is taking his hearing deficit into account. He is not developing speech at all. He is acting a bit "hyper" and seems to be "in his own world."

In reaction to feeling excluded by his wife and mother-in-law, Jake now becomes more than irritated. He is also quite fearful of Timothy's developmental delay. In his fear and anger he blames his wife for their child's slow development. He often comments on how Vera coddles Timothy, how she spends too much time with him, how Vera cannot let him act independently, and how Timothy therefore cannot grow up. Jake does search for evidence of retardation, mental illness, and so forth in Vera's family; and when he cannot find any clues, he begins to fear it may be his own genes. This is a difficult time. The family schism widens and intensifies. The coalition of Audrey and Vera against Jake takes form, as well as the enmeshment among Audrey, Vera, and Timothy.

JUNCTURE 4: DIAGNOSIS

Vernon & Andrews (1990) reported that "it is surprising to most people that children's deafness is rarely discovered until they are between 1 and 3 years old." At that time, the mother, grandparents, or occasionally friends may persist in noticing that something is wrong. In any case, a referral to the audiologist eventually occurs. It should have occurred soon after the visit to the pediatrician when the infant was 7 or 8 months old, but it is often delayed until a later period (Mertens, Suss-Lehrer, & Scott-Olson, 2000). To get up the gumption to go to the audiologist, Vera has had to work up a good anger and has had to defy her pediatrician. This is certainly an act of courage in a culture that virtually deifies doctors. (Vera is reacting against the dictums–beliefs imposed by the cultural ecological level.) Gregory (1976) observed that:

> Most mothers interviewed had thought that their child was deaf long before it was officially confirmed ... On the one side, you have the professionals emphasizing the importance of early diagnosis and early auditory training, and on the other hand, mothers feeling there is something wrong with their child and help not being forthcoming ... It is hard to admit one's child is deaf, and harder still to maintain this position against the "experts." (pp. 148, 156–157)

More than 25 years later, Pollard and Rinker (2001) echo this theme and address the effects of conflict within the professional network and its effect on parents:

> When deafness in a child is diagnosed ... parents have a myriad of questions, all of which seem critical but inadequately answered by the 'specialists.' ... Passions in the deafness field run high, especially regarding communication and educational methodologies. Few specialists remain truly objective. Many thrust their opinions on parents before they are ready to digest them or consider the alternatives carefully. Parents often express consternation at how deafness experts disagree but seem so sure of their individual opinions. This is a fair assessment of an impassioned and divisive field.

When the audiologist finally makes a firm diagnosis of deafness, there emerges a split-image of physicians, the good doctors and the bad doctors, the helpful doctors and the doctors who "didn't take me seriously." This split frequently becomes an enduring part of a family imagery, and therefore becomes a very powerful guide to action in future years, setting the stage for interacting with all professionals.

This is a very painful and complex juncture for the family. It can be a reparative experience for many couples, who had been disengaged during the previous period, too young and too much in crisis to withstand the stresses of having a disabled child. In Jake and Vera's case, they can come together during this period, can grieve and forgive each other and others. Even their anger can unite them, joining them now in a coalition against the pediatrician or potentially against Audrey (e.g., almost any mistake on her part can be used by the couple to repair the generational boundary that had broken down when the couple was fighting with each other). Alternately, they may react in anger against God (the cultural level of the ecology) whom they have come to deem as unjust. In fact, the integrity of the family, the completion of developmental stages and other dilemmas can be repaired and restored at this juncture. For clinical purposes, this, perhaps more than others, can be a tremendously important and fruitful place for intervention.

Before continuing to describe the diagnostic crisis and this particular family's response to it, the major events one is likely to see at this point are briefly summarized.

Parental (Grandparents) Grieving

Parents obviously have dreams and hopes for their children. It also is clear that these dreams and hopes, as well as the anticipation and actuality of bearing and raising an infant, fulfills basic self-esteem needs for parents. Thus, the traumatic news that their child is impaired means to parents that satisfaction of many of their own dreams and needs will be thwarted, often termed as *narcissistic injury*. Grieving is a normal and appropriate response to this crises. Although the grieving process is vitally important, it is not elaborated here. Instead, the reader is referred to extensive descriptions of grieving provided by Schirmer (2001); Allen and Allen (1979); Featherstone (1980); Greenberg (1983); Mertens, Suss-Lehrer, and Scott-Olson (2000); Luterman (1979); Moses (1976); and Thompson, Thompson, and Murphy (1979).

Parents also may grieve for reasons other than narcissistic injury. Although in our present culture it is becoming somewhat fashionable to be skeptical of professional service providers (as suggested by rising medical malpractice insurance rates), nevertheless, most parents expect their own doctor to do a perfect job. In this case, there is a transferential kind of relationship between doctor and patient in which the patient trusts the doctor much like a child implicitly trusts his or her mommy or daddy. Thus, for these parents, the news of deafness precipitates a painful letdown. They may view their infant's impairment as caused by the doctor: She or he "allowed it to happen." The infant becomes symbolic of the doctor's betrayal. Furthermore, the labeling of the cause of deafness as *etiology unknown* in as many as 50% of the cases (Moores, 1987; Vernon & Andrews, 1990) exacerbates parental fantasies of blame toward both the doctor(s) and themselves.

It is, however, important to acknowledge that parental grieving due to a loss of respect for particular professionals may have nothing to do with transference but may be a realistic appraisal. Because many physicians work under time pressures that limit the duration of direct patient contact (Bloch, 1985; Dym & Berman, 1986), parents may correctly perceive the physician(s) as rushed and insensitive. Moreover, as Katz (1984) noted, "Physicians are well trained to attend caringly to patients' physical needs. [However,] their education has not prepared them to attend caringly to patients' decision-making needs" (p. 130). He further noted that "Physicians rarely acknowledge the 'common vulnerabilities' that are part of our legacy of the human condition. Consequently, doctors retreat behind silence … make patients feel disregarded, ignored, patronized, and dismissed" (p. 120). Although this situation has recently improved somewhat, it is often, but not always, the case that physicians have undertaken years of specialized, reductionistic training to diagnose and treat problems, but have not received training in dealing with inevitable disabilities, particularly in communicating and working through those inevitabilities with those who are most affected (Christie-Seely, 1984; Dym & Berman, 1986; Katz).

Physicians may compensate for feeling the anguish of their own frustration by minimizing the problem to the parents (Mindel & Feldman, 1987). For example, a physician might reassure a parent that "the infant can certainly learn to speak and understand you … with a good lip-reading education, all will be well." Others may discuss potential of not yet developed cures, such as cochlear implants or new surgical techniques (Christiansen & Leigh, 2002).

Let us not forget grieving as a reaction to a sudden, unexpected increase in financial stressors (Moores, 1987). It costs money to fund various diagnostic procedures, to buy hearing aids and other technical devices, to take time off from work to attend medical appointments, and so on. Moreover, there is a higher incidence of physical illness with deaf children, particularly during the first 2 years of life (Freeman, 1977; Vernon & Andrews, 1990).

During this period, there is often a good deal of doctor shopping in an effort to either confirm the diagnosis or to find a cure (Pollard & Rendon, 1999; Schlesinger, 1972; Spencer, Erting, & Marschark, 2000; Vernon & Andrews, 1990). The degree to which people engage in this activity depends on the degree of the disability, on the resources available, on their own capacity to cope with the loss, or their own inclination to deny difficult realities. It also partly depends on the views and resources of grandparents, friendship networks, and of course, prevalent cultural–medical myths about what is and is not curable and how virtuous it is to cope with or to fight the fates.

Let us return to the family. Vera does grieve, although her first reaction is one of relief that she was not crazy, that she did understand her child, and that she was not hysterical or inadequate. The diagnosis of deafness vindicates her. At the same time, it is an invalidation of Jake's position and he loses leverage in the couple's relationship as a result. He has the opportunity to apologize first and then to really join with Vera and to mourn with her. However, when he begins to do so, the anger Vera had built up against him during the first 18 months bursts forth. Her anger mixed with his vulnerability to feeling attacked and incompetent in the relationship and his fear of his own strong feelings of grief cause him to pull back. So for a brief period, Vera and Jake alternate between moments of shared grief, closeness, enraged fighting, and renewed distance. This period of instability, with intermittent closeness and distance, is what makes this juncture an ideal place for intervention.

Vera and Jake do not do a great deal of doctor shopping. They are inclined to believe what the experts say. When the audiologist says that Timothy is deaf, they believe her, and she becomes a vital member of their ecology from that moment on. Few, if any, important decisions are made without the audiologist's considerations. When she later becomes unavailable by moving to another city, the entire family system is thrown off balance for several months until a substitute, a psychologist, is found—not so much to play the role of audiologist, but as an expert with credibility throughout the family—to balance the family's tendency toward schisms.

As a reaction to the instability around him, Timothy's behavior becomes very obstinate which, in turn, precipitates more parental schisms and conflict. In Timothy's case, the "diagnostic crisis" occurs during the developmental period of "autonomy versus shame and doubt" (Erikson, 1968; Schlesinger & Meadow, 1972). Thus, as expected, he asserts his autonomy and power in reaction to external controls or lack of controls around him. However, the family around him is ill-equipped to adequately negotiate issues of autonomy and power because, in some ways, the marital unit is struggling with the same issues.

JUNCTURE 5: ENTERING SCHOOL

For parents of hearing children, choosing a school is routine and usually dictated by the town or city in which the family resides; however, this is not so for parents of deaf children. These parents find themselves sucked into what seems like masses of institutions and bureaucracies, including various individuals who do not "talk to each other," who are in active conflict, or who simply do not know about the other. The parents' ecological field also immediately and dramatically expands to include may more representatives from the educational, professional, and cultural–subcultural levels. As an example, depending on the particular town and state, parents may meet the Local Education Agency (LEA) coordinator, director of special education, speech therapist, teacher of the hearing impaired, mainstream coordinator, program director, interpreter–tutor, educational psychologist, other parent groups, consumers of educational services, other deaf students, and so on. Consequently, it is common and understandable to see continued or exacerbated parental grieving as an appropriate response to the sheer multitude of people and the intimidation therein.

However, prolonged grieving can also be in response to the plethora of conflicting and dire warnings made by members of these ecological levels; warnings that "if you don't do so and so with your child, awful things will happen." As Moores (1987) stated, "[parental] decisions typically are made in the face of conflicting professional opinion, appeals to emotions, predictions of failure and 'threats' if the right advice is not followed. Opinions usually are presented in either—or terms, and the earlier sown seeds of guilt, shame, and recrimination may come to fruition during the process" (p. 139). This situation has not appeared to change significantly today (Lane, Hoffmeister, & Bahan, 1996; Spencer, Erting, & Marschark, 2000).

For example, a parent may meet a teacher of the hearing impaired from School A who directly or indirectly criticizes a teacher of the hearing impaired from School B. In part, such conflicts and tension have to do with the political oral–manual controversy or the American Sign Language versus Signed English communication controversy that is concretized for parents as needing to decide on a particular kind of educational program with a particular communication methodology. These controversies have been extensively described by Marschark, 1997; Lane et al. (1996) but are not elaborated here.

It is important to realize that the controversies about communication are only part of the story. The impetus for competing programs and competing ideologies is political and based on monetary considerations of each school district. The intense competition for students often has the flavor of commercials for household products. Thus, parents often feel quite anxious, may experience loyalty conflicts with respect to different program representatives (i.e., "but he was so nice") or between the state residential school and a school in their local district. Professionals, like salespeople, may attempt to parent the parents (the consumers), that is, "your child cannot 'survive' without our program." Here, both the process and content of the professionals' behavior are not helpful. The parents, clearly under a great deal of stress intermixed with uncertainty, may regress, feel infantilized, and invalidate themselves in favor of elevating the status of the professionals. Thus, this complementary relationship may be mutually established by both involved parties.

Moreover, in choosing a particular school placement, parents must simultaneously choose (a) a particular communication methodology (Mayberry & Wodlinger-Cohen, 1987), (b) a particular view about deafness and deaf people, and (c) a particular set of role expectations from the school about how and when they raise their child (Bodner-Johnson, 1986; Lane et al., 1996; Marschark, 1997).

Communication

Terms such as *oralism, total communication, sign language, manual communication, American Sign Language, Ameslan, American Sign Language, ASL-based, Sign Exact English, SEE2, SEE1, Pidgin Sign English, PSE, Cued Speech, Simultaneous communication*, and so on, all refer to different modes of communication that may be used in the classroom as a medium of teaching (Lane et al., 1996). These terms are often vaguely defined and often intimidate and confuse parents. For example, a father, when asked if he had any questions about his son's Individualized Educational Plan (IEP), responded negatively in an assured manner. It was only during a later individual psychotherapy session that he asked for the meanings of several terms having to do with communication. In this regard, Lane (1980) and Lane et al. (1996) emphasized how the use of language is purposely or inadvertently used to negotiate power relationships between persons. In structural family therapy terminology (Minuchin, 1974), we can say that many representatives from the educational ecological level come to exert a dominant position within the hierarchical relationship with parents, with parents in the subservient position; as if it is agreed that the professionals can "parent better than the parents."

View of Deafness and of Deaf Persons

Deaf refers to a cultural, linguistic minority, to a particular community, to a particular set of attitudes, beliefs, norms, and to a sense of pride to be part of this culture. In contrast, *deaf* also refers to a medical condition of not being able to hear well (Padden, 1980). A *deaf* person may or may not be part of the *Deaf* community; it depends on his or her attitude and stated identity (Hoffmeister, 1985). As Freeman et al. (1981) put it, "deafness can either be a difference to be accepted (*Deaf*) or a deficit to be corrected (*deaf*)." This dichotomy has profound implications for parents when they must choose a school that expounds one of these views of deafness. For example, at a seminar for parents, one mother proudly exclaimed that "School A taught my son to function beautifully in the hearing world ... few people notice he is profoundly deaf. He lip-reads and speaks almost like a hearing person!" In contrast, another mother retorted, "School B taught my daughter to be proud of her deafness, to be part of the Deaf community, to join organizations like the National Association of the Deaf." Finally, another mother enjoyed her child's abilities to travel in both worlds.

Role of Parents

Residential programs clearly assume most, if not all, of the day-to-day parental functions. Day programs only assume these responsibilities for approximately 8 hr per day, Monday through Friday. However, the unspoken apportioning of parental responsibilities between parents and school often has little to do with the explicit residential or day program schedule. As Bodner-Johnson (1986) noted, many programs are unlikely to make an organized, systematic, and continuing effort to join parents by asking for their input and providing informational evenings, and so on. Instead, they may or may not make a token effort by sponsoring an annual get-together of some sort. The tacit message here is "we do not need your involvement" and "we have given up on trying to get your involvement." Alternately, there are many schools that implicitly or explicitly seek parental involvement and cooperation and make an ongoing, concerted effort to establish more of a team relationship.

In addition, schools may communicate expectations to parents about how they should interact with their children at home (Bodner-Johnson, 1986). Most often, this has to do with a recommended or mandated mode of communication at home. An "oral program," for example, recommends–mandates to parents that they exclusively use speech and speech reading at home to communicate rather than using sign language or gestures. These programs may expect the parents to assume more teacher-like responsibilities at home, namely to help teach speech to their deaf child as additional reinforcement of what is being taught at school (Mulholland, 1981). Similarly, programs that use one form of manual communication in the classroom often recommend–mandate to parents that they use manual communication at home (Moores, 1987).

It becomes clear that parents' abilities to choose a school is dependent on achieving a particular stage of resolution of the grieving process; stated differently, a parent's interface with the educational level is dependent on his or her individual functioning within the psychological level, which, as we have seen in Jake and Vera's case, is related to the family context. School is properly viewed as an extension of the parental relationship, as an extension of home. Thus, parents naturally enlist the aid of a school to augment their efforts toward properly raising their child. Their hopes, fears, and anxieties about their child will therefore, in part, determine their evaluation of the school program and of the teachers within it.

Let us return to the family. As Timothy moves through the developmental years characterized by issues of "Initiative versus Guilt" (Erikson, 1968; Schlesinger & Meadow, 1972), both parents spend much time discussing which kind of school Timothy should attend. After sifting through several brochures, they become more confused than when they started: They ask "what is morphological development, what are visual–motor integration skills?" and so on. Vera finds out through friends about an early intervention program for parents of recently diagnosed deaf children. She asks her husband to attend an introductory group with her. Jake, sensing that his role as father has been revalidated, agrees.

The meetings are held at 10 a.m. every Tuesday. Jake and Vera attend one of the meetings and find that it consists mainly of mothers. Although the group is certainly friendly and courteous to Jake, he, nevertheless, feels awkward and subsequently becomes aware of frequently looking at the clock. He soon drops out of the program, while Vera elects to remain and also elects to invite her mother for "companionship." The women learn more about deafness. They ventilate problems and do problem solving together. They facilitate each other's mourning process. They help each other cope with the realities of raising a disabled child. At the same time, they make the reality more "normal" and palatable. Thus, it is clear that the original two-person subsystem of mother and father has not only expanded to include a third person, namely Audrey, but has also differentiated itself into two subsystems: (a) Vera–Audrey, and (b) Jake. This has come about as a result of inappropriately porous boundaries between the nuclear and extended family ecological levels.

It is important to underscore how the ecology has inadvertently contributed to this dysfunctional structure by thwarting a deviation in the patterns that showed promise of re-uniting Jake and Vera as the primary parents. Coppersmith (1982) indicated that schools may inadvertently support a dysfunctional family structure by accepting the mother as representative of the family. For example, the scheduling of "parent" support groups during the daytime hours is, from my experience and that of Mindel and Feldman (1987), fairly typical. In spite of recent changes within the cultural level resulting in both wives and husbands working outside of the home, most mothers of disabled children work in the home while the fathers work in vocational settings away from home (Mindel & Feldman).

In Vera's case, for example, she has not yet returned to her previous job and has no immediate plans to do so. Furthermore, neither Jake's idea of manhood, nor the business world in which he works, supports the value of his taking off from his work to go to these groups. Consequently, in effect, Vera and Jake are dealing with a different child because their own psychological experience of that child are so vastly different. Jake has not yet properly worked through grieving issues, whereas Vera is well on her way to doing so. The support group also inadvertently reinforces and rigidifies a split or coalition with Audrey and Vera against Jake. Thus, as with most families, it is not surprising that Vera's sign language skills are superior to those of Jake (Mindel & Feldman, 1987).

Jake and Vera agree that Vera and Audrey will visit all of the schools within a 50-mile radius of their home to look them over in person. After visiting several schools, Vera and Audrey decide that "total communication," including sign language, is best for Timothy, whereas Jake, instead, supports oralism. Night after night, the debates continue, now with Audrey firmly entrenched in her role as parent. Vera agrees with Audrey that "sign language will improve Timothy's intellectual and social functioning." Jake counters by saying that "yes ... but it's a hearing world." Vera and Audrey win the debate. In spite of some professionals advocating that they indeed made the correct linguistic decision for Timothy, that total communication is preferable to oralism, Timothy's ecology has evolved to encompass markedly dysfunctional relationships within and between several levels of the biopsychosocial systems. In this respect, Timothy loses.

While in school, Timothy continues to make consistent academic gains, and negotiates the developmental issues of "industry versus inferiority" (Erikson, 1968; Schlesinger & Meadow, 1972). Throughout his elementary, junior high, and high school years, he is placed in both mainstreamed[2] and self-contained[3] classes and, beginning in the local junior high school, often uses a note taker and an educational interpreter. He also receives weekly speech therapy. Intellectually, he is quite bright, testing in the 90th percentile on performance, nonverbal scales, and in the 50th percentile on verbal scales, both compared with hearing persons.

However, Timothy is distraught at home and at school. At home, he acutely notices that Jake spends increasing amounts of time "at work" while Vera would remain at home and, in Timothy's words, "find things to do." One of Vera's more frequent activities is to help Timothy pronounce words correctly. This not only helps Timothy develop good speaking skills, but provides Vera with a raison d'etre and a substitute for Jake. Although, for Timothy, this activity provides a way to join Vera in her loneliness for Jake, it nevertheless is fraught with much frustration and lacks intrinsic meaning for him. Furthermore, as Jake does not sign and Vera only inconsistently signs, Timothy is linguistically lost at home; he is unable to literally understand most of the conversations (Liben, 1978; Moores, 1987; Rosen, 1986).

At school, he continually feels socially frustrated as he has no real friends. Although the teacher in the mainstream classroom is linguistically accessible to him vis-à-vis an interpreter, the social chit-chat in the class-room is communicatively beyond his reach as is the lunchroom, recess, hallways, bathrooms, and the like. Very few peers approach him to talk, although occasionally someone might tease him. Timothy, unable to discern more subtle verbal social gestures, frequently acts in a manner that prompts further teasing, ridicule, and ostracism. Issues of "identity versus identity diffusion" (Erikson, 1968; Schlesinger & Meadow, 1972) become anxiety laden for him. Lacking intimate friends from whom to formulate a coherent sense of selfhood, his identity becomes diffuse and psychologically fragile. As a way of compensating for his interpersonal anxiety and his lack of social skills, he retreats by reading voraciously and by achieving high academic grades.

---

[2]*Mainstreaming* refers to the range of integration of the deaf/hard-of-hearing student in a hearing academic setting.

[3]*Self-contained* refers to an academic environment that includes only other deaf/hard-of-hearing students.

JUNCTURE 6: POSTSECONDARY PLACEMENT

Graduation from high school in the United States has long been recognized as a pinnacle event, not only for the graduating student, but for his or her nuclear and extended family. The graduation ceremony represents a concrete acknowledgment of the student's academic success and, by implication, the parents' childrearing success. It is a time when indicators of achievement become most prominent; hence terms such as *cumulative grade point average, percentile rank in the class, high honors, cum laude*, and so on. In North American culture, graduating from high school is also a time when the adolescent may leave home for the first time to attend postsecondary training or college. Thus, this time signifies both an endpoint of precollege academic accomplishment and a beginning point of transition to institutions outside of the family.

The child is faced with saying goodbye to a familiar academic environment and structure, including "security blankets" such as knowing the location of classrooms, the teachers who are easy to lip-read (in the case of a deaf–hard-of-hearing child), and the location of the best sub shop hangouts, and so forth. The child also leaves behind a familiar academic structure, including the comfort of knowing the rules for proper behavior and consequences for breaking the rules; for example, skipping classes, getting caught smoking in the bathroom, cheating on tests and the comfort of a consistent schedule for classes, breaks, lunch, and the like. Finally, and often most important, the child leaves behind high school friends. In as much as many graduating students boast of "finally leaving my school and parents," this overt relief often masks covert terror and a need to resist change (Malmquist, 1978).

This transition can be a time of joy and renewed freedom for parents: "Finally he or she is away and we don't have to...." Alternately, if the function of a child was primarily to regulate and stabilize his or her parents' marital relationship—perhaps by serving as an object of detoured marital conflict (as described by Minuchin, 1974, & Minuchin, Rosman, & Baker, 1978) or by remaining enmeshed with one parent—then this transition is likely to precipitate marked tension, fear, and anger, and to disrupt the marital relationship (Haley, 1980). This is one example of what is commonly called "the empty nest syndrome." This crisis has been extensively described by many clinicians, such as Haley and Perrotta (1986).

This transition can be much more difficult for the deaf child and his or her family (Pollard & Rinker, 2001). A deaf child in the midst of negotiating developmental issues of "intimacy versus isolation" (Erikson, 1968; Schlesinger & Meadow, 1972), the anticipation of leaving a familiar situation in which he or she feels competent may feel reminiscent of many previous circumstances that were communicatively inaccessible and therefore that were confusing, unpredictable, and often terrifying. As Rayson (1987a) noted, "particularly if the [deaf] adolescent has been shy or inept socially, the disappearance of a ready-made social world is devastating" (p. 93). Consequently, the deaf adolescent may react to the impending change by becoming overly rigid, reclusive, and depressed. If this mode of defense against anxiety proves inadequate, he or she may react by losing all controls (i.e., by excessive drinking, partying, or promiscuity).

As we have seen, fear of change is also frequently an enduring part of a family's imagery. Many families are easily able to recall countless instances when the outside world abused or neglected their deaf child. Consequently, for these parents, letting go is experienced as synonymous with participating in the abuse–neglect; it may be more difficult, guilt laden, and painful than for parents of a hearing child. These emotions may be exacerbated or mitigated by how competent or ready the parents perceive their child to be. For this reason, indicators of success at this transition often play an even more prominent role for parents of a deaf child than for hearing families.

In addition, academic success may be viewed by parents as the "fruits of their labor," as the outcome of "years and years" of academic and speech training at home; or, if their child had attended a hearing, mainstream school, indicators of success at graduation may represent "how well our child can make it in a hearing world." In a sense, many parents interpret the final academic standing of their child as a "final report card" of their own efforts (Combrinck-Graham & Higley, 1984). In this manner, many parents who receive news that their child reads English at a level similar to a 9-year-old hearing student, the average reading level for deaf students who complete a secondary educational program (Quigley & Paul, 1986), react with acute feelings of failure. Other parents view themselves as failing because of acutely perceiving their child as "emotionally immature." This news of academic and emotional standing is often either ignored–denied by parents or not communicated by teachers. Thus, around the time of graduation and the final report card, many parents experience heightened disappointment, anger, or sadness–depression over thwarted expectations. Consequently, at this time, it is not unusual for parents to re-experience all of the vicissitudes of the original grieving process which had occurred after the diagnosis of deafness.

Back to Timothy's family. Audrey had died after a long bout with cancer as Timothy entered his senior year in high school. This event had destabilized Jake and Vera's disengaged relationship that had previously been balanced by Audrey and Vera's emotional proximity to each other. Because Audrey was no longer available as a buffer between Vera and Jake, they found themselves thrust together in renewed affective contact. Although they could have utilized this crisis as an opportunity to repair and consolidate their relationship, both felt too filled with feelings of bitterness and betrayal. Jake glibly remarked that "it's water under the dam," but privately felt ill-equipped to admit that he had also participated in maintaining the marital schism. Vera, not yet recovered from Audrey's death, felt scared to reach out to Jake for emotional support, "lest he also leave me." Thus, Vera and Jake fought more and become more overtly depressed. Moreover, since Audrey's death, Jake had been going out more and more with "buddies" on Friday nights, frequently arriving home intoxicated.

Timothy's graduation from high school can be understood as isomorphic to Audrey's death 1 year earlier; now, Vera and Jake find themselves not only without Audrey as a marital buffer, but also without Timothy. Although the graduation ceremony is a happy event for them because it affirms Vera's hard work in tutoring Timothy, Jake and Vera unexpectedly experience tension between each other. Timothy, in turn, finds himself feeling strangely guilty during the graduation party that his parents have for him. When he things about his plans to attend college, his sense of guilt increases. Unable to understand or to reconcile these feelings, he thinks to himself that he must be afraid of college and that he simply might not be ready for it.

It is in this frame of mind that Timothy enters a liberal arts college for deaf students. At college, he finds a peer group in which he feels comfortable and accepted as an equal. In earlier years, in spite of having achieved laudable academic grades as a mainstreamed student, he had felt socially ostracized and therefore inferior; but "here, everybody is Deaf!" Moreover, there are no strict rules "like at home." His sign language improves, he gets drunk with his friends for the first time, and he meets a "cute" coed.

However, Timothy has a nagging awareness of whom he is leaving behind, namely his parents. It might have been different had his younger brother, Chuck, gotten in some trouble or had needed extra help in school: then Chuck could have taken over the role of marital buffer. The family structure would essentially have remained the same. However, Chuck is doing quite well in school, is extremely popular, and gives his parents no cause for concern and therefore no outlet for detouring their marital conflicts and estrangement.

Counseling at college focuses on helping Timothy develop better study habits, and provides a supportive context for him to express how he is adjusting to a new and strange environment away from home. However, when he returns to school after occasional weekend visits home and after vacations, he is more depressed than when he had left. School remains scary and his grades are in decline. The more depressed he becomes, the more he parties. Soon, he is expelled for poor grades, and he returns home.

At home, both Jake and Vera help him obtain vocational rehabilitation counseling toward formulating a training goal. At this point, Jake finds an opportunity to move in closer to his son in a context that is familiar to him—namely the world of work. Vera appreciates his input. Their marriage be comes restabilized. Timothy enrolls in a computer training program toward certification as a computer programmer.

JUNCTURE 7: MARRIAGE

At the age of 26, Timothy got married. Timothy's case, his marriage to a deaf woman, Theresa, can be understood as isomorphic to his departure from home to attend college 6 years earlier. Both events represent Timothy's efforts to individuate from his nuclear family and both threaten to precipitate a marital crisis between his parents. The wedding ceremony symbolizes a potential shifting of his loyalties from his parents to his wife. In this regard, it is significant that Timothy, as do 95% of deaf persons, chose to marry a spouse who also is deaf (Schein & Delk, 1974; Vernon & Andrews, 1990). Both Timothy and Theresa share a common culture and Sign Language. Although Theresa, having attended a residential school for deaf students, is much more proficient at American Sign Language than Timothy who had only been briefly exposed to it while at college, he quickly picks it up from Theresa. Thus, their culture and language are different from that of Vera and Jake. Timothy's marriage to Theresa represents, in part, a conscious and unconscious attempt to individuate from his nuclear family, to delineate an appropriate boundary around his marriage, which would in large part exclude his hearing parents.

However, as much as the stage is set for this shifting of loyalties, Timothy himself resolves to mitigate a marital crisis between Vera and Jake by remaining primarily loyal to them as opposed to Theresa. In addition, he is scared of the responsibility of becoming "husband and wife," of "supporting a family" (he does not expect Theresa to work), and of raising children. As he had done previously in preparation for college, he tells himself that he is not ready. Thus, although he physically leaves home following the wedding, he psychologically remains very much a part of his nuclear family as a child. Vera and Jake live only a few blocks away from Timothy and Theresa whereas Theresa's parents live over 500 miles away. Timothy calls his folks frequently on the Telecommunication Device for the Deaf (TDD), asking for advice on everything from financing options to choosing good restaurants; he even goes so far as to ensure that his wife is cooking and doing laundry "correctly" by requesting a second opinion from Vera.

There is also a unique hitch in this scenario. Because Timothy cannot use a phone without a TDD, he frequently requests that Vera either interpret telephone calls for him or make them herself. In addition, Vera often attends doctors appointments with him to interpret. Notwithstanding that Vera can neither sign or interpret, which kept important information inaccessible from Timothy, this further strengthens the enmeshment between Timothy and Vera.

It becomes apparent that, despite the unique aspects of interpreting and communication with Timothy, the family structure and patterns of interaction are similar to the family structure that characterized the previous generation; the earlier triangle that encompassed the enmeshment between Audrey and Vera and disengagement between Vera and Jake now repeats itself with enmeshment between Vera and Timothy and threatened disengagement between Timothy and Theresa. Although it is tempting to exclude Jake, who after all seldom visits the young couple, as one of the participants who supports this dysfunctional structure, nevertheless it is important to note that the marital schism between Jake and Vera influences the overinvolvement of Vera with Timothy. As illustrated in Fig 2.1 the more distance Vera feels from Jake, the more she moves toward Timothy and the more Jake moves toward work and his cronies.

There is a lot of friction between Timothy and Theresa at this time. In part, this is due to expected developmental stages attendant on building a new marriage, such as the negotiation of power, intimacy, and autonomy. However, as Jake had felt 3 decades earlier, Theresa feels slighted by her spouse and mother-in-law, and expresses her discontent. As their conflict increases in intensity, Timothy, like Vera, becomes overwhelmed, scared, and disenchanted with the marriage; he moves more toward Vera.

JUNCTURE 8: BIRTH OF AN INFANT (SECOND GENERATION)

It is during this juncture that developmental issues of "generativity versus stagnation" (Erikson, 1968; Schlesinger & Meadow, 1972) are negotiated. After 3 years of marriage, Timothy and Theresa become the proud parents of an adorable hearing infant, whom they name John (most deaf adults have hearing infants, which largely depends on the etiologies of deafness; Vernon & Andrews, 1990). They wanted a hearing child who would have access to those parts of the world that had been inaccessible to them. As outlined earlier with respect to Jake and Vera, the normal crises and stresses that couples typically experience in reaction to having a child are important destabilizing influences at this juncture. However, in the case of Timothy and Theresa, the destabilizing impact of their newborn infant is augmented by their dysfunctional marital relationship.

FIG. 2.1 Spatial map.

There are many possibilities of how the system will adapt. This stressor may trigger more dysfunctional changes in other systems levels, via what is termed *deviation amplifying feedback loops* (Umbarger, 1983). For example, Timothy may become depressed, Theresa may begin neglecting John, Vera may bring in an outside professional to provide evaluation or assistance, and so on. On the other hand, the disrupting impact of the stressor may be mitigated by becoming assimilated into preexisting dysfunctional structures via "deviation countering feedback loops" (Umbarger). Timothy and Theresa may deflect their marital struggles by one or both of them excessively coddling the newborn infant throughout his development or by increasing the degree of enmeshment between them and Vera, much like what had occurred in the dysfunctional structure of Audrey, Jake, Vera, and Timothy in the previous generation. Finally, the system may restabilize itself at a new and more healthy level; for example, the crises may prompt Timothy and Theresa to repair their relationship and to establish more functional boundaries around themselves to limit the degree of contact with their extended families. Here, there is bonafide structural change. There are many possibilities.

However, in this case, John's birth triggers the families of Vera–Jake and Timothy–Theresa–John to become more enmeshed, and the boundary that had functioned earlier to provide some autonomy for these two families now virtually disappears. The following recursive sequence becomes an enduring context that supports continued marital discord between Timothy and Theresa as well as ineffective parenting of John. As with any recursive cycle, we can arbitrarily begin at any point. John cries, misbehaves, and needs caretaking. Theresa responds in a manner that she deems fit. Timothy, feeling unsure of whether Theresa's action is correct (defined by him as in agreement with Vera), requests advice from Vera. Vera either supports Theresa to Timothy or informs him that Theresa is incorrect. Either way, Theresa get wind of this exchange, feels excluded and invalidated by Timothy and Vera, and becomes angry. The tension between Timothy and Theresa triggers John to become anxious and to cry more. This, in turn, triggers Theresa to take care of John, as Timothy is often away at work and had learned from his parents that it is "a woman's job to take care of the kids." And the recursive cycle begins again!

Timothy, like Jake before him, establishes a supportive social network to avoid the family strife. He is elected to numerous offices in the local deaf club, joins various sports leagues and frequently goes out with friends when not at work. Theresa, meanwhile, does not have a support system, feels isolated, and begins to doubt her competency both as a wife and mother. She does not share these self-doubts with Timothy or her in-laws, as she perceives them as colluding against her. Instead, Theresa finds herself becoming angry at "the stupidest things," such as a television show being preempted. Moreover, she experiences premenstrual syndrome, which greatly reduces her tolerance for stress at regular monthly intervals. She has always had somewhat of a problem handling excessive amounts of stress, which professionals had attributed to a residual effect of her mother contracting rubella during the first trimester of pregnancy, also the reason for Theresa's deafness.

Thus, the biopsychosocial context is established for child abuse (Sgroi, 1982). During one particularly stressful time, Theresa excessively and uncontrollably slaps John. Immediately following this incident, the collusion of Vera with Timothy against Theresa, now labeled as "the abuser," is more firmly established. Although the state Protective Services Agency properly charges Theresa with physically striking John, nevertheless, from a systems perspective, this action is very much entrenched in the ongoing patterns that had begun several generations ago. So in effect, everybody within this dysfunctional system is a victim.

JUNCTURE 9: ONE'S PARENTS DYING

The death of one's parents inevitably precipitates many crises at different systems levels (Crosby & Jose, 1983). Grieving certainly occurs. Psychologically, one's own mortality becomes immediately concretized as an inevitable reality; it can no longer be denied. All of one's enduring infantile dependency needs are either transformed into reliance on oneself or are simply redirected toward a parental substitute. Ambivalent and conflictual feelings toward the deceased parent abruptly come to the forefront. The deceased parent's estate is divided among the family heirs, a process that is either facilitated or confounded by the legal system. Family relationships that had been dependent on the deceased parent are renegotiated, such as in the case of pseudo-alliances that had been maintained "to make mom or dad happy." Alternately, new family relationships may finally be permitted to spring forth.

Timothy is now 42 years old. Because he had never individuated from Vera, her death forces him to face a profound sense of emptiness and loneliness that he had not felt before. He feels ill-equipped to make financial decisions—"What is life insurance?"—and to access medical and social services without Vera to serve as interpreter. Jake's death several years earlier did not have the same traumatic impact, and in fact, only served to increase Vera's involvement in Timothy's family. Now, Timothy feels abandoned and therefore impelled to reconcile his estranged relationship with Theresa both as marital partners and as parents. Although Theresa could have been available at this time to reconcile her marriage, to share Timothy's grief, and to help solve the tasks ahead, Timothy long ago had made a decision that Vera would be the primary figure in his life and that any wife would be relegated to a distant second place. Theresa therefore withdraws.

At this time, Timothy's previous routine of drinking beer on Friday nights now becomes an almost daily ritual of consuming hard whiskey; whereas Theresa, in turn, carries him upstairs to bed many nights. To feel competent, "more like a man," and to get his life back together, Timothy begins to assert himself by maintaining a rigid stance of what is "right," a value that he implicitly defines as whatever is in opposition to Theresa. Thus, they begin to argue much more about a variety of issues, such as rules for John, household tasks, the amount of time that Theresa is not at home, and about the optimal degree of extended family member involvement (Theresa's parents are now visiting more often).

As with previous junctures, the destabilizing effects of this juncture represent an opportunity for Timothy to mature and for the couple to consolidate their relationship. However, Timothy begins to regularly visit his aunt, Vera's younger sister Wendy, and requests the same kinds of interpreting assistance and advice that he had requested all along from Vera. (Wendy had coordinated Vera's funeral, incidentally, without the inclusion of an interpreter.) She now visits Timothy and Theresa, frequently on an unannounced basis, and purchases a TDD. Here, the system, which had been destabilized by Vera's death, quite quickly reequilibrates with Wendy serving the same function as had Vera. The intergenerational patterns will endure until the equilibrium within the ecology can be sufficiently destabilized so as not to continue providing a context for symptomatology.

3

Life-Span Development of the Hard-of-Hearing Ecosystem

It is a common error to minimize the psychological effects of a moderate hearing loss as merely quantitatively less than that of deafness, assuming that being hard of hearing is simply "less deaf" or that it is "almost hearing." On the other hand, as Ashley (1985) stated, it is also common for the hearing public to use the word *deafness* as an umbrella term to cover all forms of hearing loss. Although there are approximately 14 to 17 million hard-of-hearing persons in the United States (Schein & Delk, 1974), training programs, workshops, and large conferences purporting to address issues of "deaf and hearing-impaired persons" too often solely address issues of profound deafness (Diedrichsen, 1987; Schein & Stone, 1986).

In an effort to distinguish the special needs and characteristics of hard-of-hearing persons, an international organization called Self Help For the Hard of Hearing (SHHH) was founded in 1979 by Howard Stone. The preamble to the SHHH constitution reads,

> We are people who do not hear well, but are not deaf. We tend, increasingly, to be isolated. The existing pattern of community life lacks both means of communication and institutions for us to solve our special problems and live normal lives. For too long, too

> many of us have accepted a loneliness we are unable to explain to our friends or even to our families. (Stone, 1985, p. 156)

Delineating the unique characteristics of hard-of-hearing persons in an ecological context has important implications for clinicians who treat this population. This chapter is one step in that direction. It presents a clinical vignette that highlights the developmental stages of a family with a hard-of-hearing person named Joyce, presents additional transcripts from hard-of-hearing persons that highlight common clinical issues, and outlines how such persons may be similar but unique relative to profoundly deaf persons.

Like Jake and Vera in chapter 2, Jerry and Barbara and the extended family structure around them acted and reacted to the birth of their apparently normal infant, Joyce, to the times of suspicion that something was wrong, and to the eventual diagnosis of Joyce as hard of hearing at the age of almost 3. Although their grieving was not as severe as was Jake and Vera's, Jerry and Barbara were devastated by the diagnosis in much the same way. The qualitative form of grieving for parents of a newly diagnosed infant with a moderate hearing loss is the same as the qualitative form of grieving for parents with a newly diagnosed deaf infant (Pollard & Rinker, 2001; Roberts, 1984). Such parents experience all of the vicissitudes of narcissistic injury and the resultant changes in relationships with family members, friends, and professionals that were described in chapter 2. Although these effects may be quantitatively less intense than those in reaction to a diagnosis of profound deafness, it is naturally experienced as traumatic.

There are, however, some important differences that occur at the inception of a family system in which there is a diagnosed hard-of-hearing infant in contrast to what occurs at the inception of a family in which there is a diagnosed profoundly deaf infant. Jerry and Barbara, like many parents of recently diagnosed hard-of-hearing infants, were immediately and repeatedly told by physicians and audiologists what Joyce was not. "At least she is not deaf," they were reassured. The professionals described in detail the marked differences between profoundly deaf and moderately hearing-impaired persons but did not take the next step to explain the implications of a moderate hearing loss per se. In this vein, Jerry and Barbara were given clear assurances from physicians and from other parents of hard-of-hearing children how fortunate it was that Joyce would develop English language skills, have intelligible speech, make good use of residual hearing via a hearing aid, and function in the hearing world "unlike many deaf kids."

The content of these predictions was well founded. Because hard-of-hearing persons have a significant amount of residual hearing, speech and speech reading training has a much higher probability of success than with profoundly, prelingually deaf persons (Moores, 1987; Ross, Brackett, & Maxon, 1991). This provides eventual ego gratification for parents in contrast to endless years of frustration for many parents of profoundly deaf children who do not achieve oral–aural proficiency.

However, this can be a double-edged sword. It is frequently easier for parents of hard-of-hearing children to deny, in a nonadaptive manner, possible and inevitable implications of the hearing loss. The ramifications of a 50 db loss are less noticeable for the family; a hard-of-hearing person not only can hide more effectively than can a deaf person with a 90 db loss, but can more easily act as if he or she is hearing; can develop a pseudo identity as a hearing person. For example, one father was shocked to learn that his hard-of-hearing, adolescent son could not keep up with the dinner table conversation, exclaiming "but he lip-reads so well, and he is able to do beautifully when I talk [directly] to him!" Often overlooked is the fact that one-to-one, direct discourse with appropriate lighting, facial features, minimal background noise and other environmental accommodations, is usually adequate for effective communication. However, group situations, epitomized by the dinner table, frequently prove to be formidable linguistic barriers (Moores, 1987). Inevitably, the parents of a hard-of-hearing child discover, often many days, weeks, or months later, that their child did not know information had been discussed (i.e., that "cousin so and so had cancer"). Too frequently, such parents deny the true implications of this phenomenon, or genuinely do not know, and attribute it to the child's "failure to pay attention."

For Joyce's parents, as with Jake's parents in chapter 2, the diagnosis of hearing loss also provided them with a challenge, a raison d'etre. Jerry and Barbara, both having grown up poor and having worked since a young age, subscribed to the "if you can't do something, try harder" theory of life. Consequently, like many families in which there is a disabled member, Joyce's family organized itself around her hearing loss (Power & Dell Orto, 1980). Joyce's hearing loss became the focal point, an all-encompassing challenge and irritant that colored every-day activity and that took precedence over experiencing the frolic and spontaneity that, in part, characterizes healthy families. In particular, as with Timothy's family, it was Barbara who took on primary responsibility to teach Joyce to speak and speech read effectively, to "make her normal," to protect her from more harm other than already being hearing impaired, and so on. Speech training and pep talks became a well-established norm. This ongoing activity was, in part, reinforced by Joyce's noticeable progress and by a unified educational support system around Barbara and Joyce, in marked contrast to the educational controversies around communication methodology that beset parents of newly diagnosed deaf infants.

In view of the nodal position in many families that hearing loss plays, it seems ironic that the hard-of-hearing family member may also feel neglected. However, many hard-of-hearing clients report that their family would frequently avoid communicating with them: "After I asked them to repeat themselves a few times, they began to give up talking with me. It became too cumbersome for them." Similarly, an "off-the-subject" comment by a hard-of-hearing family member may be discounted or ridiculed. This phenomenon has also been described by Harvey (1998, 2001) and Schlesinger (1985) who noted that "speaking with persons who have sustained a hearing loss requires extra expenditures of energy. Such fatigue imposes stress on friends and family members and can contribute to the isolation of a hard of hearing person" (p. 109). Similarly, Ashley (1985) noted the instinctive tendency of hearing people to turn and talk to those who can hear rather than to those who cannot.

In this regard, it is important to note that frequently a person(s) attempting to communicate with a deaf–hard-of-hearing person share the handicap. The nondisabled person may become frustrated at not being understood by the disabled person or not understanding the disabled person; thus, each person is handicapped with respect to each other. However, the nondisabled person can remove him or herself from the handicapping situation and thus sigh with relief at becoming normal.

It addition, the phenomenon of many hard-of-hearing family members feeling rejected by a parent(s) also appears to be a predictable consequence of a parent(s) taking on the almost exclusive role of teacher–trainer–habilitator. As one mother put it, "after all day of taking advantage of each and every opportunity to teach him [her 9-year-hold, hard-of-hearing child] to speak correctly, I am exhausted, and I find myself shrugging him off when he doesn't understand me the first time." Similarly, one father admitted that "after a while, I don't feel like catching him up on the conversation."

The other major arena for a child's psychosocial development is school. In order to illustrate its influence, let us return to Joyce. In school, Joyce always had a vague awareness that "I was a bit off," that "there was some barrier between me and the other kids." She recalled once joining her classmates in a conversation about trucks; "when I entered the conversation, everyone looked at me weird, and then I discovered that they were talking about neighborhood parks. The other kids were not surprised, as they always knew I was different—stupid or something."

However, in contrast to how Joyce felt, the teachers were quite impressed with her. Speech therapy helped her to speak clearly, in her teachers' words, "almost exactly like hearing students." The audiologist reported that she made excellent use of her residual hearing via hearing aids and that she had an excellent English vocabulary. In summary, Joyce looked hearing. Her teachers consistently praised her tenacity, motivation, and ability to "be like all of the other [normal] kids" and prided themselves that they did not treat her special.

Perhaps what was most traumatic for Joyce was that she did not clearly understand why she was "a bit off" at school or why she misheard some conversations. Phrases like "hearing loss" or "hard of hearing," although occasionally mentioned in her home, were never thoroughly discussed, only alluded to and then with a nonverbal message to deny its reality. So when Joyce came home from school in tears because of feeling, in her words, "two steps behind," her mother admonished her to "try harder, you can do it," although she secretly feared for her daughter. The more Barbara feared that her daughter would remain "two steps behind" or, even worse, fall further behind, the more she and Jerry together insisted to Joyce that "you can do it" and recited Horatio Alger stories.

Consequently, for Joyce to openly admit and even insist that she was having trouble coping in school would be to disappoint both her parents and teachers. It would have also been a statement to her mother that she did not try hard enough. So Joyce adopted a strategy of hypervigilence, of trying her best to speech read or to pretend to understand. She became a very astute observer of peoples' expressions—she laughed when they laughed, sighed when they sighed, and so on. Nodding her head became habitual for her, whether or not she indeed understood what she was nodding at. She recalled one instance at home when her grandmother mentioned to her how beautiful the birds' singing sounded. Joyce emphatically agreed, in spite of not hearing any birds. Another frequent occurrence at home was the battle over the volume of the television; Joyce would turn it up "too loud" and her brother and sister would turn it down. Finally, Joyce gave up and left it at a volume that was convenient for her family, but that she could not hear; she pretended, lest "I disappoint my family." It soon became most important for Joyce to receive positive validation from other persons, even at the expense of her own development.

Sullivan (1953) posited that anxiety reduction is a primary motivation factor for human behavior. For Joyce in particular, as well as for many hard of hearing clients who report that they often pretend to hearing people that their hearing loss presents no problem (Harvey, 1998, 2001; Levine, 1981), anxiety reduction became the modus operandi. Rather than assertively attempting to conversationally participate in discussions (i.e., by asking for clarification) hard-of-hearing persons may feign understanding of what is going on around them to save face and to reduce the likelihood of being singled out or labeled by others (or by themselves) as dull or stupid. In addition, in an effort to reduce anxiety and to avoid being discovered not understanding the conversation, one may overcompensate by never shutting up. The more one talks, the less chance of getting caught at not following the conversation. These defensive maneuvers, although often successful on a short-term basis to reduce anxiety, frequently, on a more long-term basis, elevate the level of anxiety that "my bluff will be disclosed and I will be embarrassed."

In addition, to reduce anxiety, one may habitually avoid group situations such as meetings, concerts, dances, and social situations in which one must cope with the acoustic barrage of many persons simultaneously (Orlans, 1985). A poignant example is contained in the following excerpt from a letter sent to me by a 22-year-old hard-of-hearing woman:

> I consider myself well adjusted to my hearing impairment. I have fully accepted the loss and am aware of the limitations it poses on my communicative functioning. Yet my tolerance for having to sit back and observe rather than participate in a group conversation continues to lessen. I feel I am beginning to withdraw from certain social situations to spare me the inevitable frustration that develops. This scares me tremendously, for I am a young (22 years old), single, active, people-oriented individual. I am always interested in developing new relationships and strengthening old ones. But this is becoming more and more difficult.

As another example, consider the following transcript of a teaching demonstration interview that was conducted with a 68-year-old, hard-of-hearing man named Warren Hanna[1]:

Client: Even today, Mike, I have to fight today to go to a party, to go to a meeting. I really have a battle with myself. I still haven't overcome that.

Therapist: Can you talk about the battle? What the battle is all about?

Client: Well, I have a very excellent female friend that I've been dating for 15 years. She's very aggressive socially, or can be very aggressive socially, but she's very aware of my feelings in spite of the fact that she doesn't understand hearing loss. And often times, she'll say someone's going to have a cookout or a party and that they asked if we would like to come, subject to my okay. And this would, say, be 2 weeks away. I'd say, sure, fine, no problem. But as the hour drew closer, I would tend to get a little bit negative, to the point that I would become almost depressed by the fact that I had to go to this thing, and who wants to go to such a time-wasting thing anyway. You know, you just sort of create a black picture out there. And in going, actually, I, for the most part, enjoy it, sometimes very much. I tend to handle it for the most part, but not as easily as I'd like to.

As avoidance becomes more frequent, it may insidiously lead to chronic isolation and withdrawal which, in turn, may precipitate clinical depression (Ramsdell, 1978) and a variety of psychosomatic symptoms. In some cases, hard-of-hearing people who seek therapy have a history of medicating their depression with alcohol or other drugs that provide temporary respite but clearly exacerbate the problem. Others react to this self-imposed isolation and its resultant depression by contemplating or attempting suicide.

---

[1]I would like to express my appreciation to Warren Hanna for allowing this transcript to be included.

Individuals employ a wide array of defensive strategies to deal with anxiety or uncomfortable feelings in addition to avoidance (Ramsdell, 1978). Hard-of-hearing persons may externalize and personify their hearing loss. For example, one woman viewed her hearing loss as an "it," "as an uninvited intruder, a force that makes the world mumble and therefore impossible to hear." Another person described his hearing loss as "an interloper in my midst, and I fear no power on earth can remove him."

The fervor and high level of anxiety associated with speech reading in some ways seems greater for hard-of-hearing people than for many deaf people. Many profoundly and congenitally deaf people, having experienced since birth the insurmountable task of fully understanding spoken English, are often a bit more resigned to this limitation and, if the sound is emanating out of eyesight, sometimes do not know that they are missing conversation. In contrast, hard-of-hearing people, who have more residual hearing and who are better able to speech read, are more aware that they are missing discourse. Many hard-of-hearing clients have reported that "I almost understood what he was saying, but not quite, and felt like I was banging my head against a wall." The more one knows what he or she misses, the harder one tries; the harder one tries, the harder it becomes. It is a task that is only partially successful. Again, another transcript from the interview with Warren Hanna illustrates the subtleties of communication barriers as well as the emotional reactions associated with incomplete communication:

Client: I feel I can't cope with conversations. I feel that if—for example, I was having lunch the other day with a friend. We were talking about hearing loss, the other person had a more severe loss—it was a deaf person, actually, even though she was in the hard-of-hearing world. And she, like others, thinks I do great. I can go out and do all things I want, because I seem to function well. But I pointed out to her that, look at the table next to us, where there were like possible 8 or 10 fellows sitting around eating and talking and laughing. And I indicated to her that I couldn't participate in that type of environment. At first she really didn't understand it, but it's that kind of thing—when people are talking, it isn't just the words. You're tying together the many things in that communication process. You're tying together the situation itself; you're tying together the moods, the way something is being said; you're tying together body language; you're tying together innuendos—it all comes together as a communication process. If you're trying hard to hear, you miss out on a lot of these more subtle aspects of the communication. And even though the group—you may have heard every single word that was said, people can laugh and you're really saying to yourself, "what are they laughing about?"

Therapist: And you feel [uses the sign for inadequate]?

Client: You feel down here; you feel left out. Constantly you feel left out in one way or another.

Therapist: And the more you on the words, you ignore other aspects?

Client: Well, I think you only have so much capability. And if you concentrate in one area, it reduces your capabilities in other areas.

Therapist: Then what happens?

Client: Well, if you just start hearing the words, as I have had happen to me, people would say to me, "I was telling a joke," Not being able to pick up the innuendos or the tone, all I heard were words, and I didn't catch the impact of the joke. It's not too different than when a comedian tells a story and he builds the story up to a punch line, and tells the punch line, and almost invariably they say that at a high speed. The words come out rather rapidly. Now, if you're a hard-of-hearing person, you might say "would you repeat that again?" But he won't want to repeat it.

Therapist: Because it's lost.

Client: It's gone. The emotion that he has built up has gone entirely. And the words are just part of what the process is. I'm inclined to believe that part of the reason that we don't get the sympathy—that's a lousy word—understanding, is because everybody at some point is hard of hearing. It's true that people don't hear at cocktail parties, but they only miss like 20%. You're missing 90%, you know. But they understand it, and they think that when you say nobody hears, they're only talking about 20%. I think that tends to apply in many areas. If you start to say to somebody "I don't hear well," they'll say, "That's no problem. I have that difficulty, too." And they can't really realize the impact of you're not being able to follow that flow, that total communication package thing.

It becomes clear that hard-of-hearing people expend much energy focusing on the lips of people to maximize speech reading effectiveness and to meaningfully participate in conversations—in short, to integrate and affiliate with others. Speech reading takes attentional priority. As a result, pervasive and profound physical and mental exhaustion is commonplace (Wax & DePietro, 1984). Furthermore, I have sometimes observed that constriction of one's visual field, "I have to watch his lips," is accompanied by a similar constriction of one's psychological field, which includes creativity, fantasy life, and solo interests. For example, one hard-of-hearing client reported that "before I became hard of hearing, I had all kinds of hobbies, now my only hobby is taking lip-reading classes or doing things by myself." As a consequence, along with physical and psychological fatigue, the experiences of frustration, powerlessness, and fear are quite common.

In part, as a consequence of these emotions associated with speech reading conversations, one's abilities or perceived hearing sensitivity may actually worsen (Luey, 1987). To continue with the transcript of Warren,

Therapist: You mentioned earlier something else which many people are not aware of—that the more stressed you feel, the more you can't hear. Could you talk more about that, about how emotional factors make you hearing problem worse?

Client: Well, I don't think that it's a mystery at all. It's very simple. As I said earlier, it's a total communication process. There's not just the words. If you say something—let's say I'm using that word east. We don't take up the letter S easily, and it's easy to misconstrue that to be "eat." You might say something and say "east" and I might construe it to be "eat," and it sounds like "eat" and I have no reason to question that you said "eat," until a little farther down the road in the conversation something happens, and then I'll say, "My goodness, something's gone awry here. I didn't hear something, but I don't even know what to ask you to repeat, because that's gone, the part I missed." Then I may sort of admonish myself or say I've got to watch the words harder, watch the words. And I will concentrate on the words. By concentrating on the words, now I've reduced my sensitivities to the other aspects of the communication—the body language, the tone, the innuendo—these other areas where people normally pick up all of these things without realizing that they're taking it all in and unscrambling it and taking it for what it's meant.

Therapist: So you start off feeling left out, you focus on the words, but then that makes you feel more left out? You miss more?

Client: That's right!

Therapist: And then what happens?

Client: Well, I think as this develops you start to feel uncomfortable, you feel tense, you mind starts to wander into other things, you start to block. You're nodding "yes" but you're thinking about other areas, trying to get some comfort from the situation, but also wishing you weren't there, that you could get the hell out of the situation.

Therapist: Get the hell out.

Client: Get the hell out—be where you can relax and enjoy yourself.

Therapist: And then when you feel left out, what do you say to yourself about yourself? What's the feeling that goes with it?

Client: I don't think there's any internal communication except that I'd like to get the hell out of here.

Therapist: The reflex is to get the hell out?

Client: And why did I come here in the first place? But if I can, one of the strategies that I do try to use is to take one individual and talk to him, and maybe I can survive that way. Or if I can't do it here, in that physical set-up, I'll try to get him off to one side, off to one corner, and then I can communicate there. However, if the background noise changes even ever so slightly, it sends me through the roof!

Therapist: So part of it is almost a gut feeling of survival, the way you're describing it?

Client: Yes.

Therapist: It's being put in a situation which feels very overwhelming, impossible, and "let me get the hell out of here?"

Client: Yes. That's right. I relate it very much to—you know, Mike, I've done a lot of scary things in the war, I've had a lot of experiences, and the fear that a person can suffer from hearing loss is just as great as anything I have ever known, truly.

The strategy of coping or dealing with hearing loss has obvious implications for the development of self-concept. Theories of cognitive-behavioral therapy (Beck, 1976; Dobson, 1988) elucidate that cognitions influence emotional functioning, including self-concept, and behavior. For example, many hard-of-hearing persons, such as Joyce, report feeling embarrassed at home and at school for "not being with it." In general, this fear of embarrassment, manifested as habitual hiding, frequently becomes cognitively distorted and thus justified as needing to hide something, often in reference to an unacceptable part of oneself. As Joyce put it, "I notice myself hiding a lot. It almost seems, after years of doing this, that I have something awful to hide. It must be my deficit, or my stupidity, I hide, therefore I must be deficient."

Or, to reconcile the reasons for frequent pretending to understand conversation, I have observed many clients operate in accordance with the following cognitive algorithm:

People who lie are bad:
I lie about understanding people;
Therefore I am bad.

After several repetitions, the conclusion of "therefore I am bad" becomes functionally autonomous (Allport, 1961): "I am bad because I am bad." One then accumulates evidence to support this self-attribution of badness: "I am bad because I did X, Y, Z, and so on." Finally, as language becomes more advanced, the word *bad* gets replaced by more "grown-up" words, such as "(I am) unsophisticated, dumb, ugly, inept," and so on.

At the same time, this negative self-attribution gets reinforced by others and thus becomes one step of a recursive sequence within the ecology. As was stated earlier, it is an unfortunate truism that many hearing people, children, adolescents, or adults, often lose patience when asked to repeat themselves and to accommodate the special needs of another. Thus, the additional algorithm,

> I am bad (or other negative attributes),
> because other people react to me as bad;
> Therefore I must be bad.

Perceived inadequate support from family, friends and the larger cultural context can have profound effects on one's self-esteem, as exemplified by the following letter:

> "I'm a middle-age hard-of-hearing woman who has coped pretty well over the years. Lately, however, I've found myself becoming much more irritable with hearing people who don't seem to care! It's not so much the obvious kinds of discrimination that bother me—like no captioning, visual alarm systems, etc. It's more the subtle reactions of people: like being ignored or treated like I'm some kind of defect. Frankly, I'm beginning to feel like there's something wrong with me.
>
> Signed, Desperate and Fed Up."

Let us return to the vignette of Joyce. Early in her development, Joyce had been taught to view her world through lenses that made herself appear small and others appear large. The "others," her standard of measurement, had been hearing people; she greatly elevated the competence and power of hearing people, while devaluing her own worth. "If only I was hearing," she remembered saying when she was only 8 years old. She also recalled drawing a picture of herself as 1 inch tall and her hearing peers as about 10 inches tall. Later on in her development, her attribution of omnipotence to hearing persons would become accompanied by scorn and resentment: "I'm pissed off that [hearing] people don't know what I need."

The following transcript from Warren echoes some of Joyce's sentiments:

Client: You see, when you first get a hearing loss, you have what I now know to be a communication problem. And you know, we today, in our society, we revere people who are good communicators. They may be dumb as hell and disorganized as hell and immature as hell, but if they can communicate quickly in a conversation, we put them up on a pedestal until they prove that they're not worthy of that. If you communicate well, you're up on a little pedestal.

And the reverse of that is that if you're not necessarily a good communicator, you tend to be depressed because you have to prove yourself up to that point. And when you don't hear, you're not a good communicator. You can't participate in any of the thousands and thousands of situations that occur, whether it be a joke, a bell ringing, a door opening, or you son saying "please" or "I'm sorry," or your wife making a ca-

> ressing remark—any of these things. It isn't just a case of communication being such that you have a difference of opinion, as much as that the communication gets into the emotional aspects of your relationships with people, and that's when it starts to really hurt.

When Joyce reached the sixth grade in school (age 11), the interpersonal use of language and group discussions took on increasing importance. This represented an important "news of a difference" (Bateson, 1979) that unbalanced or destabilized Joyce's functioning at school. This was a critical juncture, for, in the past, similar feelings of being left out would become easily incorporated into the recursive cycle that included Joyce receiving admonitions to "try harder" from her parents and teachers. Her parents and teachers, in turn, would have felt that they had not tried hard enough to help Joyce try harder.

However, now her teachers and parents began to notice communication problems in the classroom. Consequently, Joyce and her parents first began to wonder whether a specialized deaf school was more appropriate than the mainstream hearing school that she currently attended. In some ways, as with many hard-of-hearing students including Jill in chapter 1, it was as if Joyce "fell through the cracks"—she was not deaf enough for the deaf school (whether it be total communication or oral), but not hearing enough for the hearing school. As another parent commented, "my child is hearing but not quite." This volleying back and forth between considering different types of educational placement naturally precipitated marked anxiety for Joyce and her parents.

Nonmedical professionals (i.e., psycho diagnosticians), assume a greater importance for families at this time whereas medical professionals took on a greater importance in the earlier years. Professionals assume, and are given by families, a certain power to define hearing loss (Bodner-Johnson, 1986). Some professionals view the hearing loss as *figural*, as the primary factor in determining the individual's biopsychosocial functioning. Others view the hearing loss as the *ground*, as only one of several factors, and perhaps a not so important one at that. This dichotomous view is paralleled by the previous description of how large or small hard-of-hearing children draw their ears in proportion to the rest of their body; as an analogy, some professionals "draw the hard-of-hearing person's ears larger than others."

Professionals who make the hearing loss figural make recommendations with the hearing loss taken keenly into account. For example, sign language training or group supportive meetings with other hard-of-hearing persons may be recommended. A specialized school for the deaf may be recommended or, at least, a number of carefully outlined supportive educational services within the mainstream setting. Alternatively, professionals who view the hearing loss as the ground diminish its preeminent importance in determining psycho–social–educational functioning. Indeed, one definition of a hard-of-hearing person is "one who, generally with the use of a hearing aid, has residual hearing sufficient to enable *successful* processing of linguistic information through audition" (Moores, 1987). From this perspective, one may also recommend a regular, mainstream school environment and use hearing norms and standards as the yardstick of academic–intellectual success or failure.

After mulling it over, both Joyce and her parents agreed that she would continue attending her current mainstream school, but with increased support services. After several meetings and negotiations with the school and town, the school agreed to install acoustic tiles, rugs, and new windows in the classroom, all of which would minimize echoing and background noise. An FM system, a special amplification device to maximize Joyce's audio reception, was put in place. Finally, a special note taker was hired who would take all of Joyce's notes in class, allowing her to exclusively focus on speech reading the teachers. Thus, Joyce, her parents, and her teachers felt prepared as Joyce continued attending junior high school. However, as prepared as they were for academic challenges, they were not prepared for the social and emotional turmoil that was to follow.

School, as a forum for meeting peers, becomes increasingly important during adolescence (Csikszentmihalyi & Larson, 1984). For hard-of-hearing adolescents, in particular, it is at this time that issues of affiliation with other hearing, hard-of-hearing, or deaf peers becomes more prominent. Most hard-of-hearing individuals identify with, and emulate, the basic values and interests of the predominant hearing society (Elliott, 1986). This affiliation with the hearing community is a consequence of how well a hard-of-hearing person is able to function in many situations among hearing persons. Communication is often effective in one-to-one situations and in some small groups. Furthermore, hard-of-hearing persons usually develop proficient oral–aural skills and command of English. As Diedrichsen (1987) stated, "Unlike deaf people, we [hard-of-hearing people] have not developed a language (ASL) or a culture all our own. Our primary methods of communication are by using our voice to express ourselves and our hearing, with amplification and visual aids, to receive communication from others" (p. 4).

This affiliation, or "pull to the hearing world," is also a consequence of an aversion to the Deaf community. Insofar as many hard-of-hearing people attribute higher status to hearing people, they attribute lower competence to the signing Deaf community. One hard-of-hearing man summed up this attitude by saying "ASL—what [nonoral] deaf people use—is too simple a language. I can't express my thoughts, I'm smarter than that." One group of hard-of-hearing persons described all deaf people "as more impaired than us." Similarly, one hard-of-hearing adult described his view of the world as divided into "the real world [hearing] and the deaf world."

However, beginning with adolescence comes the background noise of large, informal group gatherings, as well as a plethora of musical events. In addition, the darker the musical or party environment, the better. As one hard-of-hearing adolescent eloquently put it, "I can tell the difference between AC–DC and The Police [both rock groups] but understanding what my friends are saying is a pain in the ass." Stated differently, Levine (1981) observed that "Countless young hard-of-hearing people live in daily terror of being caught in the joshing camaraderie of a hearing group, of being singled out in games, of being called on in class, and, worst of all, missing the 'sweet nothings' whispered into their ears on dates." Similarly, cash registers in stores without a clear visual readout, salespersons, and telephone operators frequently precipitate marked anxiety.

Audiologically, and therefore psychosocially, hard-of-hearing persons can almost become hearing, but not quite. This stark realization usually becomes acute during adolescence when identity issues and negotiation of complex male and female relationships take on primary importance (Malmquist, 1978).

Thus, the "pull" to the Deaf community. Similar to hard-of-hearing persons, Deaf persons have an auditory disability. Both groups often wear hearing aids, may attend speech therapy, and often feel as if they are "missing something" while among hearing persons. Moreover, Deaf people certainly know what it is like to be, in Higgins' (1980) words, "outsiders in a hearing world." However, I am struck by how often the theme of feeling peripheral to the Deaf community emerges from the expressed sentiments of hard-of-hearing people. As much as hard-of-hearing persons cannot easily function in the aural–oral world, they also often have linguistic difficulty functioning in the Deaf world when ASL or some other form of manual communication is utilized. Because many hard-of-hearing persons do not learn manual communication, they experience marked isolation among signing deaf people, more acute than among a group of hearing persons.

Hard-of-hearing persons, from my experience, also seem acutely aware of the distinction made by Padden (1980) and others between either being accepted by the signing Deaf community as a Deaf person (spelled with a capital "D" to indicate membership in the Deaf culture–community), or being accepted as a deaf person (spelled with a small "d" to indicate that one has a hearing loss but is not a member of the Deaf culture–community) (Bahan, 1976). As Nash and Nash (1981) have noted, one's affiliation and acceptance into the Deaf community depends on, among other variables, one's attitudes and stated identity that "I am Deaf" and on fluency with sign language, but not solely on the presence of an auditory disability. Although there are some hard-of-hearing persons who do sign fluently, most report feeling over-whelmed and frustrated when attempting to learn sign language and frequently give up (Diedrichsen, 1987).

Moreover, as mentioned previously, many hard-of-hearing people report feeling "different" from oral deaf persons. One client expressed a common sentiment, "I may be hearing impaired like them [deaf persons], but I'm not *that* deaf." One reason for this phenomenon might be related to fear. Many hard-of-hearing clients fear deaf persons; deaf persons symbolize, or function as reminders of, the possibility of losing more hearing, becoming more impaired, "of becoming totally deaf like them (Deaf community)."

Rather than feeling different, many hard-of-hearing persons, although finding communication easier, feel excluded from oral, nonsigning, deaf groups. One client reported feeling "out of place, like not being included in a clique. I envy [the Deaf community's] togetherness, their support of each other, Deaf cultural events, National Theater of the Deaf, A.G. Bell, National Association of the Deaf, their sense of identity. But I'm not Deaf, so I'm not one of them."

As illustrated in Fig. 3.1, the delicate balance of tenuously striving to function between two worlds, the hearing and Deaf worlds, gives rise to myriad images, thoughts, and feelings. The image of "doors" has frequently been brought up. In contrast to some hard-of-hearing clients describing the door into the Deaf world as "slammed shut," many describe the door to the hearing world as "being left open only wide enough to peek in. I can sort of function in it, but feel ineffective, several steps behind, always catching up."

It therefore comes as no surprise that it is common for hard-of-hearing clients in therapy to have already experienced or to soon discover a significant amount of anger or rage around their hearing loss (Wright, 1983). Their anger may be generalized and nonspecific, as exemplified by a diffuse anger about missing a lot of information and feeling ineffective; or it may be specifically focused on hearing or on Deaf people for "ignoring me, for not giving me enough help," or for "shying away from conversing with me." One client commented that "I find myself blaming my normal hearing friends for not helping me to participate more effectively. 'Why can't they sense this feeling and the frustration and come to my rescue?' I often ask myself. It is getting difficult for me to maintain a healthy attitude and to hang on to my self-confidence in these instances."

FIG. 3.1 Between two worlds.

Negotiating the tug of war between the two worlds has implications for intrapsychic and interpersonal identity formation (Elliott, 1986). For example, as was reported in a previous publication (Harvey, 1985b), an 18-year-old male, hard-of-hearing adolescent initially complained of feeling depressed and not having many friends. During one pivotal point in treatment, I was impressed by how anxious and stuck he had consistently reported feeling. I asked him to imagine that he was standing with his arms outstretched, and that his right arm was being pulled one way while his left arm was being pulled the other way. As he imagined this scenario, he grimaced and exclaimed that "this is how I feel—pulled toward the hearing community while pulled towards the Deaf community, but I am in neither one."

As noted earlier, an individual may express anger by projecting his or her own feelings of awkwardness and self-rejection onto hearing and deaf people and be left feeling socially isolated. However, that is only half the story. There is often a recursive relationship between self-perception and the perception of others; the hard-of-hearing person's own ambivalence is, in part, due to how the hearing and deaf peer groups actually perceive him or her. In this regard, hearing people may mistakenly interpret a hard-of-hearing person's difficulty in understanding conversation or minimal attendance at group functions as aloofness or snobbishness. One hard-of-hearing adolescent reported that "hearing people don't take my hearing loss seriously. They don't believe that I'm really hard of hearing." Many hearing peers feel awkward interacting with disabled peers in general and, in fact, may experience fear—fear that "his or her hearing loss could happen to me." Finally, hearing persons may mock the hard-of-hearing person's speech. This frequently results in confusion and acute embarrassment for the hard-of-hearing person, as his or her speech is usually deemed normal at home, yet is deemed as defective at school. This can result in a split sense of good–bad in terms of sense of self; praise by parents for doing well, but put down by peers for not being normal.

Alternatively, deaf peers may view the hard-of-hearing person as "thinking like a hearing person" and perceive an attitude of superiority— "he is so stuck up." Thus, deaf peers may ostracize hard-of-hearing peers from the "in" group or clique. One reason for this is that hard-of-hearing persons frequently either communicate well orally–aurally or sign relatively poorly via an English-based visual coding system, such as Signing Exact English or Pidgin Sign English, in contrast to many deaf peers who fluently sign either English or ASL and often do not have proficient oral–aural skills. Thus, there are communication difficulties, as well as significant attitudinal differences, from the hearing world.

However, another reason for deaf people ostracizing hard-of-hearing people may not have so much to do with the differences between these two groups per se as it may involve "a third point on the triangle," namely parents or teachers. Many deaf students are repeatedly asked by their parents and students, "why can't you do as well as him [a hard-of-hearing peer]?" Hard-of-hearing students are often used as models for what deaf students can and should do, in spite of the fact that hard-of-hearing persons have a significant audiological advantage.

Thus, it is often the case, beginning in adolescence, that the hard-of-hearing individual ends up with no peer group at all with whom to identify—a disastrous situation to any adolescent who both needs and wants peer-group approval. With informal networks, as in school, hard-of-hearing persons often fall through the cracks. To make matters more difficult, many clients report that hard-of-hearing support groups in the general community are frequently attended by older persons, not adolescents. The process of falling through the cracks—being alienated from hearing, deaf, and hard-of-hearing community groups—influences, and is influenced by, individual psychological factors. It may serve as further evidence to the hard-of-hearing person that he or she is indeed somehow defective.

Joyce entered a mainstream high school. As has been described, she experienced the frustration of trying but failing to feel like a part of the informal discussions that go on in the classroom, and the chit-chat and gossip that would dramatically escalate almost every time the teacher would face the blackboard. Although she used an FM system to help her understand what the teacher would say, none of these special accommodations could help her feel part of the social group. But she kept trying. Her tenacity was a strength that she had learned from her mother. Joyce stayed clear of the deaf program in that school, often referring to it as "the Deaf ghetto." Her bitterness was most evident by her occasional references to "having enough of a problem being accepted without hanging around with them [the deaf students]." She complained that many deaf kids had labeled her by a pejorative sign that literally translates as "think hearing."

In this manner, Joyce, like many hard-of-hearing persons, in the context of familial, informal network, and other ecological factors, chose to primarily affiliate with the hearing world even though she was not solidly a part of it. After graduating from high school, she attended a mainstream, hearing college and only used technological support services, such as an infrared system for lecture halls. She continued to feel somewhat bitter against Deaf people whom she viewed as different, and as having rejected her.

Consider two other examples of hard-of-hearing persons choosing to primarily affiliate with the hearing world. To refer again to the letter that the 22-year-old hard-of-hearing woman sent me,

> I often feel like saying, "to hell with the hearing world, I'll just be deaf (with a small d)." However, since I am unfamiliar with the Deaf culture/community, I would not belong. This, coupled with my fear of isolation from the "hearing world" has kept me struggling to remain in the hearing community.

This woman's sentiments about primarily affiliating with the hearing world are also supported by Warren:

Therapist: Do you get a different kind of understanding from hearing people than from profoundly deaf people?

Client: I have only experienced profoundly deaf people to any degree over the past year and a half or 2 years, and I don't really feel I'm like them. I sense they have a great need. I sense they have a great enthusiasm, but I don't really understand them. I don't know how to relate to them other than to try to be warm, try to be helpful, but that's as far as I can go with them.

Therapist: Someone could say, well, both of you are hearing impaired, so you should have perfect understanding for each other.

Client: I feel that *hearing impaired* is a terrible term. It should never be used, really.

Therapist: How come?

Client: Well, it just confuses two totally different afflictions, and by that process of confusing the afflictions, you can be diluting all your energies, all of your directions, everything that you might be putting into a process to help to cure one thing when you're directing some of your efforts towards another, and causing nothing but a muddle in the process.

Therapist: How do you see it as two different afflictions, personally?

Client: Well, I think the most obvious way is that the hard of hearing are in the normal hearing world. They have to function with whatever is there for them to function with. The Deaf go to the Deaf culture, which is increasingly becoming sophisticated, finding ways to cope with their particular problems.

Therapist: So it's two different worlds?

Client: Two different worlds entirely.

Therapist: Culturally?

Client: Culturally and every other way, yes. Yes!

Alternatively, other hard-of-hearing persons choose to primarily affiliate with the Deaf world. One client recounted his ecstasy at first entering Gallaudet College (before it became accredited as a University) and encountering sign language for the first time in his life. He described this experience as "an awakening, as feeling alive and happy for the first time in my life!" He began to associate with a diverse range of Deaf persons, some of whom were audiologically profoundly deaf and culturally Deaf, whereas others were audiologically hard of hearing but culturally Deaf. In this context, he found a new sense of self, a sense of belonging. When introducing himself to others, he would proudly proclaim that "I am Deaf."

Vocational goals often influence, and are influenced by, one's sense of self. Its psychological importance cannot be overemphasized. For example, after graduating from college, Joyce obtained an entry level position as a programmer in a prominent computer firm. In addition to the normal drives for achievement that characterize healthy adaptations to work, in Joyce's case, it also represented a way of compensating for years of feeling inadequate among her peer group. She stated that "while I may be a bit behind at group meetings and at those after-work social–political gatherings, I am tops at what I do, because it doesn't involve my ears." She thus invested all of her energies into achieving competence.

A similar sentiment about the psychological importance of work was stated by Warren:

Client: At work, I felt confident only because I paid the price for competency. I didn't feel competent at work in terms of social things as they related to work or even in verbal communication things. One of the biggest struggles I had was to build my company big enough that I could hire other people to go to meetings for me, to do what I couldn't do.

Therapist: But what area of work did you feel competent in?

Client: Technically. I was very, very technically oriented. I knew how architects thought, smelled, breathed. Engineers the same; owners the same. And I was an excellent letter writer. I probably am a man of letters of this state. I used to find that if I could draw a conflict into a letter-writing process, 9 times out of 10 I'd win.

Therapist: So you became competent in those areas that were not affected by your hearing problem?

Client: That's right.

Therapist: And I'm going to assume—and let me check this out with you—that it was terribly, terribly important for you to feel competent at those things, particularly when socially, interpersonally, communicatively, you didn't feel competent at all?

Client: That's right. Well, you see, you're drawing into an area that I've never thought much about. I guess that is true. I sometimes have thought that I committed myself to that because I wanted to make money, although I was not a money-hungry person directly. But I guess maybe that is true, that I wanted to feel competent and that was my way of doing it. True.

Unlike 95% of deaf persons who marry other deaf spouses (Schein & Delk, 1974; Vernon & Andrews, 1990) most hard-of-hearing persons marry hearing spouses. Consequently, the normal marital process of negotiating the explicit–implicit rules regarding distance, intimacy, and power that characterize hearing couples, has a slight twist to it when one spouse is hearing and the other is hard of hearing (Sonnenschein, 1987). For example, to continue with Warren,

Therapist: Let me ask you, if I may, about your marriage. You were married to your wife prior to becoming hard of hearing, and during and after it. How does being hard of hearing affect your marriage?

Client: It's strange, but people that are close to you, like my wife, didn't seem to realize you have a hearing problem, really. I don't understand that. If I say to my son, "I have a hard time hearing under this circumstance," he would seem to turn around and say, "Oh no you don't."

Therapist: So your wife would say essentially, "it's no big deal, you can overcome it?"

Client: Yes, that's almost always been the way. It can also be very demeaning too, when we go to restaurants, for her to have to hear the order for me. And at some point, she can get a little tired of that, or a person can, and then make a remark to me. I think what I'm trying to say is that I'm increasingly depending on that person, and that kind of thing tends to build on itself, and then that person will get tired of it and make some remark as if to say "get off my back." It could just be a momentary remark but it can destroy a whole process that may not be right to begin with. But this dependency, nevertheless it's there and it's part of what we consist of, and it can be, I would think, kind of shattering to a person. It hasn't happened to me that much because in most cases I try to do my own thing.

Therapist: But it's tempting to become quite dependent on a hearing spouse, for example.

Client: Oh, yes. Oh, yes. We were out to dinner, a few of the hard-of-hearing people, back some months ago, and this fellow who has a hard-of-hearing problem—I ordered something and he said, "Why don't you order for me?" I thought, "Oh-oh, here we go. This dependency thing." I don't know what I did at the moment. I was thinking more about that than his remark and what specifically was to be done.

4

Treating the Hard-of-Hearing Individual in Context

Mary, a 35-year-old, single, hard-of-hearing woman, recounted the following recurring dream to me during the first session of individual treatment:

> I was leaving my house to take a walk, when suddenly the whole world became a Trivial Pursuit® board and all of the people I met became Trivial Pursuit® cards. And the only way I could continue my walk was to answer the questions on all of the cards correctly. I became terrified, because there was no way I knew most of the answers. Then I woke up in a cold sweat.

For Mary, and for many hard-of-hearing persons in treatment, this dream served as a metaphor for what she wished to change about her mode of being in the world, her presenting problem of anxiety.

Discussing the significance of Mary's dream led to a series of memories about her early childhood, which included developmental experiences such as those outlined in chapter 3. For example, Mary vividly recalled her terror at school when she was asked to play games such as "Concentration®," "Jeopardy®," or "Hollywood Squares®." First of all, she reported, "even if I could understand the teacher (which was not all of the time), I often could not understand the other kids. They would yell out of turn, mumble, or have gum in their mouths." Second, even when Mary could understand what others were saying and could competitively "jump in," she frequently did not know the answers. Although she was average in intelligence, her moderate hearing loss significantly reduced the number of opportunities for "incidental learning" (Moores, 1987; Schirmer, 2001). *Incidental learning* refers to the process of "naturally picking up" information from the environment, which occurs, to a large extent, through the auditory channel, as exemplified by overhearing conversations. Thus, games such as Trivial Pursuit®, which are designed to measure incidental learning, precipitated marked anxiety and feelings of self-deprecation for Mary, and her experiences connected with Trivial Pursuit® came to serve as a metaphor for how she viewed herself and her world.

After describing her dream and her associations to it, Mary outlined her view of her hearing loss:

Mary: It's a constant cloud hanging over me which prevents me from doing so many things with my life.
Therapist: What is the "it"?
Mary: Being hard of hearing, of course!
Therapist: Are you sure? Nothing's that simple.
Mary: (Elaborates in detail how her hearing loss has thwarted her life.)
Therapist: I appreciate all of those feelings, and you are certainly not alone in feeling them. They are common sentiments of many hard of hearing people. But somehow it seems like something(s) is attached to "it," to your being hard of hearing.

One possible goal of psychotherapeutic intervention is to show clients other possibilities for viewing themselves and their world than what they know at present, to challenge their belief systems or epistemologies. In fact, Montalvo (1976) defined *therapy* as "an interpersonal agreement to abrogate the usual rules that structure reality in order to reshape reality" (p. 333). The clinician first joins a client in conveying accurate understanding of his or her would view and then, at an appropriate time, challenges it and attempts to demonstrate the viability of other more adaptive and flexible views. Immediately sensing a therapeutic alliance with Mary, I therefore quickly challenged her by introducing confusion and complexity into her heretofore solid set of beliefs and images around her hearing loss; namely, her view that being hard of hearing inevitably meant remaining incapacitated.

As for many persons, there is no doubt that a severe hearing loss presented real problems for Mary. Moreover, the therapist attempting to deny the enormous impact of a moderate hearing loss is clearly acting counterproductive to treatment. However, hard-of-hearing persons in treatment too frequently accept a wide array of self-deprecatory feelings, beliefs, images, thoughts, and so on, as self-evident truths that are beyond scrutiny. Such cognitive statements have been learned from significant others in the past and often are reinforced by others in the present ecology. They have become internalized as a set of beliefs, assumptions, and images about oneself.

Given that the clinician is able to track the recursive cycle that supports the particular presenting problem, the clinician has distinct choices about at what level(s) to intervene to be most helpful. In Mary's case, neither her family nor significant others were immediately available for intervention. With Mary, however, it was clear that the psychological systems level, her intrapsychic functioning, was the most responsive to therapeutic intervention. First, she reported significant anxiety, and therefore, significant motivation to change. Second, she was new to therapy, and therefore, relatively open to new ideas, as contrasted with someone who has received years of insight-oriented therapy that has become repetitive and that has resulted in minimal behavioral changes. Third, she immediately responded to my initial probes at challenging her internal set of beliefs and images about her hearing loss.

Consequently, I chose to begin systemic treatment by intervening in the psychological level. The specific body of therapeutic strategies or techniques were, in part, derived from cognitive-behavioral therapy (Beck, 1976; Dobson, 1988). The underlying assumption of cognitive-behavioral therapy is that a client's emotional disturbance follows from distortions in thinking, or so called "irrational beliefs." Cognitive distortions influence emotional functioning that, in turn, influences behavior. Consequently, cognitive-behavioral therapy targets interventions toward modifying a client's set of irrational cognitive assumptions or beliefs about him or herself and the world. "Although I was using individual cognitive-behavioral therapy techniques, I was thinking systemically." The systemic perspective posits that cognitive distortions precipitate behavioral responses that then trigger reactions from others: which, in turn, validate and reinforce the individual's cognitive distortions. It is by way of this recursive process that the dysfunctional cycle is maintained. Thus, with Mary, it was vital to track not only the intrapsychic but also the interpersonal effects of my interventions.

After having initially challenged Mary's set of cognitive beliefs and assumptions as represented by her metaphor of "it [hearing loss] is a constant cloud hanging over me," I began to inquire about what internalized connections to being hard of hearing she made and how she learned to think this way.

Therapist: I want to figure out with you how you came to define being hard of hearing as the cause of your problems. For example, what did your friends at school attach to "it"?

Mary: You mean how did they react? They laughed, thought I was "out to lunch" all of the time, when I would answer the wrong question.

Therapist: Did you believe them, that you were "out to lunch"?

Mary: After a while, you have to. I felt reduced to nothing. (demonstrates this with her hand)

Therapist: Yes, and that is what I mean by attached. In a way, you have been taught to view your hearing loss as a "package deal": you being hard of hearing came 'delivered' with being 'out to lunch,' not too bright, stupid. All that got attached, connected, to how you defined your disability. It was as if being hard of hearing also meant being stupid.

Mary: I see. But you know, the fact is much of the world does respond differently to me because I'm hard of hearing.

Therapist: You're absolutely right. And I think many people may have thought you were "out to lunch." But you continue to believe them. That is the part that you can change.

It had become a self-evident truth for Mary that her hearing loss was synonymous with stupidity—being "out to lunch," a conclusion that she correctly pointed out was also reinforced by the culture. Mary had come to see these discrete and unrelated phenomena of "being out to lunch" and of being hard of hearing as one and the same. She did not consciously realize making this psychic connection.

The case of Mary clearly exemplifies the common phenomenon of a disability "spreading" to become a handicap. Wright (1983) defined a *disability* as an objectively measurable medical condition, such as an audiologic impairment; she defined a *handicap* as the experienced difficulties that one has functioning in the environment that may or may not be an inevitable result of one's disability. In Mary's case, her disability was clearly her 50 db hearing loss. However, one of her reasons for initiating treatment was to examine her need to do things perfectly or not to do them at all. She experienced no joy in venturing forth into the world, making mistakes, learning from them, and maturing. Instead, every potential challenge became a test, replete with all of the evaluation anxiety and stress that normally accompanies being put on the line. She thus began to retreat more into herself. This was her handicap. Her audiologic disability was a given; her handicap—her withdrawal and straining to achieve perfection—did not have to be a given. However, up to this point in treatment. Mary unconsciously meshed her disability and handicap together. The disability of a moderate hearing impairment spread to encompass her whole being, her whole mode of functioning in the world. As an analogy, being hard of hearing became a noun for Mary, not an adjective; as if to view herself as "I am hard of hearing," rather than "I am a person who is hard of hearing."

Consequently, Mary had come to view every situation as a critical test of her competence; a chance meeting with a friend at a beach (where she did not wear hearing aids) terrified her—"what if I do not understand what she is saying?" Group situations on the job, social gatherings in (dark & noisy) restaurants and bars—in short, any group event that inevitably is noisy—elicited similar anxiety. Her self-deprecatory cognitions and therefore affective terror and feelings of incompetence became habitual and naturally generalized to acoustically appropriate situations in which she could have easily functioned. Thus, what could have been her modus operandi of being in the world remained that of looking at the world. It was psychologically easier to look at "Trivial Pursuit® cards" rather than to risk "losing the game." This experience is common among hard-of-hearing persons (Harvey, 2001, 1998; Myers, 2000).

To shed some light on how Mary's disability spread to become a handicap, we continue with a transcript of a later therapy segment.

Mary: I guess I can remember many people—my mother, father, teachers, friends—teaching me to make those connections, that being hard of hearing meant being inferior. I read what you gave me about disabilities and handicaps. I had always gotten them confused. So I guess I was taught to feel stupid!

Therapist: What did you do when you sensed that your classmates thought that there was something else wrong with you?

Mary: I tried to find the darkest corner of the room, I guess to hide, sometimes literally, or sometimes just by how I acted.

Therapist: And what did your classmates, teachers do when you hid?

Mary: I guess they felt sorry for me, some laughed, others tried to help, some yelled. I noticed I didn't get asked the difficult questions, maybe they (teachers) didn't want to embarrass me.

Therapist: And when they didn't ask you difficult questions, when they talked louder, what was that like for you?

Mary: I felt reduced to nothing! Really like nothing, really lousy. I knew what they were thinking, that I was some kind of defect. But they didn't have to pity me because I hid in the corner. Shouldn't they have known what was going on?

Therapist: Perhaps. And as you allow yourself to feel angry at your teachers and others for labeling you as handicapped, do you feel yourself becoming stronger or weaker?

Mary: Definitely stronger. Not so down on myself. But down on them, for sure!

Therapist: So you had been taught to make this connection—being hard of hearing is like being nothing, stupid. It is an erroneous connection. But this is only one half of the story. It sounds like you were part of a dance.

Mary: (smiles) What are you talking about?

In the context of our positive, working relationship, it was again helpful to introduce complexity: Namely, that Mary was part of a "dance" that included significant others around her. I have found this metaphor useful as a psychoeducational tool to introduce the tenets of systems theory in treatment. A dance requires at least two partners. One cannot do the waltz without a willing and cooperative partner who coordinates his or her every step with the other partner. Mary had correctly identified one half of the dance, namely situations in which people taught her to view herself in a negative manner. She had punctuated a linear sequence of A causes B; namely that "other people caused me to feel out to lunch." In fact, she was not incorrect, for, as outlined in chapter 1, children in many ways are passively molded by the environment around them to think, feel, and act in certain ways. Mary's early environment molded her to define herself by "connecting" some inevitable disabling effects of being severely hearing impaired, such as not being able to completely follow many conversations, with viewing herself as "nothing." Helping Mary to first realize this connection and many similar kinds of connections that were taught to her, and then to question the validity of these internalized connections, were the first steps towards helping her elevate her self-esteem and her overall sense of happiness.

However, this was only a first step. Although Mary's linear punctuation of causality was not incorrect, it was incomplete. Children, as a function of their psychological development, also begin taking the lead in the dance; they are not only molded but begin to mold others around

them. If the therapeutic work with Mary had stopped when she only consciously realized how others had influenced her cognitive beliefs (their part of the dance), she would have had insight into her psychological development and, in particular, would have been more able to separate the disabling and handicapping effects of being hard of hearing. However, she would not have had many of the necessary tools to help her take responsibility for change in the present. It is also necessary for persons to realize their own part in training others to act toward them in a certain manner.

As exemplified by Mary, one does not operate solely from an internal locus of control or from an external locus of control, but rather a combination of the two; a person continually acts and reacts to the environment that, in turn, continually acts and reacts to the person. It is a dance. Specifically, Mary felt inadequate in school and indeed acted the part: She "hid in the corner." In this manner, people came to believe that there was actually something wrong with her and reacted by showing pity or avoidance: They "looked down at her." Mary reacted to their responses by hiding more. The more inferior Mary felt, the more she hid, and the more people in her environment viewed her as deficient and pitied–avoided her; and, in turn, Mary's perceptions of those peoples' actions prompted her to feel inferior and hide more.

Therapist: You felt like nothing and hid, so your teachers and peers looked down at you, so you felt like nothing and hid. Or we can start by saying that your peers and teachers looked down at you, so you felt like nothing and hid, so they looked down at you. Other people acted; you reacted. Or you acted, and they reacted. In one sense, it doesn't matter which came first, the chicken or egg. Do you think it would have changed the dance between you and your teachers, if you proudly stood up instead of hiding?

Mary: Definitely. But my teachers could have changed their part, too.

Therapist: Absolutely If either person changes, the whole dance changes.

Mary: But as a child, it was difficult for me to change my reactions to people when they kept acting the same towards me, and it's in the past anyway. Hindsight is 20–20.

Mary was correct. However, elucidating the dance in the past paved the way to change the dance in the present. Consequently, at this point, the therapy focused on helping Mary to clarify her insights about how she had acted and reacted with significant persons in her environment in such a way as to spread her disability to become her handicap. Treatment then focused on helping her to utilize those insights to change how she acted and reacted in the present.

Therapist: So back in grade school, you hid in a corner and helped train people how to define who you were. What do you do now?

Mary: I just feel really lost, under pressure.

Therapist: And what do you do to show that?

Mary: I guess I withdraw, sometimes pretend to understand what people are talking about.

Therapist: And how do other people react?

Mary: Hmmm, by not pressuring me too much, I guess, or shying away maybe.

Therapist: I'm impressed with how similar the dance is now to the dance before; and with how you actually train people to look down on you. You withdrawing and looking dumbfounded helps them think you are, in your words, "out to lunch." Can you change your part of the dance in the present?

Mary: That's easy on paper, I guess, but do you know how it feels to jump in a conversation and say something that has nothing to do with what people are talking about?

Therapist: Tell me.

Mary: It's humiliating. I remember a long time ago, all of us [siblings and her parents] were yacking about something or other; and my grandmother, who was hard of hearing at the time, said something way off the subject, she couldn't really hear our conversation. And we all laughed at her, it was pitiful. And now I know how she must have felt!

Therapist: How?
Mary: Oh, embarrassed, inept, stupid, foolish, scared ...
Therapist: So I'm beginning to understand how admitting to people that you don't understand a conversation got attached to feeling humiliated. You have learned that through watching your grandmother and by the other experiences we discussed.
Mary: Yeh. (Describes in detail several situations in which she withdraws to save herself from risking humiliation, etc.) Yeh, and I guess my dance in the past *is* like my dance in the present!
Therapist: And if you change your connection between assertively asking for clarification during a discussion and feeling humiliated, what would you do differently?
Mary: (describes that she would confidently ask for clarification)

As discussed in chapter 3, one function of Mary avoiding many hearing-group situations and feigning understanding was to preserve her persona that she was just like any hearing person and did not have any special needs. Openly admitting her needs was viewed as synonymous, connected to humiliation. All of her ego functions became subverted in favor of hiding from others. Mary evaluated a social gathering as a success if nobody took care to ask "can you hear me?" and if "everybody treated me exactly like everybody else." Convincing others that she enjoyed herself took on greater importance than actually enjoying herself. Intellectual pursuits, such as learning from the environment around her, became delegated to having secondary importance in favor of maintaining this facade, or false self. Her modus operandi became "I am what I appear to others"; a task that required enormous energy and that depleted her resources and motivation to adequately function intrapsychically and interpersonally.

Mary's mode of coping also could not succeed. She frequently exposed herself by responding to what she thought someone said. Moreover, her speech was inevitably different than that of hearing persons. People frequently asked her from what country she came and commented on her "different accent." For these reasons, she correctly perceived that other people saw through her veneer of acting like a hearing person. Thus, her mode of coping made for a tenuous hold onto the hearing world and therefore for a tenuous sense of self.

Mary's one solace was that she was not profoundly deaf. Each time she felt humiliated, she felt relief that "I'm not that bad off." However, this solace or rationalization fueled her fears of losing more hearing. In contrast to deaf people who for the most part know that they will remain permanently deaf, hard-of-hearing people frequently experience fluctuations in their level of hearing (Orlans, 1985). Consequently, visiting the audiologist, who confirms this biological–audiological information, may precipitate fear; because fluctuations in hearing can then no longer be easily denied. In addition, a common head cold or earache (or other biological phenomena), with resultant diminution of hearing, can be frightening: "Will I permanently lose more hearing?" Particularly in Mary's case, she described her hearing loss as an omnipresent threat to expel her from the hearing community and "sentence me into the Deaf community."

To more directly deal with her fears of facing and accepting her hearing loss, at an appropriate time in treatment in accordance with her emerging confidence and strength, I suggested some tasks that she could do on her own. First, I asked her to go swimming (which she loved), which necessitated taking off her hearing aids. While at the beach or pool with her hearing aids off, she was further instructed not to avoid friends as she had done previously, but to actively seek them out and chat with them. She reported completing this task and was quite jubilant with her new found "freedom." She reported that "telling my friends that I couldn't hear them, but I wear hearing aids, and that I am hard of hearing was nowhere near as bad as my fantasy of how it would be!"

Mary's initial success and enthusiasm with this homework compelled me to suggest a related, but more difficult, task, namely, for her to purposely remove the batteries from her hearing aids before a relatively unimportant business meeting. During the meeting, she was asked to state to her colleagues that her batteries were dead and to be more assertive about getting clarification on what was being said. Again, she returned the next week jubilant and with new insights and experiences, such as the respect that she had, from her point of view, surprisingly received from others by being assertive. Other persons lost some of their vindictive power. Moreover, her change in behavior, her demonstrated ability to face and to overcome her "worst fantasies," rapidly increased her level of respect for herself and her self-esteem. Whereas she previously was, in a sense, phobic about becoming deaf or appearing deaf to others, she again learned the distinction between a disability and a handicap. In her words, "not hearing what someone says does not have to be a big deal." No longer ashamed, Mary emerged from her corner.

Therapy with Mary continued for approximately 1½ years. One theme of our work had to do with untangling Mary's web of unconscious connections that had served to spread the disabling aspects of her hearing loss to encompass many handicaps, and then helping her change her behavior. As treatment progressed, we encountered several more connections in her web. These included Mary fearing the wrath of others if she dared to fully participate in conversations. In regard to her self-esteem, she asked herself "am I even entitled to participate?" If so, "how much?" "Will I burden other people by speaking up?" "Dare I exchange the safety of looking at the world for, instead, being in the world? I would then be expected to contribute, and I am scared I won't be able to."

Another theme in treatment had to do with helping Mary stop "waiting for Godot," for other people to initiate change; and to realize that, in spite of living in an oral–aural world that is often insensitive to her hearing loss, she at least in part, was treated in a way that she taught others to treat her. Mary became more aware of the many choices she could actively make in changing her part of the dance even though she could neither change the whole world nor make her hearing loss go away. Moreover, she became selectively committed to educating and therefore changing the responses of only certain persons in her environment. Now much more accepting of herself, she did not deem it as urgent that everybody respond affirmatively to her. She began to choose on whom she wished to expend effort at achieving their acceptance and intimacy.

Selected others did respond to Mary's change, to her "coming out." Initially from Mary's verbal report, the reactions of other persons in the ecology to her changes of behavior were carefully monitored and tracked; how other levels (i.e., family) coevolved with her changes. In Mary's case, other family members and acquaintances reacted quite supportively. Her parents had for the first time purchased a telephone amplifier so Mary could comfortably use the phone when she visited them. Prior to this time, Mary was too ashamed to ask for this, and her parents had not offered. Her new found assertiveness at work was met with official sanction in the form of a job promotion, and was met with unofficial sanction by several men noticing her, apparently for the first time.

Given that individual change had triggered changes at other levels, it was important to support and to amplify these deviations with respect to her mother and father. They were invited to attend two meetings. During these meetings, I introduced complexity into how her parents' behavior had been punctuated by Mary as having caused Mary's problems. As illustrated in this book, it is tempting but fallacious to linearly view parents as *toxic entities*—as the reason for any observed problems with an identified patient. Consequently, the meeting focused on helping Mary to view her parents' earlier role as indicative of having done the best they could, given that they, like her teachers and others, were limited by their biopsychosocial context.

As Mary experienced increased joy and elation, in her words, "for the first time," she also paradoxically experienced increased sadness, interspersed with frequent crying. This was a very important therapeutic juncture. It represented Mary beginning to grieve about how much happiness had been denied to her, and that she participated in denying her own happiness prior to realizing that there was more to life than constant anxiety and faking it. In her words, "what I had been missing all of my life, all the wasted time, suddenly hit me like a ton of bricks." Fully experiencing joy was "news of a difference" (Bateson, 1979); it provided her with a yardstick with which to measure the quality of her life up to the present. With this news of a difference came a profound sense of sadness.

This phenomenon seems analogous to Plato's parable of the prisoners in the cave, as depicted in *Plato's Republic Book VII* (translated by Grube, 1974). Plato depicted several men who had been restricted since birth by being tied up in a cave with their backs toward a fire. To them, ordinary reality consisted of shadows made by them and by the fire. This reality was comfortably accepted without question until one man freed himself, climbed up a tunnel, and saw the outside world for the first time. He then came back and reported the "news of a difference" to the men. As a result, they acutely realized that their reality had indeed been constricted; and therefore, began to feel saddened, anxious, and angry, as well as curious about new forthcoming experiences.

It is important to distinguish the grieving and sadness that Mary experienced at this juncture from clinical depression. Beck (1976) described sadness as the usual consequence to loss and therefore adaptive to the individual, in contrast to depression that is "a different emotional state, [feeling] totally defeated, dead inside" (p. 121). Thus, her sadness and grieving were reframed as productive, as both necessary and helpful.

Consider the following transcript that addressed this grieving process. In this session, anger as one component of grieving, not sadness, was most figural.

Client: I remember not going to the school dance, not speaking up in class, not feeling like anyone gave a shit about me. I can't believe all the stuff I missed.

Therapist: You couldn't see the "forest through the trees" and couldn't act on the choices you actually had ... and others were also in the same predicament.

Client: I know that now, but it makes me angry ... cheated. It pisses me off!

Therapist: Yeh. We all actually make choices, and are also victims of our circumstances. It's sort of contradictory. You can't change the circumstances until you realize that there are other possibilities.

Client: It stinks!

Therapist: Yeh, it does. [pause] But keep on describing other choices, other parts of your life that seemed inevitable but were not.

Client: [Describes other areas]

Therapist: You need to grieve over the loss, this loss of an illusion of stuckness, before you move on.

As Mary and I began to prepare for termination of treatment, I asked her to list some of the "trail markers" that she felt had signified progress toward her dealing with and better accepting her hearing loss. I am impressed with their generic applicability to the kinds of issues that, from my experience, have been frequently brought up by hard-of-hearing persons in roughly the same order during psychotherapy as they work toward adjusting to hearing loss. The indicators of adjustment are presented here in the order that the items were brought up and addressed by Mary during the 15-month treatment, with the exception of the first four items that she completed prior to our first meeting:

1. seeking an understanding of the biological–audiological aspects of hearing loss through discussions with professionals, in particular, physicians and audiologists;
2. independently reading material on hearing loss;
3. obtaining hearing aids;
4. wearing hearing aids;
5. obtaining other technological assistive devices as needed, such as a visual doorbell system or phone amplifier;
6. learning to be alert to social cues from which she could deduce the content of conversations and therefore increase her chances of successful lip-reading;
7. admitting to others when she could not hear;
8. recognizing and labeling feelings associated with coming to terms with her hearing loss (i.e., grieving);
9. discussing her feelings about hearing loss with the other hard-of-hearing persons;
10. realizing that *ipso facto* she is not burdening all acquaintances or significant others by being hard of hearing, but instead, learning how to discriminate among persons whom she can and wishes to trust with her intimate feelings;
11. discussing her feelings about hearing loss with nonhearing impaired persons;
12. reducing the phenomenon of spread—changing her experience of herself as hard of hearing from a noun to an adjective, thus redefining her sense of self;
13. increasing assertiveness: realizing that, in part, she must train many hearing people how to properly react (i.e., not to leave her out of conversations) rather than waiting and hoping that they will change.

As an example of this last step, consider the following letter, sent by a 61 year old hearing impaired woman:

> In my middle years, when I joined SHHH, I developed a new self-image of a person who must self-advocate whenever I join the company of "normally hearing" others. In my case, I wear a hearing aid which has a DAI (Direct Audio Input) microphone and wire. I then make my hearing loss "visible." I call the DAI my "neon wheelchair." People tend to be sympathetic and accommodating when they see a wheelchair, but not a hearing aid when they can't see it.

> I make it a point to wear my DAI at all meetings and social events. When asked, I explain that it helps me to understand speech a little better in groups. I've gotten over the vanity issue, and I wear my long hair pulled back behind my ears so my BTE/DAI aid is visible. I realize that the more I advertise my hearing loss, the more people become aware of my needs and include me in discussions. My then "visible" hearing loss forces others to modify their behavior and communication strategies. Unless we ourselves call attention to our needs and wear our "equipment" visibly, the "hearing normally" others won't acquiesce to our needs. "It is better to beat one small drum, than to curse the silence."

Intermittently, during the course of our work together, I would ask Mary about her recurring dream of her world becoming transformed into a Trivial Pursuit® board. She would repeatedly state that the dream had remained the same. However, after approximately 14 months, her answer changed:

> As before, I was leaving my house to take a walk, when suddenly the whole world became a Trivial Pursuit board, and all of the people I met became Trivial Pursuit cards. But unlike before, when one of the cards attempted to force me to answer the questions correctly, I stared at it and said "I won't play your game; but I'll teach you one of my own!

It was then that I knew our work together was coming to an end.

5

Treating the Deafened Individual in Context

Sam was a 35-year-old male who had normal hearing until the age of 20 when he, in his words, "became afflicted with a rapidly progressive hearing loss" leading to profound deafness by the age of 22. He requested psychotherapy because of symptoms of depression and anxiety. Having only worked with prelingually deaf and hard-of-hearing persons prior to Sam, I was surprised how taxing communication was, although his receptive oral skills were excellent due to his adventitious hearing loss. Repetitions were often necessary. I found myself not only talking slowly and carefully, but also using more simple language, as well as nodding my head more and conducting a more passive form of therapy than was my usual style. As Schlesinger (1985) reported about her own initial experience with deafened persons, "I soon noticed myself feeling somewhat impotent. I daydreamed about my next client who was prelingually deaf and who signed ASL beautifully." With her, communication would be no problem, and I might learn some new ASL idioms and nuances of Deaf culture. I also recalled the client before Sam with whom one-to-one communication was also no problem, as he only had a 50 db hearing loss.

This scenario of initial frustration and avoidance is common among clinicians who first encounter persons who sustain a significant adventitious hearing loss. A similarly implied scenario is evidenced by the dearth of material devoted to describing persons with acquired hearing loss, as contrasted with the plethora of literature devoted to describing prelingually deaf persons. Although the clinical literature on the congenitally hard-of-hearing population is also relatively sparse, SHHH serves as a lobbying and supportive network for hard-of-hearing persons and also provides a regular publication for its members (Stone, 1985). However, persons with acquired hearing loss tend to fall through the cracks to an even greater degree; they tend to be isolated from each other and have no well-established network. Although there are some important unique characteristics of this population, the literature has erroneously subsumed them under the broader label *deaf and hearing impaired*.

The following therapy transcript from a session with Sam highlights some of the unique and traumatic psychological effects of traumatic hearing loss, including the initial experiences of helplessness:

Client: It was like the rug got pulled out from under me. I tried to hold on to the last bit of hearing I had, my one thread of contact with reality. I tried meditation, visualization exercises, lost count of how many doctors' appointments. But I lost it, and became deaf.

Therapist: It was impossible for you to hold on to it, to prevent it from going away.

Client: Damn it! And now I'm at the mercy of ... I don't know what. I can't understand a lot of discussions, strain so much I get headaches. Feel lost. I enter conversations sometimes but end up saying something off the subject, because I miss some key words. [proceeds to discuss insurmountable linguistic barriers—situations in which he is unable to understand what is being said—and his inevitable fatigue after a long day trying to lip-read].

Therapist: You certainly often can't control being linguistically behind or left out among groups of hearing people. What else?

Client: [recounts other situations of helplessness, including fatigue, loss of many friends, and encountering patronizing reactions from some persons]

Because prelingually deaf and hard-of-hearing persons have never experienced first the presence and then attenuation of sound, it often becomes an integral facet of their identity. In contrast, as the transcript with Sam illustrates, persons who have experienced traumatic hearing loss experience a loss of sensory capacity from which they had defined themselves (Glass, 1985; Myers, 2000; Ramsdell, 1978). J. Ashley (1985), who became deaf as an adult, emphasized that "the born deaf are denied the advantages gained by the deafened before their hearing loss, yet they are spared the desolating sense of loss" (p. 61). As Elliot (1983) said, "prelingual deafness is a sensory deficit. Acquired deafness is a sensory deprivation" (p. 119). Consequently, whereas many congenitally or prelingually deaf persons may consider their deafness a "difference to be accepted" and part of a cultural phenomenon, deafened people may consider their deafness as a deficit, a disease or, as Sam put it, an "affliction."

Meadow-Orlans (1985) suggested that the variables of age (particularly whether the onset of hearing loss occurred before or after the development of speech), severity and rapidity of loss, and the amount of residual hearing exert important biological influences toward shaping the functioning of the particular individual. In addition, Schlesinger (1985) described the myriad of possible psychological reactions to acquired hearing loss as related less to the nature of the disability than to its meaning to the individual. As an example, coping with a major life crisis, such as acquired hearing loss, frequently includes revising one's view of how life is or should be. One meaning of the traumatic loss may be that life is not necessarily fair. Life need not conform to the axiom that good things happen to good people, and bad things happen to bad people, a sentiment that is echoed by Kushner (1981) in his book entitled, *When Bad Things Happen to Good People*. Life also need not follow the rule that rewards are divided up in accordance with how much work one puts in. The sorting out of these and other beliefs and feelings occurs during the process of grieving (Elliott, 1986; Moses, 1986).

Similarly, Humphrey, Gilhoma–Herbst, and Faurqi (1981, cited in Meadow-Orlans, 1985) stated that a person's "attitudes to a disorder first suffered at a stage in life when it was felt to be untimely and exceptional are different from the response to the same disorder encountered at a stage where it is conventionally expected as part of a 'normal running down'" (p. 29). Becoming deaf or significantly hearing impaired at the age of 30 is phenomenologically distinct from becoming deaf or hearing impaired at the age of 70, secondary to presbycusis, a loss of hearing associated with aging.

The emotional trauma or grieving associated with "untimely deafness" also varies widely (Harvey, 1998; Luey & Glass, 1995; Luey & Per-Lee, 1983; Rousey, 1970). J. Ashley's (1985) list of adjectives about his own progressive 90 db hearing loss included "thunderbolt of deafness," "tortured months," "shattering beyond belief," "plummeting of my happiness, aspirations, and hope for the future," and "existing in misery." Sam also exemplifies these feelings of despair and desperation; to "hold on to the last bit of hearing I had" in reaction to having "the rug pulled out from under me." Indeed, depression is a common reaction to late-onset hearing loss (Carmen, 2001; Larew, Saura, & Watson, 1992; Pollard, 1998; Trychin, 1991).

Given the intensity of affective reactions to acquired hearing loss, it comes as no surprise that denial holds a pivotal role in shielding one from that realization. Denial plays an important and adaptive function towards preserving the intrapsychic sense of self (Kyle et al., 1985). This period of initial adjustment through denial prior to or following the actual diagnosis may vary from a period of a few days to 20 or 30 years or more! In Sam's case, although the rate of his hearing loss was rapid, the duration of this period of denial was 9 years. It was only after this period that he requested an audiology appointment to test his hearing. In a sample of hearing-impaired persons compiled by Kyle and Wood (1983), of the 89% of interview respondents who reported difficulties in street conversations, 79% reported that they would not publicly tell people that they had a hearing problem! Whether these respondents had intrapsychically acknowledged it to themselves but not yet publicly is unclear.

Kyle, Jones, & Wood (1985) further observed that it is easier for one to deny hearing loss with stimuli over which volume control can be exercised, such as watching television or using a telephone. In contrast, it is usually in situations when such control cannot be exercised, that is, when telling people to speak up is socially unacceptable, that awareness of hearing loss rises. Although it is common for one to initially accuse others of mumbling or of talking too softly, such rationalizations, after repeated confrontations by others, eventually succumb to a realization of hearing loss.

The variables of *control* and *information* are useful in conceptualizing how to psychologically assess and assist deafened persons. Schlesinger (1985) defined lack of control or powerlessness as "an individual's self-perception as not having the cognitive competence, psychological skills, instrumental resources, and support systems needed to influence his or her environment successfully" (p. 105). Receiving information from the environment can be conceptualized as occurring on three levels, as delineated by Ramsdell's (1978) tri-level description of the psychological functions of normal hearing: (a) the symbolic level, which encompasses understanding language; (b) the signal or warning level, which encompasses having access to direct signals of events to which one makes constant adjustments in daily living; and (c) the primitive level, which encompasses what is loosely described as the auditory background or rumble of daily living. Clearly, all of these levels of information are affected by loss of hearing.

Kyle et al. (1985) described the process of an individual coming to terms with acquired hearing loss as a function of these variables of control and information. They listed eight axioms:

1. Individuals live and work in information environments governed by social and personal norms as well as access features such as speed, intensity, and density of information.
2. Individuals, through personal and social adjustment, attempt to control the access features of the information they receive.
3. In normal circumstances, most people have adjusted to a specific level of control of these features, which varies from one individual to another but is negotiated and agreed upon in any social circumstances.

4. The onset of hearing loss disturbs the control that the individual can exert.
5. In terms of access, the individual's initial response is to increase the intensity, the repetition, or the concentration level to maximize the information being received.
6. This overt additional control may be unacceptable to others in social situations and produces a realization of hearing loss.
7. There are at least three solutions: (a) increase the level of control at all costs; (b) accept or expect a reduced level of control and flow of information; and (c) reject or avoid situations in which the level of control is threatened. All three can be adopted by any individual.
8. The degree to which an individual can tolerate the reduced and varying access to information at home and work will determine the degree of adjustment (p. 122).

To return to Sam, it becomes apparent that his self-attribution of helplessness, or of absolute noncontrol, reflected his intolerance and inability to cope with reduced levels of control and information flow. Sam's attempt to increase the intensity and repetition of his efforts toward maximizing the information that he receives from the environment proved fruitless. He could not understand or control aspects of his environment that he had previously taken for granted, such as television, conversations, and music. However, the generalized dichotomy of success or failure—control or noncontrol—is a cognitive distortion, as is illustrated by the following therapy segment with Sam:

Therapist: [After Sam had recounted numerous situations in which he felt helpless] Okay, that is half of the story, but it's tempting to think that it's the whole story. What in your life, since becoming deaf, are you able to control?

Client: Uh (pause) ... I'm taking classes to learn how to lip-read better. And I've gone to the audiologist a few times for a hearing aid adjustment. That's it.

Therapist: It's a lot easier for you to think about what you can't control. You talked a lot more about that. But try to keep going.

Client: (after a while) Maybe I should take sign language classes.

Therapist: Maybe. That's a choice, and you can control it. And what else is controllable?

Client: Well, at work I asked a coworker to listen to the walkie-talkie for me, so I won't have to pretend that I understand it. I also finally requested different seating during meetings, better lighting, and I got my boss to buy an infrared audio system.

Therapist: So you do have control about how you present yourself, your assertiveness with colleagues and your boss, whether you say 'I need assistance because of my deafness' or act as if you do not have special needs.

Client: Yeah, I certainly have control over that, and before, I couldn't be assertive at all for a long time. (Discusses different situations of control and noncontrol.)

Therapist: You actually did (and do) have control over several areas but have acted as if you didn't.

Client: Yeah (ha), if you want to get philosophical about it.

Therapist: Actually, (ha) I do. You know, you also do have a choice about how much you change your body, mind, and soul because of your hearing loss. Some people redefine their whole being, their essence, because of their disability. Other people purposely separate out, compartmentalize, parts of themselves. You do have choices.

Client: Well, I still like hiking, I always enjoyed hiking ... and ballet ... and my humor! I still have that.

Therapist: Right.

In Sam's case and others, it was helpful to clearly differentiate, or compartmentalize, those aspects of himself that he could control—such as his attitudes, beliefs, behaviors, and emotions—from those that he could not control; and those aspects that were and were not affected by his hearing loss. Elliott (1986), in reference to her own hearing loss, stated that "shifting gears is a process by which we choose change. Now that may seem crazy because we sure didn't 'choose' hearing loss. But we can choose how we manage it" (p. 23). This process of compartmentalization reduces the effects of spread, as is described in chapter 4.

In this regard, it is important to note that one typical reaction to hearing loss is a pervasive feeling of helplessness. The helplessness literature initiated by Seligman (1975, cited in Schlesinger, 1985) suggests that sustained inability to avoid negative outcomes prompts individuals to give up and become passive, to habitually operate from an "illusion of incompetence." Persons such as Sam, who have recently lost a significant amount of hearing, certainly operate from an illusion of incompetence by minimizing their capacity to influence or impact their environment.

In addition to reducing the effects of spread, namely to differentiate what about oneself is and is not inevitably affected by deafness, one also has choices about what value to place on the experiences of feeling out of control—as bad or good, helpful or nonhelpful, tolerable or intolerable, and so on. The following segment with Sam ends with a hypnotic, indirect communication for him to view his hearing loss differently:

Therapist: And to get even more philosophical, you also have a choice about how you view things which are in reality beyond your control. You can view loss of control as nothing but horrendous. Or you can surrender more to it—accept it, learn from it, not need to be in control so much over everything.

Client: It's awful to not to have control.

Therapist: Okay. How would things change if you chose to view loss of control in a different way? Or to view it in degrees instead of absolutes?

Client: It's still awful.

Therapist: Let me tell you a story. I know a person who recently lost his sight. And he therefore had trouble knowing where to walk, knowing who was in the room, knowing what people were thinking. And he became scared, he became angry, very depressed, felt very sorry for himself, very nervous. He wasn't, of course, wrong to feel those feelings. It is quite natural; it is quite healthy. At a point in time, later, and I'm not sure how much later, he did a sort of switch. He found a crazy kind of thought, one which a supportive friend suggested to him. He thought of how he could also learn from it, how he could benefit from it, how he could experience the grieving, the fear, depression, anxiety, and many other feelings; and only when he is ready, begin, not only to feel and think about the negative, but to do that switch, too. How to learn from it? Things are not that simple. Bad or good. How to benefit, become smarter, more sensitive? Things are often both, and [pause] can control the switch both ways, not only one way.

The reader experienced in hypnosis will recognize this as an example of an Ericksonian, indirect hypnotic induction procedure (Haley, 1967) with which I indirectly communicated to Sam that there is a flipside to the negative aspects of becoming deaf. I indirectly alluded to Sam as "a person who recently lost his sight" and to myself as "a supportive friend." This is not to be Pollyannish and over emphasize "the silver lining in every cloud" nor is it to wish that another person become disabled. However, it is to acknowledge the bipolar complexity of traumatic events and to gain a sense of respect and appreciation for both its positive and negative aspects. For example, Milton Erikson, who has been acclaimed as the master of indirect hypnosis, attributed the reasons for his skill to having been rendered paralyzed for much of his childhood by polio; this gave him the opportunity to develop astute concentration and observational skills. Through his long and painful ordeal, he also learned to view or "frame" his disability, in part, as an invaluable gift (Rossi, 1982). This represents the metalevel of feeling powerless.

The degree to which an individual with progressive or traumatic hearing loss can come to compartmentalize, tolerate, or reframe the overall reduced control and flow of information is, in part, related to ego intactness. For example, P. K. Ashley (1985) described how she perceived her husband, Jack, adjusting to his hearing loss:

> Self-confidence is key. What they [friends and colleagues] have noticed is that Jack does not feel inferior because of deafness, and therefore he never behaves in the

> slightly humbled way that the struggle to understand so often induces in the deaf person. With a temperament that is a mix of aggression, warmth, and humor, he is constitutionally incapable of allowing others to dominate him. (p. 81)

There is also a recursive relationship between "self-confidence" and "not allowing others to dominate him." With self-confidence comes egalitarian relationships with others; with egalitarian relationships comes self-confidence. As is illustrated by Mary in chapter 4, an individual who views him or herself as inferior sets the context for others to become dominant and to show pity. The reactions of others, in turn, become the yardstick by which that individual affirms his or her own feelings of inferiority.

There is a strong precedent for a person with acquired hearing loss to punctuate the beginning of the linear cause and effect sequence with oneself as reacting to external influences (i.e., "I feel X because others do Y towards me"). In this regard, J. Ashley (1985) reported that it is a reality that many hearing people patronize deaf people; "it is not easy to accept the fact that some people look down on the deaf, but it is so. They tend to equate loss of hearing with loss of reason, perhaps because of the invisibility of the handicap or a result of difficulty in communicating. It is one of the heaviest burdens deaf people have to bear" (p. 69). However, this represents only one option of punctuation. One could alternately punctuate the linear cause and effect sequence, beginning with external forces as reacting to oneself. As an example, later in treatment, Sam was able to realize how he trained other people to help maintain his own sense of ineptness; in his words, "I made it easy for my colleagues and supervisors to pity me, for other people to avoid me, because I feel inept." Whether a person reacts to the environment or the environment reacts to the person is a moot question, for systems theory teaches us that we control our context that controls us.

EFFECTS OF ACQUIRED HEARING LOSS ON FAMILY

In terms of how a person who has recently sustained a hearing loss affects his or her family, Orlans (1985) suggested that the impact is similar to other significant stressors and is related to the severity of hearing loss, the characteristics of the individual, the family's integrity, and the family's stage of the life cycle, such as the age of the children. As an example of the latter influence, in a family with both old and young children, the hearing loss of one parent represents more of a loss for the older children rather than for very young children. Therefore, greater effects of loss, such as depression, would be predictable with the older children. However, this will be mitigated by the extent to which they receive support from within the family, outside family supports, and by the extent of their individuation from the family.

In general, Kyle et al. (1985) observed that the hearing children frequently turn to the hearing parent and avoid the parent who has sustained a hearing loss. As an example, P. K. Ashley (1985) stated that "one of our few unsolved problems has been the effect of fatigue, which deafness so easily brings. When Jack is tired, inevitably his lip-reading skills decline, and the extra effort required adds to his exhaustion. This spiral places the family in a quandary. We hesitate over whether something is worth saying or not" (p. 78). She further elaborated that "there is an instinctive tendency for hearing people to turn and talk to those who can hear rather than to those who cannot, even when the conversation concerns the deaf person. [Thus the children may] turn to me and say, 'tell him what I said'" (p. 80). It is also not unusual for the hearing parent and children to gossip about the deafened parent in front of him or her.

Kyle et al. (1985) also noted that families frequently come to view the manifestations of anger and frustration by the deafened family member as being indicative of self-centeredness and as failure to adjust or adapt to the loss of hearing. Consequently, members of the family might be apt not only to avoid the deafened parent, but to also manifest anger toward him or her. Schein and Stone (1986) noted that "the disability [of hard-of-hearing or late-deafened persons] often generates hostility within their own family. Family members, including spouses, sometimes become annoyed when their requests are ignored or their conversation misunderstood. Anger and resentment, loneliness and bitterness, can build to barely tolerable limits" (p. 13). It becomes apparent that these common reactions of avoidance within families may support dysfunctional intergenerational affiliations and coalitions that include the family feeling victimized and antagonistic toward the deafened member.

The other direction of the punctuation—how the family affects the deafened individual—is illustrated by frequent comments that "my family just doesn't understand my plight" (Kyle et al., 1985). Many such individuals, frustrated in their attempts to gain support from their spouses and, to a different extent, from their children, often withdraw and may become clinically depressed or may abuse alcohol or drugs. The more an individual does not feel understood, the more he or she withdraws, and the more the family may come to view him or her as egocentric and angry, and the more that individual does not feel understood. And so on.

This circular reciprocity of causation is also relevant to examining dependency issues that arise in the marital relationship (Harvey, 1998; Sonnenschein, 1987). Consider the following therapy segment in which a 42-year-old woman, who recently became profoundly deaf as a result of the herpes virus, discusses her marital relationship:

Client: I finally told my [hearing] husband not to always jump in and interpret for me when we're with other people.

Therapist: How was it that you two got into that rut?

Client: I guess he felt protective of me, I guess he wanted to save me from not understanding people, but I don't need his protection all of the time. For a long, long time, I couldn't figure out why I felt like a little baby who couldn't do anything herself. I came to realize that his interpretation became sort of selective—you know, he edited what was being talked about. It reminds me of reading those Readers' Digest condensed novels!

Therapist: So after your hearing loss your husband became sort of your gate-keeper to the world?

Client: I guess so. But out of good intentions, I know! But in many ways, he shut me off from people, and I remember many times he would deliberately not interpret insensitive or patronizing remarks people would say about me. I know where he was coming from, and I appreciate it. But goddamm it, I don't want to be filtered any more from the world! I'm a big girl!

Therapist: Could you tell your husband that how he treats your hearing loss makes it easy for you to feel like a baby?

Client: (Ha.) I already did last night!

A similar issue is also illustrated by the following transcript of another couple that included Tom (35 years old), who recently became deaf, and his hearing wife Sue (33 years old):

Therapist: What has changed between you two since you [Tom] lost your hearing?

Tom: We never seem to go out and socialize like we used to.

Sue: That's right. Most of our previous friends lose patience.

Therapist: With whom?

Sue: With Tom. He can't lip-read some of them, particularly when he gets tired and when it is noisy.

Therapist: And then what do you do?

Sue: I help out by interpreting.

Therapist: And what's that like for you [to Tom]?

Tom: Well, I appreciate it, of course, except when my friends say to Sue, 'tell him that ....'

Therapist: And what do you then do?

Tom: Nothing, except sometimes Sue says to them, 'tell him yourself.'

Therapist: And do they?

Sue: Sometimes, but it reverts back after a while.

Therapist: (to Sue) It must be hard to try to be the link between Tom and potential friends.

Sue: It sure is! I wish people would be more considerate. That's why it's tough for Tom at parties.

Therapist: And for you, too?

Sue: Of course, it's tough for me, too.

Therapist: Are they related? I mean, when Tom and people aren't connecting easily and Tom looks as if he's having a lousy time, you sort of feel obliged to give up your good time and help him out, and you have a lousy time?
Sue: Yeh. I can't enjoy myself unless Tom is.
Therapist: (to Tom) And what's that like for you?
Tom: I didn't know that until now. I only knew that Sue was having a lousy time.
Therapist: So given this new information, what are your thoughts or feelings?
Tom: I don't want that arrangement! I don't want Sue to be so busy interpreting for me and helping me have a good time that she has a miserable time herself. I guess though she usually knows when I'm having a tough time of it, lip-reading, feeling lonely, and so on. Ugh—And then we'd go home, and it would be tense. And I couldn't figure it out.
Therapist: And you (to Sue)? Do you want to continue this arrangement between you two?
Sue: No, I'm tired of it.

Their friends losing patience was one of several factors that contributed to Tom and Sue becoming socially isolated. However, what was of greater systemic significance, in terms of their marital relationship, was that Tom and Sue together had established implicit rules that (a) Sue is to intercede when there are linguistic communication problems between Tom and another person; (b) the reason for social isolation is to be attributed to other insensitive, impatient hearing persons; and (c) Sue cannot enjoy herself socially unless Tom is also enjoying himself. The goal of therapy with this couple was to modify these implicit rules.

Finally, consider the following letter that was sent to me by a 39 year old female (Harvey, 2002):

> "I am progressively slipping into further deafness. I am experiencing continued lack of support on the home front and at times I become so overcome with emotional pain that I cry and feel as though I am drowning. My husband says snap out of it and its all my fault that people at work ignore me the way they do because of my loud voice ... How do I make my family see how painful it is to be a hearing person one day and then for almost 11 years be slipping away slowly from the ability to hear?"

My answer was as follows:

> "With all due respect to your husband, I cannot believe that people at work treat you the way they do *because of* your loud speaking and tone of voice. Your voice can't be strong enough to force people to act discriminatory and aggressive. It also sounds like you might understandably be angry at him for telling you to "snap out of it" (if you figure out how to do that, let me know) and for his "lack of support on the home front." A common

scenario would be for you to accuse your husband of being insensitive and inpatient; he may, in turn, accuse you of being stubborn and not appreciating his help; and your strife would escalate, leaving both of you feeling alienated and betrayed by the other.

"Let me suggest another scenario. It is very tough for a spouse to *vicariously experience* the emotional pain and helplessness—in your words, "drowning"—that the other spouse experiences directly. When one member of a system is in crisis, each and every other member is also in crisis, albeit in different ways. Your husband and family may feel overwhelmed and helpless by seeing you "slip away slowly from the ability to hear." (When my daughter was stung by a bee, I swear it hurt me more than her). It may hurt them so much that they deny it, prematurely suggest solutions, and/or immediately give platitudes or advice.

"Rather than express anger and outrage toward your husband, you can first thank him for his efforts and then clearly spell out what you need from him. You are speaking of a universal need to feel understood, supported and validated, particularly when traumatized by loss. Your husband can "simply"—it's not simple to do in practice, only in theory—listen to your pain, understand as much as possible, hold you, soothe you and much later, give advice. (There is an old English saying, "*Shared joys are doubled; shared sorrows are halved.*")

"However, it is not solely your responsibility to get others to listen; in your words, "to *get* [my emphasis] my family to see how painful it is" or "to get [my emphasis] my coworkers to stop mistreating me." Just as you cannot *get*—a.k.a. force—people to act in a discriminatory way, you also cannot *get* people to understand and respect your pain. Stated differently, it's not your fault if your family, coworkers, insurance companies, etc. never come forward in the way that you hope.

"You can however set the stage; make it more comfortable for others to reach out and come forward. Most hearing persons—including significant others, family and coworkers—do not understand how hard-of-hearing people—who, after all, do not look disabled—are often subtly excluded from communication loops. For your family, you could play audio tapes of simulated hearing loss, share articles about the effects of hearing loss and on communication tips (all available through the S.H.H.H. bookstore). Family therapy or couples counseling may be helpful to resolve issues of loss, hurt, betrayal and frustration that everyone undoubtedly feels."

ACQUIRED HEARING LOSS AND THE INFORMAL NETWORK LEVEL

Luey (1980) deemed it almost inevitable that the newly deafened person would lose some hearing friends who will not submit to labored communication and who are "threatened or repelled by the sheer intensity of the deafened person's feelings" (p. 258). Sam, for example, prior to the age of 28 when his hearing loss became quite severe, recalled having "several informal buddies with whom I could get together and 'chew the fat'." Now he "schedules meetings"; friends do not drop in as they had done in the past.

Moreover, social encounters become tests to measure how long the conversation could last and remain comfortable. J. Ashley (1985) also described a similar kind of social encounter:

> I took my cup of tea to a table to join four friends. When one of them asked me a question which I could not understand, the others repeated it for me but I was still unable to lip-read it. They paused while one of them wrote it down and I was aware that the easy-going conversation they had been enjoying before my arrival was now disrupted. Within a few minutes two of them left and after a brief pause the other's explained that they had to go because of pressing engagements. They were genuinely sorry and I understood, but it was small solace as I sat alone drinking my tea. (p. 149)

In the previous quotation, Ashley referred to feeling alienated from four hearing friends. However, many deafened persons also feel alienated from the Deaf world. Similar to the feeling described by many hard-of-hearing persons, deafened persons also frequently report feeling "stuck between two worlds" with resultant identity confusion. Consider Elliot's (1978) description about her own identity confusion as a deafened person:

> Even now I find myself wondering from time to time who I really am. Hearing people often think I am hearing because my speech is good; deaf people often think I am hearing because my signs are bad. Identity crisis. Hearing people have their culture based on spoken language and we are caught between incomprehensible speech on the one hand and incomprehensible signs on the other. If only those hearies would talk more clearly! If only those deafies would sign more slowly! (p. 1)

Many deafened individuals resolve their internal tug of war between the hearing and Deaf worlds by opting to primarily identify with the hearing world. However, their resolution often represents an end point of a series of changing relationships with the Deaf world. Specifically, I have observed common patterns of deafened persons coming to terms with their degree of affiliation with the Deaf community, and finally arriving at a comfortable identity with respect to the world in general. Consider the following therapy transcripts that are taken from five different intervals during a 2-year treatment of Amy (age 41), who became profoundly deaf at the age of 37. The transcripts illustrate the vicissitudes of this particular woman's feelings of affiliation with the Deaf world. Here, themes of affinity with respect to the Deaf community can be labeled as infatuation, frustration, anger, rejection, and acceptance of marginality.

It is important to note that I am not implying that these degrees of affiliation are necessarily sequential stages of optimal development, nor that one stance is necessarily more adaptive than the others; nor is it implied that this sequence is universal among deafened persons. Although I have frequently observed these stances in roughly the same sequence with approximately 25 deafened individuals who have attempted to become members of the Deaf community, the sample size is too small to permit generalization. The sequence is presented here to spark further study and verification using a larger clinical sample.

Infatuation

During the following segment, Amy seems to be infatuated with deafness and the Deaf community; in her own words, like a "crush":

Client:	I really want to be part of the Deaf community, can almost taste it! Been doing a lot of reading about it. I read Carol Padden's article about capital D. Would you teach me about it? I mean like how you become a member?
Therapist:	I don't know. I'm a hearing person and am not part of the Deaf culture. Have you met many Deaf people?
Client:	Well, I have gone to many community functions, to practice signing with several Deaf persons. I also became a member of the state association, just paid my dues. Maybe I should join some committees. They [Deaf persons] sign so beautifully, but so fast! I remember almost feeling this way when I had my first crush, felt so nervous, like I wasn't going to be accepted.

Frustration

Approximately 4 months later, Amy's frustration begins to surface and threatens to overshadow her initial enthusiasm and excitement:

Client:	It's sooo slow. You know, I sit and watch and try to figure out how to break in, break into the circle. But I did volunteer to be part of a committee on ... [recounts all of her attempts to break in].
Therapist:	What feelings come up for you as you do this?
Client:	Well, that definitely feels good. And there have been a number of very supportive people, one person in particular, who kept asking me if I understood [the sign language during the meetings]. But they [the Deaf people] would often have to repeat. After a while, they forgot to do that and forgot about me ... and I felt like an outsider. And I felt so damn awkward ... really clumsy.
Therapist:	And how are your sign language classes coming?
Client:	Slow, but good. I'm getting a tutor.

Anger

Later in treatment, Amy's initial frustration shifts to become anger. Amy discusses the implications of a particular sign that some Deaf persons had made in reference to her. It is made by signing "hearing" over the forehead, to indicate that a person thinks like a hearing person.

Client: What the hell do they [Deaf community] expect? I can't help it if I "think hearing"—I grew up hearing! It's ironic that people who are outsiders, who know what it's like to be outsiders, treat me as if I'm doing something wrong. You know, I have skills they can use, too. I'm tired of their stuck-up attitude!

Rejection

In this segment in which she explains her analysis of culturally Deaf persons, Amy psychologically backs off from the Deaf community and moves toward the hearing community. Her efforts to preserve her thwarted self-esteem and previous feelings of rejection from some Deaf persons are apparent:

Client: The Deaf may well be proud of their language but I think relying on ASL can further isolate the Deaf. To get all the services they need, the Deaf have to do their own lobbying: to take advantage of captioning, of books, of newspapers, of almost everything, they need to read. But I regret that ASL seems to be more popular than lip-reading and speaking or at least signed English, because I have met few of the Deaf who exclusively use ASL who can also read and write well. And, it's a hearing world. Let's face it. It's a hearing world.

Marginality

This segment occurred after I had asked Amy to draw a sociogram of herself relative to all of her Deaf and hearing friends and acquaintances (see Fig. 5.1). I used this tool in order to facilitate a discussion about her degree of comfort and affiliation with both worlds. She concludes that she is "basically hearing but really in a class of my own," a realization that both saddens her but ends a painful period of amorphous feelings about her "belongingness" to informal networks.

Client: It looks like I'm way out here, and the Deaf crowd over there [points to one corner of the page], and the hearing crowd over there [points to the other corner of the page]. Almost like I live a marginal existence to either group. Sort of in the hearing world; sort of in the deaf world. I think hearing, though. But really, I'm in a class of my own!

The process of an individual psychologically dealing with acquired deafness and maintaining family and peer relationships can be helped or hin-

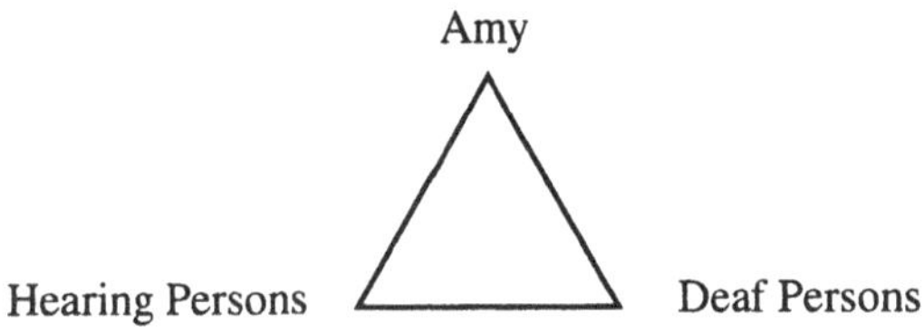

FIG. 5.1 Amy's drawing.

dered by professionals. As an illustration, consider the following segment of an interview conducted with a middle-aged man who first experienced profound and then moderate hearing loss at the age of 21 as a result of proximity to loud bombshells and artillery during WWII:

Client: I went twice to a psychiatrist when I was 26 years old, 5 years after I lost my hearing.

Therapist: How did you find that experience, of going to a psychiatrist?

Client: I found it very confusing. It would almost have been better if I hadn't gone. Because I found that he was almost trying to direct my thinking into certain channels. I used the expression "it didn't amount to peanuts" which was an expression that seemed to be used at that time. Although my speech was perfectly clear, he kept having me repeat that word "peanuts," "peanuts," until I realized he somehow was construing the word "penis" from "peanuts," and was drawing a relationship. And that kind of thing made me feel like saying "see you later." I just couldn't deal with that.

Therapist: What do you wish the psychiatrist would have done, knowing what you do now?

Client: Well, I wish that he would have gotten into the stress, the accompanying stress, that normally goes with losing your hearing, and go into how it affects family and friends around you. And go into detail how the stress develops, where it will happen, and even though there's no easy answer, the basis for its being there. Just knowing that would provide a great deal of support in itself.

Therapist: To know that there are psychological reactions, stresses, anxiety because of hearing loss. It affects you; it affects those around you.

Client: That's right.

Therapist: To know that it's not in your head, it's not made up, fabricated.

Client: That there are very positive reasons for it, and deafened and hard-of-hearing people everywhere need to know that.

ACQUIRED HEARING LOSS AND THE SPIRITUALITY LEVEL

As noted in the first chapter of this book, spritual issues have finally been acknowledged as vitally important in reference to coping with hearing loss. As an example, the following reader's question and my response is included verbatim, taken from a column "What's On Your Mind?" which I do for the *Hearing Loss* journal.

> "Dear Dr. Harvey, In your column so far, you haven't talked about the most valuable help that we hearing impaired people can ever receive: the Gospel of Jesus Christ. For example, Matthew 11:26 says "Come to Me, all you who are weary and burdened, and I will give you rest." Isaiah 41:10 says: "So do not fear, for I am with you; do not be dismayed, for I am your God. I will strengthen you and help you; I will uphold you with My righteous right hand."
>
> Every waking minute, I thank my Lord and Savior for blessing me after I lost most of my hearing at the age of 55. Many people think I'm obsessed because I preach the Gospel every chance I get. But it has saved my soul and has helped me cope with my hearing loss. I wouldn't be the least bit surprised if you don't print this letter, but it would surely help a lot of people.
>
> God bless, B.D.
>
> Dear B.D., Obviously, it would be inappropriate for me to comment on your particular religion or spiritual path, nor do I have the wisdom to do so. Although I cannot speak about souls, I can say a few words about coping. Spirituality—*however one defines it*—has always been among the two most important ways that people have coped with loss, including hearing loss. (The other way is via peer support.)
>
> Although avoiding the topic of God is often considered safer for polite conversation, ironically, God occupies an inordinate amount of our attention. I'll never forget my then 5-year old daughter's astonishment when she learned that the Bible has sold more copies than even *The Cat in the Hat*! In the face of trauma, suffering or loss, it is often God that is held accountable, even when one questions the existence of a deity. For example, a group of prisoners in a Nazi death camp put God on trial and found God guilty for permitting the atrocities. They condemned God to death. But when the trial was over, the leader announced that it was time for the evening prayer.
>
> A story with a similar message was told by Woody Allen: "There was a guy who goes to a psychiatrist and says, 'Doc, uh, my brother's crazy. He thinks he's a chicken.' And the doctor says, 'Well, why don't you turn him in?' And the guy says, 'I would, but I need the eggs.'"
>
> Like eggs, God is "something" many of us also need, although our definitions of him/her/it vary widely. Perhaps, as many psychologists speculate, human beings are "wired" to at least *consider the question* whether there is some *indefinable* power beyond us. As adults, we often continue to ask ourselves that question, particularly surround-

ing a crisis or major loss. And what answer we *choose* for the "God question" strongly influences the way we interpret our experience, including hearing loss.

But whereas many in crisis, like yourself, feel solace by experiencing God's presence, others feel betrayed. I'm reminded of another man about 55 years old who, prior to his hearing loss, held spiritual beliefs which did not account for undeserved suffering. Bad things could *not* happen to good people. He did not find solace in Scripture or in biblical stories, such as Job, which would have justified and even deified his suffering. Instead, he deemed God as having committed the ultimate sin against him. His outrage marked a beginning of his redefining his spiritual beliefs.

As the topic of God is sensitive and often misunderstood, permit me to again emphasize that I'm *not* endorsing or proselytizing a particular spiritual path or, for that matter, any path at all. There's an old query: "Is God a figment of our imagination? Or are we a figment of His?" At least for the purpose of our present dialogue, it need not matter. From my experience, typically people who have experienced any major loss strive to articulate what influence spirituality does and does not play in their lives. There are many possible outcomes to this struggle: our imagination of God may lead us to feel comfort, gratitude, anger, or fear; some of us are "re-born"; some feel connected to a "larger whole" or "higher power"; some regularly chant versions of "May the force be with you." And a statistician colleague of mine—himself a self-proclaimed atheist—defined God as "error variance."

I once worked with a woman who had awoken from her sleep to find herself profoundly deaf. She, too, struggled with defining God and concluded that "it would be so easy to believe that God will take care of everything; but I don't believe there is one." She defined her spirituality differently. In her own words,

> "As the sun rose, I took a walk in the woods. The sun came up over the trees, through the mist, exposing the splendor of greens and other colors of the woods. Although I guess it may sound corny to you, it was an *epiphany* for me ... It was then I knew that everything would be okay."

So there are many possible answers to the "God-question." Rather than label certain answers as right or wrong, we can illuminate our struggle to formulate spiritual questions and answers; for it is this inquiry, this process, this struggle—regardless of the specific outcome—that is so important for those who have incurred any major loss, including hearing loss. In other words, all of us. With that caveat in mind, I am happy to print your letter. (Harvey, 2001b)

6

On Joining the Deaf Client

The process of therapeutic joining with a deaf client has been extensively described in the deafness literature. For example, Langholtz and Heller (1988), Sussman and Brauer (1999), and Sussman and Stewart (1971) stressed the importance of the therapist communicating with the client via his or her primary and preferred mode of communication, of understanding facts of deafness and of understanding the impact of special problems that deaf persons often experience. Dickens (1983, 1985), Holt, Siegelman, and Schlesinger (1981), and Pollard (1998) discussed the importance of therapist and patient expectations, involvement of third parties, problems of diagnosis, and modifications of therapeutic technique. Anderson and Rosten (1985), Christensen (2000), Glickman (1983, 1986), Glickman and Gulati (in press), Glickman and Harvey (1996), and Leigh and Lewis (1999) have delineated cross-cultural counseling issues; such as attitude, distance variables, eye contact, and information sharing. Moreover, Leigh (1999) described theoretical and practical issues of providing cross cultural treatment to a variety of populations within the deaf community; for example, African American, Asian American, Latino people, as well as those with specific conditions, such as HIV and Ushers syndrome.

This chapter incorporates conclusions from previous literature and from my clinical experience to provide an ecosystemic perspective of joining a deaf client during the initial stages of psychological treatment. This framework focuses specifically on joining considerations that influence, and are influenced by, the environmental context—ecology—in which both the therapist and client function. For illustrative purposes, this chapter is divided into several "components" of joining that must occur either sequentially or simultaneously with other components: linguistic matching, differentiation from the referrer, differentiation from the level of culture, and matching of a client's construction of reality.

LINGUISTIC MATCHING

The most obvious component of joining is that the client and therapist use the same communication mode—they establish what I term, *linguistic matching*. This may be American Sign Language (ASL), Pidgin Sign English, Signed English, spoken English, and so on. If the deaf member prefers to use Signed English, the therapist should follow suit and match it (to join him or her); if the former prefer to use Pidgin Sign English without voice, the therapist should match it; if the former prefers to communicate orally, the therapist should match that also, and so on. Finally, if the deaf member uses ASL, the therapist should also use ASL. Not only is therapy ineffective if the therapist and client do not use the same language, but it may prove harmful, as exemplified by frequent cases of psychiatric misdiagnoses (Mindel & Vernon, 1971, 1987a; Pollard, 1998 ; Vernon & Andrews, 1990). In addition, as many deaf persons report that hearing professionals evaluate them on the basis of their speech quality, Anderson and Rosten (1985) and Nash and Nash (1981) point out that deaf persons respect hearing people partially on the basis of their signing skills.

Regardless of the particular mode of communication between therapist and client, it is important that the therapist ensure that explicit rules are established for what to do if the client and therapist are not understanding what is being communicated. Rather than the therapist asking, "Do you understand me?" the question can be more appropriately phrased as "Am I clear?" There is a distinction between whether "you [deaf client] are capable of understanding me [therapist]" versus whether "[therapist] have done an adequate job in expressing myself to you [client]." Deaf persons frequently report that hearing people, even when communicating inappropriately, put the onus of responsibility for assuring adequate communication on the deaf person. A hearing person (i.e., therapist) asking "Do you understand?" to a deaf person (client) may be perceived as insulting and condescending.

In individual treatment, it is preferable for a therapist and client to communicate directly without the use of an interpreter. The reasons for this have been well described in the literature: An interpreter affects transference factors (Harvey, 1982, 1984a, 1984b; Roach, 1979); may introduce discomfort about confidentiality (Stansfield, 1981); and often results in logistical scheduling problems, especially as it is preferable to work with the same interpreter consistently for the duration of ongoing therapy (Stansfield, 1981). Moreover, including an interpreter, per se, does not assure an optimal linguistic situation; a great deal of subtle contextual material gets lost in the process of interpretation (Harvey, 1985a). For example, humor, sarcasm, plays on words, metaphors, and idioms are often lost in interpretation between different languages and cultures. However, if a therapist does utilize an interpreter, it is mandatory that a solid background and understanding of all these nuances is obtained (Taff-Watson, 1984).

Because the linguistic considerations of conducting therapy with deaf clients has been thoroughly reviewed in the literature noted above, it is not explicated here, other than to emphasize that linguistic aspects are clinically and ethically vital (Pollard, 2002).

DIFFERENTIATION FROM REFERRER

Most deaf clients are referred by hearing professionals (Burke, Elliott, & Lee, 1987; Holt et al., 1981). This is due to several factors. Glickman and Gulati (in press), Langholtz and Heller (1988), and Pollard (1998) noted that deaf people have less knowledge than hearing people about what therapy is and how it can be beneficial; the deaf person may view counseling as being for "bad" or "crazy" people; the deaf person may have knowledge of a friend's negative experience with hearing clinicians; and the deaf person often lacks knowledge about sliding fee scales, which is especially relevant because, in general, their level of income often precludes the means of self-referral to private practitioners. Moreover, there are rarely Telecommunication Devices for the Deaf (TDD) in most private practice offices or agencies.

However this is not the full story. Often deaf adolescents may be referred because of behavior problems in the school. Behavior problems, by implication, are usually more disturbing to others than to oneself; youths and adolescents, resenting control by others, may deem the environment or situation to be at fault, not themselves (i.e., "I just wish my teacher would get off my back"). A typical student with behavior problems would not be expected to refer him or herself for treatment; rather, a teacher or guidance counselor typically initiates the referral.

All of these factors contribute to the likelihood that the initial therapeutic situation will consist of a triangle made up of the referrer, the therapist, and the deaf client. It is the therapist's immediate task to avoid the inherent pitfalls of functioning as part of a triangle that is, in turn, intimately woven into the ecological fabric. Stated in systemic terms, the therapist must avoid becoming part of the interactional sequences which include the presenting problem. As has been described by Harvey and Dym (1987, 1988), dysfunctional sequences may be supported by the complex and often conflictual relationships between a deaf person and myriad professionals (such as clinicians, vocational rehabilitation counselors, teachers) who, in turn, refer the deaf person for psychological treatment. The therapist must differentiate from the referrer(s), and thus become, "meta" to the triangle (see Fig. 6.1). There are specific tasks involved in differentiating from a referrer(s), depending on from which characteristics the therapist wants to differentiate.

One such characteristic has to do with *role confusion* among the therapist, referrer, and the multitude of other counselors in the deaf client's ecological field. The client often does not know how the therapist's role–qualifications differ from those of, for example, the dorm counselor, school counselor, vocational rehabilitation counselor, speech therapist, interpreter–tutor, and so on. To achieve differentiation, it is necessary to accurately portray the process of psychotherapy as distinct from other helping disciplines. As a psychologist, I have found it useful to assign the sign for "psychology" to me with my name sign; assign different job signs to all of the counselors with whom the client is interacting; and then spatialize them separately from each other. This can be done by spatial referencing, drawing pictures of the respective professionals, writing poster signs designating their jobs, or by inviting the respective counselors to the session. Finally, it is important to differentiate them from each other with examples, and then explain and compartmentalize what job description–function each type of counselor performs.

The sequence just mentioned sets the stage for more detailed elicitation of the client's expectations from therapy. Questions that may be helpful to elicit the client's expectations of the therapist include: What have you (client) heard about therapy? What does the therapist do and not do for you? Will the therapist interpret for you? Assist in making phone calls? Get you a job? Be a source of information? And so on.

After eliciting expectations, as with hearing clients, it is necessary to provide information about what therapy is, and is not. However, this procedure is often particularly important for deaf clients as they often have not been privy to knowledge of the process of therapy. Clarification of expectations includes identifying that it takes time to identify problems and accomplish

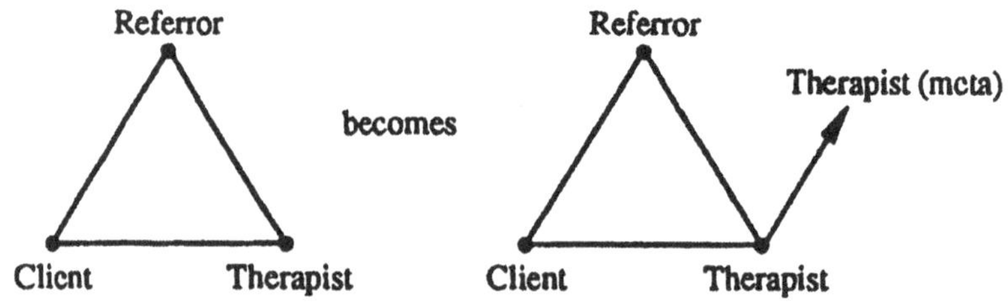

FIG. 6.1 The therapist as meta to the triangle.

change; that talking about thoughts, feelings, behavior is helpful toward promoting change, and so forth. This includes, for example, that therapy does not mean advocacy. This issue of information giving has been described by Langholtz and Heller (1988).

Confidentiality issues, as conceptualized in this framework, represent an important move by the therapist to differentiate him or herself from other participants within the deaf client's ecology. As Falberg (1985) noted, there is a mistrust on the part of many deaf clients concerning hearing professionals maintaining confidentiality. In addition, the need for clarity and reassurance about confidentiality is also a reflection of the vast number of persons who typically comprise a deaf person's ecology (Harvey & Dym, 1987, 1988). Communication among service providers may be necessary to be helpful. However, clear parameters of how, when, and if this communication occurs is critical. The therapist must explain issues of confidentiality in detail, not only to provide requisite information to the client but also in order for differentiation to occur.

In addition, as Falberg (1985) stated, specific rules need to be established in regard to unplanned social encounters between the therapist and client. Deaf and hearing clinicians are likely to attend functions, such as Deaf community events and workshops, whether it be for social or educational–cultural reasons, sign language exposure, and so on. Some clients prefer me to "look through them" as if I have never met them, others prefer a short "hello," and still others may think nothing of talking about personal therapeutic matters. Rules for conduct during out-of-session encounters clearly need to be established ahead of time.

A second ecological characteristic of the referrer–therapist–client triangle is related, not to role confusion, but to possible explicit or implicit conflicts between the referrer and client. The prevalence of such conflicts is understandable in light of what Chough (1983) termed as the *trust–mistrust phenomenon between deaf and hearing persons:* A long history of many deaf people feeling oppressed by the hearing culture (Mindel & Vernon, 1971; Pollard, 1998; Rosen, 1986). Many such historical precedents occurring at the cultural–political level of the ecology sets the stage for conflict between the hearing referrer and the deaf client that threatens to pull in the therapist to take sides.

There are many cases when the therapist is tempted to agree with the referrer and disagree with the client about the need for treatment. Consider the case when a referrer mandates psychotherapy for deaf parents, who have previously been abusive to their children and who are properly deemed at risk for committing further abusive acts. Although the parents are not presently abusive nor neglectful and do not wish treatment, the necessity for treatment is justified as a means of improving their parenting skills and preventing further abuse. Whether legitimate or not, there is a complementary relationship established among these two parties in which the deaf parents likely feel bullied by the (hearing) agency.

Here, adequate joining between the therapist and client is essential, as it is the basis for establishing a therapeutic contract to explore other more germane concerns of the client, perhaps not directly related to the reason for referral. However, it is likely that the referrer and the therapist may be perceived by the deaf client as in collusion against him or her, and that this perception may impede joining and precipitate premature termination of therapy. In this manner, the presenting problem that may have prompted a referral may become worse. The therapist should be particularly sensitive to the possibility of becoming entrenched in these dysfunctional transactions and take active steps toward becoming meta to the conflict.

There are at least three specific steps toward joining the client and becoming meta to the referrer–client conflict. First, it is necessary during the initial meeting to explicitly ask the client whether he or she agrees with the referrer about the benefits of psychotherapy. If the client disagrees with the referrer about the need for treatment, it is important for the therapist to explicitly solicit from the client his or her perceptions of the disagreement; for example, specific "bones of contention," affective reactions, dates of expressed conflict, and the like. This process of helping the client to differentiate the two positions ipso facto helps put the therapist meta to the conflict.

However, this is only a first step. Second, the therapist must then be clear about his or her loyalties in regard to the conflict. The therapist must assume a stance of neutral curiosity (Cecchin, 1987) that only enlists the client's aid in teaching the therapist more about the conflict. Here, the therapist assumes a one-down and student-like position, as opposed to immediately trying to be overtly helpful. In the special case of when therapy is mandated (which often implies a conflict between client & referrer) it is also helpful to acknowledge the "stuckness" of the situation, while emphasizing that although "we have to meet, what we do together is up to us."

Third, the therapist, having achieved a neutral and curious stance, then needs to elicit, from the client's point of view, his or her characteristics, beliefs, or feelings that are independent from the conflict or coalition within the triangle and that justify treatment. If successful, this process elevates the dyadic, therapeutic interaction to another level, in which the client is more personally committed to treatment. For example, in the previously described case of a referrer persuading deaf parents to receive psychotherapy to improve their parenting skills, the therapist may elicit from the clients that "it is obviously important to you to have a final say about the welfare of your child" and then can discuss "how, from your point of view, you feel your authority gets undermined. Is it by Protective Services, is it by your child?"

Another possible triadic configuration involving the referrer and therapist inadvertently colluding against the client may occur when a vocational rehabilitation counselor attempts to persuade a deaf person to become gainfully employed when that person wishes to continue collecting Social Security benefits. When their conflict reaches a specific level of intensity, the vocational rehabilitation counselor may respond by referring the client for treatment. Again, whether gainful employment is or is not desirable over collecting SSI has been debated elsewhere (Pimental, 1981) and is a moot point in this context. Here, what is important is the existence of a conflict in goals between the vocational rehabilitation counselor and the client that has prompted a referral to the therapist; that the VR counselor requested, persuaded, or mandated the client to receive treatment when it may or may not have been indicated. The importance of the therapist becoming meta to this conflict is apparent. (The important concerning who has the right to mandate improvement for another are beyond the scope of this book.)

Alternatively, there are many cases when therapists may be tempted to collude with the client against the referrer. For example, one teacher referred a deaf student for treatment to "make him less prejudiced against speech." The deaf student himself refused to use his voice and prided himself on his ASL fluency and on his leadership within the Deaf community. Having ascertained both sides of this conflict, the therapist privately felt that the deaf student was correct; that the teacher was "motivated by her own ethnocentric needs to make the deaf student adopt hearing norms rather than motivated by a desire to help him make independent decisions."

The situation of the therapist finding it easy to agree with the deaf client's adversarial position against the referrer, at first glance, appears less problematic than when the therapist leans toward siding with the referrer. After all, in the former case, an immediate therapeutic alliance is established. However, if one conceptualizes the ongoing referrer–client conflict as possibly supporting dysfunctional behavior of the client—perhaps in that the conflict restricts necessary information flow between referrer and client—then it becomes clear that their relationship must be modified. Colluding with the client against the referrer may simply provoke a counter, symmetrical response from the referrer, may escalate the conflict, and may prove counter therapeutic. Here, the therapist simply becomes incorporated into the dysfunctional triangle and essentially becomes part of the problem. For example, a therapist colluding with a deaf client against an independent living skills (ILS) trainer may precipitate anger and defensiveness from both parties and inhibit both the client and the ILS trainer from working together at a later time, even at a time when it would be to the client's benefit.

Moreover, many apparent disagreements between referrer and client at a content level are not as dichotomous as they first appear and are often supported by and entrenched in dysfunctional transactions at a process level. Furthermore, a client's resentment may also be a function of his or her intrapsychic perceptual distortions that are not emanating from the referrer.

Thus, the therapist should not to be too quick or absolute in his or her assessment of the conflict. I may scratch my head, verbally indicate my confusion, and request further meetings to enlighten me; only at a later time, would I reframe the conflict. For example, I might later reframe a referrer's (in one client's words) "intrusiveness" as "loving concern but perhaps too much of it."

A third ecological characteristic that frequently occurs within the client–therapist–referrer triangle is an enmeshed, overly dependent relationship between referrer and client. This has been described in a classic article by Palazzoli, Boscolo, Cecchin, and Prata (1980) entitled "The Problem of the Referring Person." Written over 2 decades ago, it is still relevant today. Consider the example of a client and a counselor who have worked together for a number of years and have become friendly over time, so that the boundaries between them have become blurred. They have developed a shared, mutually supported view of the problem. Both of them may have explicitly or implicitly agreed that the client initiate psychological treatment with an outside therapist, but if, and only if, the outside therapist agrees with their definition of the problem. Alternately, a conflict in their relationship may have precipitated a referral to an outside therapist by the client or counselor. In this sense, the client overtly or covertly initiating this referral, or agreeing to it, has the same function as may an extramarital affair within a marital relationship; despite an apparent conflict between referrer and client, this conflict may still be superficial and there may remain a strong bond between them that functions to exclude a third person (see Fig. 6.2).

In either case, the therapist often finds him or herself overtly or covertly barraged by two people to agree on the definition of the problem (and solution). For example, hearing parents frequently refer their deaf child for treatment, while labeling the presenting problem as "our child does not accept deafness." There is often an implicit or explicit request for the therapist to agree with their definition of the problem. Families often resist accepting the existence of psychological problems having nothing to do with deafness because of years of trauma dealing with deafness (Dickens, 1985).

In general, Palazzoli (1985a) and Palazzoli et al., (1980) pointed out that a referring person often occupies a nodal homeostatic position in relation to the individual client or his or her family; the pattern of interaction between refer-

FIG. 6.2 Structural map of referrer-client-therapist relationship.

rer and client may maintain the problem. Thus, if the therapist does not initially join the referrer, the referrer may gain a lot of power—the power of an absent member. The referrer, perceiving the therapist as a threat, may subtly persuade the client to become resistant to therapy or to terminate from it.

Consider the case of a referring ILS specialist, who demonstrated a need to be needed, and a deaf client, who demonstrated a need to be supported. The new therapist correctly diagnosed their dysfunctional relationship, but erred by immediately stepping in to help the client become more independent from the ILS specialist. Because this tactic threatened the original dyad, the client promptly terminated treatment. The ILS specialist, in turn, telephoned the therapist to indicate his disagreement with the particular approach and with the therapist's "insensitivity." The therapist then justified the clinical approach, a response that only served to escalate the conflict.

As Palazzoli (1985) also pointed out, this scenario commonly occurs when a person is referred to treatment by his or her sibling. The homeostatic transactions between the client and sibling may be threatened by the client having begun therapy with a new therapist despite the fact that the sibling initiated and encouraged the referral. The potential for a dysfunctional triangle must be considered by the therapist accepting a referral from siblings who function as parental children in the family. Such a case is exemplified by Marsha in chapter 4.

In general, it is important that the therapist first assess the present psychological position of the referring person within the client's ecology: Is the referring person an important member of the deaf client's family, informal network, professional network, and so forth. The therapist can then establish—negotiate a position within the triangle. It is frequently beneficial for the therapist to invite the referring person to a meeting that includes the client. The therapist can then join the referring person in the client's presence and all three persons can agree on and coordinate therapeutic goals. Clear differentiation of roles is also greatly facilitated.

For example, I was asked by a referring audiologist to treat her 29-year-old deaf client who was having trouble individuating from her nuclear family. On meeting the client individually, it became clear that both the client and audiologist were having difficulties individuating from each other because the latter had provided important emotional and audiologic assistance for several years. When the deaf client was asked about various thoughts and feelings that the client was experiencing, she would often make references to "how well the audiologist knows me." Assessing that the audiologist and client were enmeshed and that the audiologist functioned as the gatekeeper, she was invited to the next session with the client's permission and, in fact, relief. We then negotiated our individual roles and fields of expertise, and I was careful to explicitly recommend that the audiologist and client continue their important relationship. Thus, I supported the dyad, easily joined the client, and later in treatment discussed individuation issues with respect to the family and the audiologist, and later with respect to myself. Meetings were also occasionally set up with the audiologist and client (& others) as treatment progressed.

Unfortunately, for a variety of reasons, it may not be possible to involve the referring person in any way, however entrenched he or she may be in occupying a nodal homeostatic position that serves to maintain the presenting problem. There may be logistic scheduling difficulties or simple refusal by the referrer or client. In such a case, the therapist may have to simply pay verbal homage to the referrer when the client brings up the subject, or compete with the homeostatic bond inherent in the relationship between the client and the referrer by beginning dyadic treatment. However, this arrangement is often less than optimal for joining to occur.

DIFFERENTIATION FROM LEVEL OF CULTURE

Differentiation from the level of culture is a more general case of differentiation from specific referrers in the ecology. The task here is to differentiate from culturally based preconceptions and role expectations that the client may have about the therapist and vice versa, whether or not the client was self-referred or referred by others. A deaf client's preconceptions of a therapist who is hearing is determined by transference factors, from previous positive and negative experiences with the hearing culture (Harvey, 1996; Pollard, 1998). A deaf client may revere the therapist because of a history of viewing hearing persons as superior to deaf persons, including him or herself. Alternatively, a client's preconceptions may be negative. The ethnographic research by Nash and Nash (1981), in which deaf persons rated hearing professionals as untrust-worthy, remind hearing clinicians that a deaf client may demonstrate initial distrust and suspicion because of what Vernon and Makowsky (1969) term *minority group dynamics and oppression*. These dynamics have also been discussed by Chough (1983), Glickman and Gulati (in press), Glickman and Harvey (1996), Kannapell (1983), Pollard (1998), and Sussman (1976). Moreover, they are illustrated by the case in chapter eleven, referred to as "ordinary evil."

Similarly, a deaf client's preconceptions of a therapist who is deaf is determined by transference factors, derived from previous positive and negative experiences with the Deaf culture (Harvey, 1996). Here, the dichotomy between *deaf* (audiologically hearing impaired) and *Deaf* (a member of a cultural group) is relevant to understanding the therapist–client dyad, although this dichotomy does not account for the plethora of nuances of perception found in clinical practice. Furthermore, as Glickman (1986) and Leigh and Lewis (2000) noted, there are varying degrees of enculturation within the Deaf culture. Nevertheless, for heuristic purposes, we can posit that the attitude of a audiologically *d*eaf of a culturally *D*eaf client toward a *d*eaf or *D*eaf therapist is influenced by perceived similarity factors. Although the degree to which perceived similarity enhances rapport remains somewhat equivocal (Anderson & Rosten, 1985), nevertheless anecdotal reports suggest that similarity often facilitates joining (Elliott, Bell, Langholtz, Nguyen, & Peters, 1987). For example, the decision of a prospective client to function more distant to the Deaf community, as a *d*eaf person, or more proximal to the Deaf community, as a *Deaf* person, will likely influence his or her emotional proximity or rapport with a *deaf* or *Deaf* therapist.

Again, however, the influence of perceived similarity factors on joining depends on the specific context and previous experiences. Indeed, as Leigh and Lewis (2000) aptly note, there is a "significant burden on the deaf therapist who works within the deaf community because the intricacies of living within this small community place the deaf therapist in a fishbowl for all to see." (p. 60).

Attention to differentiation from the culture and appropriate interventions must necessarily be in accordance with the idiosyncrasies of the chemistry between a particular therapist and client. One self-labeled *d*eaf therapist reported having marked difficulty establishing a therapeutic alliance with a client whom he perceived as *d*eaf, in spite of the ease of communication and their common disability. The difficulty in rapport made sense only when the therapist ascertained that the client had earlier been negatively labeled as *deaf* by a group of *D*eaf persons, who mockingly compared him with hearing persons. In contrast to the therapist's self-perception, the client had perceived the therapist as *D*eaf, and thereby experienced negative transference toward the therapist. Thus, ascertaining both the client's and therapist's attitude about deafness and relationship to the Deaf community and culture, along with previous and current experiences with the various cultures, provides important information about transference factors for predicting successful initial therapeutic joining.

Apart from similarity factors, it has been my experience and others (see Anderson & Rosten, 1985; Sue, 1981) that the process of differentiating from the wider cultural context often requires a bit more self-disclosure on the part of the therapist. Because some vagueness or tabula rasa increases the likelihood of transference or displacement (Colby, 1951), it follows that self-disclosure will increase the likelihood of differentiation. For example, a therapist might recount his or her unique process of choosing to enter the field of deafness (i.e., "I initially wanted to work with deaf persons because I found sign language to be a beautiful language, and because I found cross-cultural dynamics to be interesting"). However, although a bit more self-disclosure is often helpful, it must be balanced with vagueness, for too much self-disclosure by the therapist might jeopardize the therapeutic relationship. One client summarized her initial session with a therapist by complaining that "I learned more about him than he did about me!"

It is extremely important for therapists to ask themselves some hard questions having to do with how or if they are indeed differentiated from the cultural context, both deaf and hearing, in which they function. Boyarin, Burke, Evans, and Lee (1987), Langholtz and Heller (1988), and Sussman and Brauer (1999) noted the high prevalence of countertransference issues among hearing therapists who work with deaf clients. In addition, Levin (1981) underscored that patients with handicaps generally arouse powerful countertransferences in their therapists. Some therapists may even begin their work with handicapped clients out of identification with the damaged patient. Feeling damaged themselves, such therapists will struggle internally to 'cure' others of problems that in some way remind them of their own (p. 121).

Some fundamental questions for the therapist, deaf or hearing, to ask include: What ecological expectations are on me? How will I handle them? How can I satisfy the people who refer clients to me in order to keep up referrals? Do financial considerations constitute a conflict of interest between therapeutic goals and referral sources? What motivated me to choose the field of psychotherapy in general, and the field of deafness in particular? Am I a therapist to obtain praise? As Glickman (1986) aptly stated, it is important to ask who is helped more, the giver or the receiver? These are difficult but important requisite questions.

Questions about countertransference and differentiation from the ecological context, including culture, naturally lead us to the issue of the therapist's attitude toward deaf persons, and to the therapists behavior during the session. It is obviously vital that therapists have respect for clients in the context of the clients' experiences and culture (Evans, 1987; Sussman & Brauer, 1999). However, if one assumes a priori that the client who is from the Deaf culture must therefore have x, y, z characteristics, that "I know about Deaf culture, therefore I know about you," then one is guilty of stereotyping. As Sue and Zane (1987) noted, this is a common misunderstanding, or bastardization, of cross-cultural therapy. Although the cross-cultural emphasis has properly elevated many peoples' view of deafness from a pathological condition to a culture (Lane, 1984), the misuse of cross-cultural counseling is equally as dangerous. For example, it is often described as a "given" that deaf people who sign value a hearing therapist quite positively if that therapist has good sign language skills. Although this is quite often true, it is also true that some clients who are aversive to identifying with the Deaf community, and therefore who are aversive to sign language, favor a therapist who does not sign well.

A related example of what I consider to be a misuse of cross-cultural counseling relates to a commonly cited supposition that there is a specific psychology of deafness and of Deaf persons, as opposed to common patterns of relationships occurring within the ecology. In this regard, Moores (1987) criticized many professionals for their paternalism and acceptance of myths, distortions, and half-truths about deafness and deaf individuals [and for their] glib generalizations.

Related to stereotyping of deaf persons is the common misconception that there are specific modes of treatment that are appropriate and inappropriate, that is, that deaf people cannot benefit from insight-oriented therapy because they are concrete and therefore need a less abstract kind of treatment (e.g., Glickman & Gulati, in press; Happ & Altmaier, 1982; Rainer, Altshuler, & Kallman, 1963; Stewart, 1981; Sussman and Brauer, 1999). Some can, others cannot; like hearing persons, it depends on the client. Deaf clients with average intelligence and who have grown up with an adequate language base that fosters conceptual and abstract reasoning skills can often benefit from insight-oriented approaches. In contrast, clients with limited language and conceptual skills require more concrete approaches. However, Sussman's (1988) statement is well taken:

> The reported failures and difficulties in psychotherapy with deaf individuals are more a reflection of the therapist's clinical skills, understanding of deafness, attitudes, personality, cultural sensitivity, experience with deaf clients, and sign language competency, rather than the imputed or stereotyped limitations of a deaf client. (p. 5)

There are several other examples of therapists viewing a deaf person in what appears to be a disrespectful manner that retards or prevents joining. One such example was a hearing therapist attempting to initially join a deaf client by saying, "Deafness sucks, doesn't it?" Quite rightly, the client interpreted this therapist's attitude as "hearing equals health, deafness equals nonhealth." In a similar vein, many deaf clients recount with anger previous therapists implying that "I (the deaf person) have a communication problem," rather than "we have a problem communicating that must be solved together." In these cases, the therapists defined deafness as an impairment. Although their definition of deafness may match that of some *d*eaf clients, it does not match that of *D*eaf clients, for whom deafness represents a cultural difference (Lane, 1984). However, as previously noted, in terms of the kinds of clients of present themselves for treatment, the dichotomy of *d*eaf and *D*eaf is an oversimplification; for many client's attitudes and identities in reference to deafness fall somewhere in between these two poles. Consequently, this distinction should properly serve as a starting point to guide the therapist's questioning and learning about a specific client.

This attitude on the part of the therapist can best be summarized by the term, *therapeutic naivete*. It seems self-evident, but vital to remember, that the therapist does not know a prospective client prior to a meeting. It is most helpful in initiating treatment to state that "I don't know you," and ask "would you be willing to teach me who you are?" In this regard, Anderson and Rosten (1985) noted that the therapist's hearing status is not as important as the therapist's sensitivity to the client as an individual. Similarly, Sue (1981) emphasized the therapist variables of expertise and trustworthiness as primary determinants of an optimal therapeutic relationship between therapist and client.

To summarize, the idea of cross-cultural counseling is helpful and humanistic if, and only if, it offers the therapist a series of questions and hypotheses to ponder. It is important to ask whether or not a particular client has those x, y, z culturally based characteristics, and how that person may view the world in ways influenced by cultural factors. The therapist must be able to frame such assumptions as questions, as possibilities as opposed to givens. As Sherlock Holmes said (cited in Minuchin & Fishman, 1981, p. 50), "It is always a mistake to theorize ahead of the data."

MATCHING THE CLIENT'S CONSTRUCTION OF REALITY

There is an old story about a child who was learning how to become an umpire. One day, the child lined up three experienced umpires and asked them to explain their individual techniques. The first umpire replied, "I call them as they are." The second replied, "I call them as I see them." The third replied, "They *are* as I see them."

This section on joining focuses on the process of the therapist assessing and matching what is termed the client's construction of *reality or world view.* We are all "third umpires." We must understand how a client's experiential history, current life context, and future goals mold his or her view of the world and then communicate that understanding to a client. It is consistent with Grinder and Bandler's (1976) description of "anchoring," Erickson's dictum to "begin where the patient is at" (Bandler & Grinder, 1975; Haley, 1967), techniques of framing and reframing (O'Hanlon, 1984; Watzlawick et al., 1976), and Meichenbaum's (1994) use of metaphors in establishing client rapport. Indications of successful matching of a client's construction of reality may include a client's smile or nod of the head following a remark of the therapist, as if to indicate "yeah, that's it." More explicitly, one client exclaimed, "Yes, now you know where I'm at" after the therapist had summarized the session.

A therapist, deaf or hearing, does not need to communicate directly with a deaf client in order to achieve linguistic matching as described earlier in this chapter. This can be successfully achieved through an interpreter. However, with an interpreter, to the extent that some of the more subtle clinical material gets lost as an artifact of interpretation per se—perhaps in proportion to the interpreter's own idiosyncratic world view—direct communication is preferable, if not necessary, for precise third umpire matching of the client's experiential world.

Matching of a client's construction of reality is essential, particularly when a therapist from the hearing (majority) culture is treating a member of the Deaf (minority) culture. On a macrolevel of analysis, there exists a wall between these two groups of people that may impede the necessary matching from occurring. Therapists and clients are from two somewhat antagonistic groups, in that the Deaf culture is a minority group which has been oppressed by the hearing culture (Gannon, 1980; Glickman & Gulati, in press; Padden, 1980; Sussman, 1976). Minority groups have different world views, shaped by their subordinate status: Each group sees or understands the world in markedly different ways. Moreover, each group may affectively and negatively react to each other's view of the world. Sussman (1976), for example, noted that "it is a rare deaf person who has not as a child been ostracized, ridiculed, and denigrated by nondisabled children. Such memories are painfully poignant" (p. 10). Finally, as Glickman (in press) noted some deaf clients present as psychologically unsophisticated, that is, as unfamiliar with the constructs of psychotherapy.

Although on a macrolevel it appears that deaf persons who present themselves for psychological treatment view the world differently than hearing persons, it should again be emphasized that this situation is much more complex than a simple dichotomy would suggest. The clinician who works with individuals should interpret this result with caution. As emphasized in the preceding section, on a micro level, the therapist should operate from a position of therapeutic naivete; that is, commonly observed world views of deaf clients offer possibilities—hypotheses—to guide the therapist's questioning of a particular client. The therapist wonders aloud about the degree to which various schemata are meaningful towards constructing and organizing a client's world. Earlier, this process was referred to as the therapist asking whether a particular client operates from x, y, z characteristics.

Thus, what follows are speculative descriptions of four prevalent ways that deaf clients whom I have treated have described or framed their third umpire constructions of reality. I have observed these themes presented with a high degree of regularity; and, although the following themes are by no means idiosyncratic to deaf persons, they nevertheless appear to be more prevalent among deaf clients than among hearing clients. However, it is emphasized that these descriptions are based on the limited sample of my clinical experience and therefore are presented as tentative in terms of their generalizability. In reference to clinical practice, the four themes, or frames of reality, are presented only with the intent of guiding the therapist's mode of inquiry; they are not presented as a priori facts.

Distance Variables: Close–Far, Disengaged–Engaged

The schema of psychological distance from other persons has frequently been used by clients to describe the quality of their relationships with specific others. For example, a deaf person may depict a group of hearing people by pointing five fingers upwards on one hand and pointing one finger upwards on the other hand to depict him or herself as a deaf person. The distance between the client's "hearing persons hand" and "deaf person hand" represents the degree of engagement or intimacy that the client experiences with them. One's experience of engagement or disengagement is represented by the physical distance of the hands.

Often distance variables are related to linguistic accessibility. For example, one deaf client depicted his nuclear family by five fingers and localized one finger quite far away to represent himself. He them mimicked his parents and siblings talking incomprehensibly to him, emphasizing that he does not feel included. He similarly described many hearing situations in this manner. Linguistic engagement and disengagement, as with many clients, was an important schema that molded his perceptions.

Equivalence Variables: Same–Different

This schema is related to clients' perceptions of their similarity or dissimilarity to others in the environment. In my experience, this has most often been in reference to whether others are deaf or hearing. One side of this dichotomy is exemplified by the comment of Benderly's (1980) that "to be deaf is to be not hearing ... is to be one of us and not one of them." On the other hand, one deaf student who was mainstreamed with other hearing students, far from viewing himself as fundamentally different from his hearing classmates, proudly exclaimed "all of us are basically the same."

A client's attribution of similarity with reference to hearing or deaf persons appears related to whether he or she identifies with the hearing or Deaf community. For example, within a hearing environment in any context, does the client consider him or herself as similar to or as different from others, and to what degree? Specifically with reference to the deaf client–therapist context, does the client consider him or herself as similar to or different from the therapist (who is either deaf or hearing)?

Gestalt Variables: Figure–Ground

This schema is a consequence of many deaf persons experiencing a pervasive sense of being different from the wider ecological, hearing context. Given that a client feels different from others in the environment, he or she may feel in the foreground or in the background relative to the crowd. This dichotomy is a basic tenet of Gestalt psychology, which teaches that the mechanics of perception require the separation of images into figure and ground. Consider one client who described her experience of feeling in the background: "I felt alone, lost, almost like I disappeared when I went to the rally [among hearing people], like I evaporated." Here, the client reported feeling insignificant, indeed nonessential, an amorphous part of a hearing crowd which she perceived as figural. However, during another point in therapy, this client described experiencing herself as in the foreground, as figural, among hearing persons in a mainstream, academic setting: "I could never daydream, skip class, or doodle in school. The interpreter would notice instantly, and the other hearing kids would roll their eyes." This phenomenon has also been described by Falberg (1985).

Competence Variables: Powerful–Powerless

Themes of empowerment and powerlessness are frequently present in the discourse of deaf client in therapy (Harvey, 1989; Schlesinger, 1985). Although hearing clients also frequently bring up this theme, deaf clients often make particular reference to the larger hearing world in which they function. For example, the play "Children of a Lesser God" poignantly illustrated themes of control and competence, power and powerlessness, between deaf and hearing persons. Sarah, the lead deaf character, continually attempted to exert control and demonstrated her competence with respect to the hearing characters. She felt thwarted and powerless among hearing persons throughout most of the play–movie, because of communicative isolation and discrimination. In contrast, she felt quite competent among her deaf peers.

The so-called "Deaf President Now" Gallaudet Revolution is perhaps the most well-known example of successful advocacy of Deaf rights. In 1988, Gallaudet University's Board of Trustees announced that a hearing person had been selected as their seventh president, despite all the evidence and support for a Deaf president. This oppressive act prompted long overdue national attention for the rights of deaf people and set the stage for that wonderful success story.

Powerlessness with reference to hearing persons was also illustrated by Benderly (1980) who noted that

> In more cases than not you will find, surprisingly close to the surface and barely hidden by education, good manners, humor or experience, the running scores of anguish and resentment, the gaping, unstaunchable wounds of wrongs done decades before, a bottomless fury: an identical litany of slapped hands, tied wrists, punishments, scoldings, tedium, humiliation. (p. 229)

Self-attributions of powerlessness may also be a result of the client him or herself distorting reality because of previous maladaptive experiences, as in the case of a deaf person deifying and attributing omnipotence or omniscience to hearing people. As an example, two deaf parents, because of previous maladaptive experiences feeling one-down to hearing persons, began a therapy session by timidly asking in what direction should they set the clock for daylight savings time. Although this question per se would not necessarily be indicative of the one-down, one-up complementarity, in this case, their question appeared to be one of several examples of this pattern. I therefore replied (truthfully) that I too always get confused about which direction is correct. We figured it out together.

7

Communication Logistics of Family Treatment

Unlike families consisting solely of hearing members who communicate in the same language, families in which there is a deaf member present unique challenges for the therapist. For many deaf persons who have a prelingual,[1] profound,[2] or bilateral[3] hearing loss, the efficacy of receptive comprehension of spoken English via speech reading is grossly inadequate (Liben, 1978; Perry & Silverman, 1978; Pollard, 1998; Pollard, Miner, & Cioffi, 2000; Vernon & Andrews, 1990). It is, therefor, likely that manual communication would be a deaf family member's primary and preferred means of fully understanding discourse in any environment, in particular, within the family (Lane et al., 1996; Moores, 1987). Because approximately 90% of deaf persons have hearing parents and siblings (Schein & Delk, 1974; Vernon & Andrews, 1990) and many families resort to spoken communication as opposed to achieving proficiency in manual communication (Lane

---

[1]Prelingual hearing loss refers to a hearing loss that has occurred prior to the development of language (Moores, 1987).

[2]A profound hearing loss refers to a hearing loss over 90 decibels. This results in extreme difficulty not only in understanding shouted conversation but even in hearing the sound of the voice (Levine, 1960).

[3]Bilateral refers to affecting both ears.

et al., 1996; Rawlings, 1971; Stuckless & Birch, 1966), there is often a linguistic communication barrier within the family.

Although one could properly apply Watzlawick et al.'s (1976) dictum that "one cannot not communicate" to the communication that occurs over a period of years between deaf and hearing family members and conclude that communication therefore happens adequately; this dictum primarily applies to nonverbal communication. It does not apply as well to verbal communication, which includes vocal language and a signed language. Within such families, much verbal information frequently does not get exchanged between deaf and hearing members; thus the frequent complaint of communication problems. The deaf member frequently is not able to understand fully what others are saying orally; and the hearing members often have trouble understanding the deaf member.

Although families consisting of all hearing members also often get labeled, or label themselves, as having communication problems, here, the clinician assumes that verbal communication is adequate and therefore assumes that such problems refer to dysfunctional interactional patterns that cause distress. For families in which there are deaf members, however, the problem is frequently two-tiered. Such families may experience these same kinds of dysfunctional interactions plus verbal communication difficulties. To make matters more complex, it is often problematic to separate generic dysfunctional patterns from those emerging from linguistic difficulties. Consider the frequent remark of parents that "my deaf child really does understand, but he or she is just pretending not to." Indeed, as with totally hearing families, this may be legitimately the case.

Given that the genesis and maintenance of a presenting problem for families in which there are deaf members is frequently not as simple as inadequate linguistic communication, the remedy, in turn, does not solely comprise of sending them to sign language classes. It is like simply recommending to an anorexic person that he or she should eat more. In the context of ecologic factors, which have been described in chapters 1 and 2, linguistic communication difficulties are frequently related to nonadaptive levels of denial operating both intrapsychically among various family members and interpersonally vis-à-vis implicit rules (Ford, 1983; Jackson, 1965) that prohibit open acknowledgment of certain disabling and handicapping effects of deafness. Such rules serve the function of encouraging the members to pretend that linguistic communication problems and other differences do not exist. For example, there are families in which all members, including the deaf member, deny such communication problems; families in which the deaf member emphatically states that communication is inadequate only to encounter resistance from his or her parents; and the reverse situation in which parents insist that there are communication difficulties only to encounter significant resistance from the deaf member. Harvey

(1998a, 2001) and Mendelsohn and Rozek (1983) have documented instances of families who have been taught to nonadaptively deny implications of deafness.

Consequently, when initially meeting a hearing, nonsigning family in which there is a deaf member whose primary and preferred language is sign language, a clinician is immediately faced with the tasks of establishing the verbal communication logistics of the treatment session; and ferreting out verbal communication difficulties from other dysfunctional interactional patterns. This chapter focuses on the first task by delineating the pros and cons of several options for enacting verbal communication during the session with the previously mentioned kind of family.

Table 7.1 lists six options for the hearing, hard of hearing, or deaf therapist's mode of communicating with each family member.

As can be seen from Table 7.1, the first three options are implemented in conjunction with an interpreter; the therapist communicates either orally, by way of a visually coded English system without voice, or by ASL (naturally without voice). Here, the interpreter voices for the benefit of the hearing members when the therapist signs without voice, and signs for the benefit of the deaf member when the therapist is voicing English without signing. The latter three therapist's communication options are implemented without interpretation: the therapist communicates orally, by way of a visually coded English system simultaneously with voice, or by way of ASL. Naturally, the mode of communication that the therapist chooses will, in part, depend on his or her proficiency. For example, a hearing or deaf therapist who is not skilled in ASL would not opt to use the third option—ASL without voice. Similarly, a deaf therapist who is not proficient with oral communication would not opt to use Options 1 and 4, which involve oral discourse.

It is shown that for every logistic decision that the therapist makes about communication, there is, on one hand, therapeutic advantages; yet, on the other hand, compromises. Thus, the therapist can continually vary which option to use during a given session and between sessions, in accordance with the particular therapeutic goal. The therapist is not restricted to following one option but should flexibly vary them as the need arises.

OPTION 1: THERAPIST COMMUNICATING ORALLY WITH VOICE-TO-SIGN INTERPRETATION

The oral method is the natural way of communicating for hearing persons, including hearing parents and hearing siblings. The hearing therapist or oral deaf therapist using this first option voices to hearing family members, whereas an interpreter signs in whatever form of manual communication is preferred by the deaf family member: transliteration (spoken English to manually coded English system), ASL, fingerspelling, or some other means.

TABLE 7.1

Logistics of Verbal Communication Between Therapist and Client

Persons with Whom the Therapist Communicates Directly	*Therapist's Mode of Communication*	*Interpreter's Mode of Interpreting for the Therapist*
Option 1		
Hearing family members	Oral without sign language	Voice-to-manual communication
Option 2		
Deaf and hearing family members	Manually coded English without voice	Voice-to-manual communication
Option 3		
Deaf and hearing family members	ASL without voice	Manual-to-voice communication
Option 4		
Hearing family members	Oral	No interpretation
Option 5		
Deaf and hearing family members	Manually coded English with voice ("sim-comm")	No interpretation
Option 6		
Deaf family member	Manual communication without voice	No interpretation

Although the therapist communicates in the presence of both hearing and deaf members, the therapist communication is direct for all hearing persons, although it is indirect (mediated through an interpreter) for the deaf member. Although this places the deaf member at a greater disadvantage than if the therapist communicated directly to him or her via manual communication (such as with Option 2), the deaf person is significantly more able to understand what is transpiring in the session than if there were no interpreter present to interpret oral dialogue.

The decision of the therapist to use this first option of oral communication is predicated on the fact that he or she primarily wishes to join with a hearing family member at a given time. Therefore, the therapist chooses the direct mode of communication via a common language, spoken English. If a therapist uses a signed language without voice (Options 3 & 6) while communicating with hearing family members, in some cases, it precipitates some discomfort on their part. The discomfort may be due to their resistance accepting sign language or awkwardness about having the interpreter voice for the therapist. (This is elaborated later in this chapter.) In any case, the parents' discomfort would be counter therapeutic until therapeutic joining has properly occurred.

The rationale for viewing this choice of oral communication as a joining operation between the therapist and a hearing family member an be clarified by further elucidating the problematic aspects of this option with respect to the deaf member. Here, the linguistic input is indirect, one step removed. The addition of an interpreter per se does not create a situation of equivalence or of equal accessibility for the deaf member. Although interpreters provide accurate interpretation as much as possible given their extensive training, it is subject to minimal levels of temporal and content distortion. These are artifacts to interpreting between any two languages in general, and are not idiosyncratic to interpreting for deaf persons in family therapy sessions.

In regard to temporal distortion, it is impossible for interpreters to provide identical simultaneous interpretations of an oral dialogue. There is a required time delay. Interpreting from spoken English to ASL, for example, requires first listening to the phrases and their meanings, then manipulating the information according to the syntax of ASL, and finally expressing the phrase through ASL. This process requires at least several seconds and increases in duration when the interpreter does not immediately understand the discourse. Therefore, the deaf member conversationally falls a little behind and cannot participate in perfect temporal synchronicity with the hearing family members.

Thus, as a result of the inevitable time lag between a phrase being voiced by a hearing person and being signed by an interpreter, a deaf client may always be at the edge of his or her seat waiting to jump in the conversation at an appropriate time. The therapist may erroneously assume that the deaf person is exhibiting a verbally passive stance. The deaf person, in turn, may inadvertently be learning to remain passive in the family. In one situation, a deaf client exclaimed, "By the time I could think of what to say, someone else was halfway through his next sentence. I finally gave up!" It is apparent that this situation may reinforce a deaf client's feelings of passivity and inferiority.

An additional drawback with interpretation is content distortion. It is not feasible to interpret everything—the subtle nuances, innuendoes, body position changes, facial cues, and so forth. Moreover, the level of content distortion would theoretically be a consequence of the inevitable level of distortion in the perception of the message by an interpreter; how much data an interpreter misses or modifies. Such distortion would be expected to increase in direct proportion to interpreters' conscious and unconscious needs, desires, and defensive structure, and to decrease in proportion to their training and experience. In other words, interpreters, as human beings, would be expected to perceive inaccurately—and therefore interpret inaccurately—content that is highly emotionally loaded for them. However, one would expect this tendency to lessen as interpreters receive further specialized training and certification with the Registry of Interpreters for the Deaf (RID, 1976).

The process of joining a hearing family member vis-à-vis this option of communicating can best be illustrated by Erickson's techniques of indirect hypnotic trance induction (Bandler & Grinder, 1975; Haley, 1967). The effectiveness of these hypnotic techniques is facilitated by one-to-one, direct communication, without temporal and content distortion. The therapist frequently matches a prospective client's body posture, rate of speaking, use of metaphors, and use of unconscious and conscious symbolism; to borrow a phrase from neurolinguistic programming (Grinder & Bandler, 1976), the therapist communicates with a client simultaneously on nonverbal and verbal levels to match his or her "map of the world." The verbal and nonverbal subtleties—certain body positions, winks, smiles, metaphors, symbolism, and so forth—are impossible to convey completely through an interpreter.

The following is an example of a family that included an enmeshed hearing mother–deaf child dyad and a disengaged hearing father. For several sessions, the mother had complained of feeling overwhelmed and lonely. This transcript contains an indirect and metaphorical therapist communication about her tendency to take on too much responsibility and becoming overwhelmed:

Mother: [begins the session by chatting about her garden] ... With this drought, I need to water it almost every day.

Therapist: Where do you get the water? [matches mother's seating posture]

Mother: Well, there are no hoses or faucets nearby, so I carry it in by pails. Sometimes a neighbor lets me borrow his hose.

Therapist: So you need the water to help your garden grow—without the water, you cannot make this happen? [therapist smiles]

Mother: Uh huh. [looks confused]

Therapist: And if you were asked to help the plants grow without the help of water, what would you do? [slows down pace of speech to match that of mother]

Mother: Well, I couldn't.

Therapist: Maybe you could attend all of the horticultural meetings, support groups, maybe attend different garden clinics? [therapist winks]

Mother: Yeh, I wish ... [laughs, pauses, slowly nods head]

Therapist: That you could help the plants grow in this way?
Mother: Yeh. [smiles]
Therapist: But you couldn't do this even though you may try? [smiles]
Mother: Right, I can't do it all myself. [nods more emphatically]
Therapist: I don't blame you for needing the water, who up to now has been difficult to find. Are you ready to ask the water for the help you need?
Mother: I think so.
Therapist: And as you picture doing that, how do you feel?
Mother: [begins to sob]
Therapist: Could you share that with your husband?

I had joined with the mother by symbolically discussing her need for her husband (the water) to help her raise the children (the plants). By matching the mother's usage of symbolism and by matching her nonverbal behaviors, I was simultaneously communicating on a surface and deep structural level (Grinder & Bandler, 1976). The probability of success of this technique was increased by one-to-one, direct communication. Many of the subtler and indirect hypnotic suggestions would have been lost if they were communicated via an interpreter.

OPTIONS 2 & 3: THERAPIST COMMUNICATING VIA MANUALLY CODED ENGLISH OR VIA ASL WITH SIGN-TO-VOICE INTERPRETATION

In these options, the therapist uses a manually coded English system, such as Signing Exact English or Pidgin Sign English without the use of voice (Option 2), or ASL without the use of voice (Option 3). The interpreter interprets sign to voice for the benefit of the hearing family members. These options represent the reverse linguistic situation of the previous option of oral communication: Here, the therapist communication is direct for the deaf person via sign language and indirect (mediated through an interpreter) for the hearing persons. Thus, communication is accessible to the deaf member even when the therapist is communicating with the hearing family members. There is no information lost through interpretation.

It is important that the therapist utilizes the mode of manual communication, which is the deaf member's primary mode.[4] To join the deaf member, it is appropriate to use Option 2 if he or she uses Pidgin Sign English or Visually Coded English, as opposed to ASL. However, if ASL is the deaf member's primary and preferred language, this method will prove to be linguistically

[4]There are instances when deaf clients may resist acknowledging and using their primary mode of communication, such as Manual Coded English or ASL. The sources of their resistance may be intrapsychic or in reaction to a family denial system.

inaccessible to him or her. In that case, the therapist should use Option 3 in order to increase linguistic accessibility to the deaf member.

Because there is maximal visual contact between the therapist and the deaf member, the deaf member becomes privy to all of the subtle verbal and nonverbal nuances of the therapist even when he or she is communicating with other family members. This option greatly increases the probability that the therapist can join the deaf member, because it conveys an attitude of respect for linguistic accessibility and provides a common language base. In the case of a hearing therapist, the message is "I am altering my usual mode of communicating with hearing members out of respect for you [deaf member]."

Although this option is used primarily to converse with and join the deaf family member, it also may be used as an intervention for conversing directly to hearing members, when proper joining has occurred and when it is therapeutically helpful to risk introducing some discomfort. Communicating to hearing parents in sign language through an interpreter models for them that communication need not be vocal to be intelligible; that signed language is a sophisticated verbal language. Once the initial awkwardness subsides, this intervention is effective in conveying a sense of awe that their deaf son–daughter, who may be nonvocal, is nevertheless quite linguistically competent in manual communication. Vocal communication is not equivalent to verbal communication.

In addition, the following transcript illustrates that these options also pave the way for more subtle intervention strategies with respect to the deaf family member, as analogous to those mentioned in the previous section. In this transcript, I was attempting to help Amy, a 25-year-old deaf female, "come out" as a lesbian to her parents. Throughout this transcript, I used Pidgin Sign English without voice, Amy's primary and preferred mode of communication, and the interpreter interpreted sign to voice. Amy also used Pidgin Sign English without voice when conversing with me and with her parents. Incidentally, prior to this session, much time was spent with Amy to help her prepare for this moment:

Therapist: [to Amy] Well? [Therapist smiles slightly]

Amy: [to therapist]; [Also smiles slightly] I guess this is it, huh?

Father: [oral, with voice to sign interpretation] You're not pregnant, are you? Using drugs? What is it?

Amy: [laughs, looks at therapist]

Therapist: [also laughs] What help do you need from me now? [maintains eye contact longer than usual in order to emphasize message, and to support it nonverbally]

Amy: [breaks eye contact with therapist]; [to father] No, I'm not pregnant, no I'm not using drugs. [looks down and becomes silent]

Therapist: [while looking at Amy intermittently, therapist converses with her parents through the interpreter] Can you find a way to support Amy in what she is trying to tell you? [therapist nods head slightly to Amy to indicate that she can "jump in" when she's ready, but to take her time]

Amy: [to parents] Do you love me no matter what?

It was clear that Amy needed to feel that the therapist was primarily allied with her, as opposed to being primarily allied with her parents. Therefore signing directly to her, and communicating to her parents indirectly through an interpreter, was therapeutically important.

OPTION 4: THERAPIST COMMUNICATING ORALLY WITHOUT INTERPRETATION

In this option, the therapist communicates orally without interpretation to the hearing and deaf members of the family. Assuming that sign language is the deaf member's primary and preferred mode of communication, it is immediately apparent that, from the perspective of deafness with its emphasis on accessible communication, this option is inappropriate at best and perhaps can be construed as unethical. Stated differently, the therapist reinforces a dysfunctional sequence that occurs across levels of the ecology; the therapist communicating ineffectively is isomorphic to the case of some parents communicating ineffectively, to the case of some educators communicating ineffectively, and so on. Details relating to the debate about effective communication methodology—the "oral–manual controversy"—were mentioned in chapter 1 and are not elaborated here. Interested readers are referred to Lane et al., (1996) and Moores (1987).

Although this option is linguistically inappropriate for the deaf family member, it may be systemically appropriate in terms of the pragmatics of intervention. Although the therapist insisting on signing "so the deaf member can understand" is certainly, politically correct in terms of Deaf cultural considerations, premature politicizing on behalf of the deaf member may precipitate premature termination of treatment by the family. The therapist who suggests the use of sign language or a sign language interpreter to a family who ardently denies linguistic and other implications of deafness, is introducing a restructuring intervention. This intervention immediately confronts a common family rule prohibiting the use of manual communication that has been supported by the ecology, as described in chapter 2. Such families may have implicitly or explicitly agreed that "we will not talk with our hands to our deaf child," using the justification that he are she "is more intelligent than those other deaf people who need to sign."

For example, consider the following excerpt from an initial interview in which it seemed therapeutically inappropriate to ensure linguistic accessibility for the deaf client; signing had threatened the homeostatic balance of the family which served to deny the implications of deafness.

Therapist:	[introduces himself using Simultaneous Communication]
Father:	[voice] I wish you wouldn't sign, doctor. We don't do that. He [12 year-old deaf son] has been educated well, and is quite intelligent.
Deaf son:	[Simultaneous Communication]; [to therapist] Wow, you sign! [proceeds to sign in ASL without the use of voice]
Therapist:	[Simultaneous Communication] Yeh, but your father is older than you, he deserves respect ... [now therapist changes to only voicing, without an interpreter] so we'll begin by only talking.

In this example, the immediate therapeutic task, which would ultimately be helpful to each family member, was to join the father. Signing was a premature restructuring intervention (Minuchin, 1974). Accommodation must precede restructuring. Stated differently, it is sometimes necessary to sacrifice short-term linguistic accessibility ethics, as delineated by the field of deafness, in favor of long-term therapeutic benefits. However, this should be done with extreme caution.

When using this option of oral communication without interpretation, the therapist can conduct treatment in the usual manner as with a hearing family, but privately keeping in mind that the deaf member is probably conversationally lost and may be pretending to understand much of the conversation. In a family of five members and a therapist, for example, there are 360 possible permutations of dyadic communication: father to mother, mother to father, brother to sister, sister to father, and so on. Thus, even if the deaf member could understand the spoken communication, he or she has no way of localizing a person's voice when he or she begins talking. Furthermore, people in groups often talk at the same time!

It is vital for the therapist to carefully time when and how he or she points out the child's lack of comprehension of the content of the discussion; the therapist must first join the family members who hold the power to influence other family members to communicate using a given methodology. (The importance of joining the most powerful member of a family system was illustrated in chapter 1.) Assuming that the therapist has already begun to establish rapport with the protagonist of the family, and has begun to earn the family's respect as an expert, he or she can engage the family in figuring out ways of communicating more effectively. It is common that the therapist who first points out inadequate verbal communication with families at the proper time, and then "works through their feelings about it" often precipitates the family's expression of pent-up anger at professionals who in the past "steered us wrong ... told us not to sign."

It is sometimes, but not always, the case that the therapist, to join the family, must use this option for several sessions or several months, during which time the deaf member essentially is conversationally lost. However, my experience suggests that the deaf child is implicitly aware and approving of the therapist's intent, provided that initial joining has occurred between therapist and deaf child. However, after appropriate linguistic communication in the session has begun, it is therapeutically vital for the therapist to explicitly acknowledge the deaf child's plight by eliciting and clearly explaining the reasons for not having signed and for the family (& deaf child) having participated in a game of "make believe everyone understands each other." This, of course, is the essential therapeutic work. This work serves as an effective catalyst towards helping the family to examine their conflictual thoughts, feelings, and behaviors about having a deaf family member.

There are other instances when it is not therapeutically appropriate to add signing or interpretation to facilitate intrafamilial communication, even when it is linguistically useful. Adding sign language frequently may thwart the development of functional interactional sequences in which family members are struggling to recognize and ameliorate verbal communication difficulties. The following transcript depicts a father struggling to communicate effectively with his 15-year-old deaf daughter. Here, the father is attempting to explain abstract concepts by using English metaphors, as opposed to Sign rules, and the daughter is not comprehending their meanings.

Father: [voicing] I don't mind you getting perturbed at me. But I want you to know that your mother and I have had marital difficulties, you might say interpersonal problems, and I guess I felt overwhelmed, work pressures, I couldn't go to your mother so I, uh, dumped it on you. Like a soda bottle, you know, shaking it up, comes out all over.

Daughter: [shrugs and appears not to understand]

Father: [pauses and appears anxious; voices to therapist] She doesn't understand me.

Therapist: [Simultaneous Communication to daughter] Mary, your father really wants to say something to you. Would you help him?

Daughter: [Simultaneous Communication] You angry when I spilled Coke in house?

Father: [voices] (ha) No. [attempts to explain again, but looks frustrated]

Therapist: [Simultaneous Communication to father] You really want Mary to understand how you feel, and you're trying real hard. Would you ask Mary how you can explain it more clearly?

[Father and Mary struggle together. Father eventually succeeds.]

Daughter: [Simultaneous Communication] So you and Mother were fighting and that's why you yelled at me more?

Father: [looks relieved and jubilant] Yeh! That's it!

Either the therapist or an interpreter could have easily signed to Mary what her father was saying; however, in this particular interaction, it would have needlessly insulted and disempowered the father by depriving him of an emotionally important and therapeutically helpful struggle to communicate with his daughter. Moreover, this intervention paved the way for developing an important and new interactional sequence, in which the father asks the daughter for help on how best to communicate with her. Supporting the functional sequence had a ripple effect in the system; in this particular case, many of the conflicts between the father and daughter were significantly resolved once it became an implicit–explicit rule that it was permissible to acknowledge and address linguistic communication problems.

OPTION 5: THERAPIST COMMUNICATING VIA SIMULTANEOUS COMMUNICATION WITHOUT INTERPRETATION

In this option, the therapist voices for the benefit of the hearing members, and simultaneously signs in a Pidgin or Manually Coded English system for the deaf member. Thus, no assistance from an interpreter is required, whether the therapist is directly communicating with the deaf family member or with the other hearing members; in both cases, the therapist uses simultaneous communication, often abbreviated as "sim-comm." In contrast to Option 2, when the therapist's communication is via Manually Coded English without voice, but with voice-to-sign interpretation, this option is initially a bit less awkward for hearing family members. The therapist simultaneously communicates to all family members and has adequate control of both signed and vocal factors. For example, when the therapist communicates with parents using sim-comm, the parents will hear the therapist's voice, not that of an interpreter as in Option 2. Furthermore, assuming that Manually Coded English is linguistically accessible to the deaf member, another advantage of this option is that the therapist can more easily convey a message to the deaf member while talking to a hearing member.

For example, in the following therapy segment, I was simultaneously voicing and signing with a father in front of the deaf son, Steven. An interpreter translated voice to sign when the father was speaking:

Therapist: [sim-comm to father] Steven may not understand the pain you feel.

Father: [voice; interpreter signs] He is selfish. I'm sick and tired of him thinking only of himself.

Therapist: What would Steven need to do to show you that he feels concern for you? [therapist looks toward Steven]

Father: Leave gas in the car, etc. [lists]
Therapist: I wonder if Steven is grown up enough to do some of those things before the next meeting? [therapist glances at Steven]

One possible disadvantage of this option has to do with clarity of communication, as described from the perspective of the field of deafness. First, Manually Coded English is often not the deaf member's primary mode of communication. ASL may prove to be more accessible. Second, some members of the Boston Deaf community and many interpreters assert that it is clearer to sign without voicing, and report that both modes of communication suffer when speakers attempt to use Simultaneous Communication. This observation has been confirmed by Strong and Stone-Charlson (1987) and Marmor and Petitto (1979). Thus, it is a common occurrence at Boston conferences for deaf persons to request that the speaker choose between signing or voicing and that an interpreter be used. In addition, Lane et al. (1996), Nash and Nash (1981) and Woodward (1982) and many deaf people suggest that it is a cultural norm to sign without the use of voice. However, such preferences do not seem to be uniform in the Deaf community; in fact, many deaf and hearing speakers across the country regularly sign while voicing at conferences, and so on. This is an unresolved issue that merits further study.

A final disadvantage of this option is that it carries less impact than the therapist signing without voice. It is often helpful to demonstrate the sophistication of sign language with drama and impact, best accomplished by signing without voice. However, as emphasized earlier, the effectiveness of this "demonstration" with a particular family member assumes that the therapist has properly joined that person. As with all of the communication options, it becomes apparent that timing considerations should dictate the use of this option.

OPTION 6: THERAPIST COMMUNICATING VIA MANUAL COMMUNICATION WITHOUTVOICE AND WITHOUT INTERPRETATION

In these options, the therapist communicates directly with the deaf family member by using the client's primary and preferred mode of communication, such as Manually Coded English, ASL, or various pidgin modes. There is no sign to voice interpretation for the benefit of the hearing family members. This option represents the reverse situation of Option 4, which uses oral communication without voice-to-sign interpretation so the deaf member is conversationally isolated; here, the hearing members are conversationally isolated. Consequently, as with Option 4, this option must be used carefully and judiciously in order not to needlessly exclude participants of the session.

The impact of this option on the deaf member varies. It may promote effective joining as this option solely takes the deaf member into account, even excluding other members; it is akin to a "private club." One deaf child, eager to pursue a private conversation with me, exclaimed, "it is like hidden gossiping but in front of my father!" In contrast, some deaf members, in an act of loyalty (or manners) to their parents, resist this intervention, and do not wish to be rude by "whispering in front of other people."

Reactions of hearing family members to the therapist using this option also varies greatly. If, and only if, this intervention is timed carefully, in accordance with a mutually respectful relationship between therapist and hearing members, the latter will not be offended but will often report amazement and new found respect. However, if this intervention is not done carefully, it may needlessly insult and exclude other family members. Implemented carefully, this communication option is very effective for demonstrating and educating hearing parents about what linguists have known for over two decades, namely that ASL is a bonafide language with its own syntax (Baker & Battison, 1980; Baker & Cokely, 1980).

As an example, enactment of this communication option prompted one parent to state his sudden realization of "how complicated ASL is. I couldn't understand any of what you two [therapist & deaf member] were talking about for 5 minutes!" Similarly, following a long conversation between a deaf adolescent and me in ASL without interpretation, I asked the family to discuss how it felt to be linguistically excluded. The younger sibling commented that "I felt stupid," a sentiment that was also echoed by the parents. It then became much easier for the family to empathize with the deaf adolescent's continual experience of linguistic exclusion.

An additional effect of this option is that it immediately, although temporarily, rigidifies the boundary between the deaf child and parents and quickly promotes an open, fluid exchange between therapist and child. The parent is excluded by virtue of not knowing sign language, whereas the therapist and deaf member know sign language. For various therapeutic reasons, the clinician may wish to begin promoting such a boundary. The therapist and deaf family member communicating with this option during the therapy session can serve as a microcosm of other more general interactional changes that need to occur between child and parent having to do with distance regulation or boundaries, changes specifically having to do with privacy needs. This option is an in vivo demonstration of a private discussion between therapist and deaf child, even though other family members are present.

In this regard, the therapist can balance private signed communication with the deaf child, as delineated by this option, with private oral communication with hearing parents, as delineated by Option 4, to further emphasize needs for separateness. In the context of achieving specific clinical goals, enactment of various private dialogues can serve as metaphors for what needs to occur outside of the family therapy session. In particular, this technique may be useful for deaf adolescents or young adults who are attempting to emotionally separate from their parents.

8

The Use of an Interpreter for the Deaf in Family Therapy

Whereas the focus of chapter 7 was the logistics of therapist communication with different family members and only alluded to intrafamilial communication, this chapter specifically focuses on intrafamilial communication in deaf-member families during the therapy session. How does a therapist enact communication among deaf and hearing family members in a family in which the hearing parents and siblings do not sign, and the etiologic factors and audiologic configuration of the deaf member's hearing loss are such that his or her primary mode of communication is manual communication rather than spoken English? Does the therapist neglect to comment on the words and sentences that the deaf member misses, in favor of focusing on other interactional factors of the family system? Does the therapist modify the conversational pace of the meeting (e.g., by instructing people to speak slowly & in sequence, etc.) to increase the deaf member's verbal participation in the session? Does the therapist attempt to sign some or all of the discussion for the deaf member? If the deaf member has unintelligible speech, does the therapist attempt to voice for him or her for the benefit of the hearing members? Should an interpreter be present?

There are no absolute answers to these questions. As discussed in chapter 7, introduction of sign language or a sign language interpreter must be done judiciously in the context of the therapeutic goals. Consequently, the appropriateness of how, or if, a therapist should intervene to influence the mode of verbal communication among family members is dependent on the specific therapeutic objective aimed toward modifying the intrafamilial transactions that maintain the presenting problem—the family's reason for seeking therapeutic assistance.

As described in earlier publications (Harvey, 1982, 1984a, 1984b, 1985a, 1986), with a deaf-member family in which there is a verbal communication barrier, an interpreter is often included in family therapy both to modify intrafamilial linguistic and systemic transactions. Including an interpreter in treatment has also been described by Dean and Pollard (2001), DeMatteo, Veltri, and Lee (1986), MacEachin (1982), Marcos (1979), Sluzki (1984), Stansfield (1981), Sussman and Brauer (1999), Taff-Watson (1984), and Pollard (1998). As a linguistic intervention, an interpreter facilitates verbal communication, vocal or signed communication, among family members. The interpreter interprets voice to sign to enable the deaf family member to understand the hearing member's vocal communication, and interprets sign to voice to enable the hearing members to understand the deaf member's signed communication. Even though a therapist may be fluent in manual communication and certified as an interpreter, it is usually neither feasible nor therapeutically prudent to interpret for family members while simultaneously providing treatment. It is best for the therapist to communicate with family members via the six options listed in chapter 8. A clinician cannot provide effective therapy and be concerned, at the same time, with accurate interpretation or transliteration of manual communication and spoken English. Both are discrepant, complex, and energy consuming tasks.

It is important to note that, as illustrated in chapter 2, families are often taught to nonadaptively deny implications of deafness and, therefore, do not adequately cope with the demands of raising a deaf child. With these families, simply including an interpreter in treatment to facilitate verbal communication would not result in systemic change; the linguistic effects of an interpreter would not help the family solve the problems that brought them to therapy. However, the effects of including an interpreter in treatment are not restricted to linguistic factors. In spite of the fact that the "only function of an interpreter is to facilitate communication" (RID, 1976, italics added) and by implication not to influence the participants' behavior beyond what one would expect from making effective communication possible, an interpreter inevitably affects the interaction in many additional subtle yet important ways. The therapist can view the interpreter as part of the family-therapist system and use an interpreter in a systemic manner to precipitate systemic change.

The purpose of this chapter is to provide illustrations and ramifications of appropriately including an interpreter in family therapy, particularly as a systemic intervention toward modifying transactions that are assessed to support the presenting problem. This chapter primarily addresses therapists, hearing and deaf, who are skilled in sign language and who are knowledgeable about deafness, although some of the proposed interventions can be used by nonsigning therapists.

This chapter does not address families who are productively denying certain implications of deafness. Denial of the impacts of deafness at the time of the initial diagnosis is psychologically healthy. In this case, denial serves an important function of enabling parents to psychologically prepare to deal with painful emotional reactions, as well as many logistic stresses that are part of having a deaf child (Moses, 1976; Vernon & Andrews, 1990). This chapter is restricted to describing interventions with families who exhibit dysfunctional linguistic and denial characteristics; it, for example, does not address families in which there are "successful oral" deaf members.

Moreover, as described in detail in chapter 7—(Option 4) therapist communicating orally without interpretation—I do not always include an interpreter in family therapy. For example, including an interpreter with a family who recognizes communication barriers and who is taking steps to ameliorate them would block those functional transactions and, therefore, would clearly be counter therapeutic. Similarly, including an interpreter before a family is able to recognize and adequately deal with the necessity for more adequate verbal communication is counter therapeutic and would frequently precipitate unnecessary resistance and often premature termination from treatment.

This assessment is typically made during the first session of family treatment when there is often no interpreter present. The determination of whether or not the inclusion of an interpreter would be advisable either immediately or later in treatment is made by the therapist first asking each family member to state his or her preferences and reasons, pro or con, in terms of including an interpreter; then requesting the family members to discuss this among themselves; and then making a clinical judgment of the systemic effects of introducing this intervention, using the principles described in chapter 8.

When it is therapeutically appropriate to include an interpreter in family treatment, I typically go through a standard sequence. The interpreter and family, including the deaf member, arrive and wait in the waiting room together; I then invite the interpreter in the office for a presession meeting; the session takes place; and, at the end of the session, the family leaves while the interpreter remains for a postsession meeting. The interpreter and family waiting together is a function of scheduling logistics; the preceding hour is usually booked with another appointment and the interpreter and family members often arrive early. The occurrences of presession and postsession meetings with the interpreter, however, are purposeful and have been described in detail by Stansfield (1981) and Taff-Watson (1984). The content of these meetings is elaborated in the final section of this chapter, which describes the relationship between the interpreter and therapist.

INITIAL REACTIONS TO INCLUDING AN INTERPRETER

It is important to note that a complex series of verbal and nonverbal exchanges immediately take place between the therapist and the family in connection with the initial introduction of an interpreter. The acute observation of cues, such as the family members' comments about the interpreter, their avoidance or frequent observation of the interpreter, and their body posture relative to the interpreter all provide a wealth of clinical data that can be used to therapeutic advantage. It is therefore important for systemic diagnosis that the therapist elicit the family's reactions, both during the initial encounter with an interpreter and throughout the duration of treatment.

As an example, a deaf family member may state that the presence of an interpreter is unnecessary, but on closer examination, may occasionally peek at the interpreter during a conversation. Here, the therapist can acknowledge this event to then examine the child's conflict between breaking the family rule (Jackson, 1965) that "we do not need to use interpreters" versus being able to comprehend what is being spoken. Alternately, a deaf family member may openly look at the interpreter to understand what a family member is saying, prompting the parents to react by feeling a combination of inadequacy ("we do not know Sign Language"), guilt ("we should have learned to sign"), and relief ("we can finally communicate!"). Other possible reactions from parents of overt anger (i.e., "our child is not dumb—he or she can lip-read") or passive anger (i.e., while smiling, the father asks, "doctor, is an interpreter really necessary?") certainly indicate that the therapist's intervention of including sign language or an interpreter may be violating implicit–explicit family rules. In many cases, these reactions may be prognostic of a more flexible and destabilized family homeostatic structure and therefore more readiness to change.

Reactions of the Deaf Family Member

We now more specifically turn our attention toward the deaf family member's initial reaction to the presence of an interpreter. Stansfield (1981), Taff-Watson (1984), and others have pointed out several factors that determine whether the deaf member's reaction is positive or negative: the quality of the deaf member's previous experiences with interpreters, his or her perceptions about the reasons for including an interpreter, his or her perceptions about who the interpreter "belongs to," and his or her comfort with confidentiality parameters.

The importance of comfort with confidentiality, although self-evident, deserves special emphasis. The RID Code of Ethics regarding confidentiality should be clearly explained, and the deaf (& hearing) members' reactions and comfort levels should be carefully elicited. If, for whatever reasons, the deaf (& hearing) member does not trust the interpreter to maintain confidentiality, treatment will be immediately and irreparably thwarted. Issues of confidentiality become particularly important with deaf family members because of the interpreter's probable affinity with the Deaf community.

Assuming that the family is comfortable with confidentiality, the presence of an interpreter usually facilitates the process of initial joining between the deaf family member and therapist, particularly if the therapist signs for him or herself with the deaf member. Including an interpreter in treatment serves as a concrete acknowledgment to the deaf person of the therapist's commitment to ensure adequate intrafamilial linguistic accessibility during the meeting. For example, at the end of one particularly difficult session for a deaf adolescent who was getting reprimanded by his father for staying out too late, the adolescent commented in ASL that "at least with an interpreter, I understood why he [father] was so pissed off"; the adolescent then directly thanked both the interpreter and therapist.

However, with a hearing therapist, in particular, it is occasionally the case that the deaf member experiences initial affinity with the interpreter but guardedness with the therapist. Why is this sometimes the case? In part, it is fostered by the logistical setup of the family and interpreter waiting in the waiting room prior to a session. Prior to the initial session, the interpreter often utilizes this opportunity to informally assess the deaf member's communication by chatting with him or her. Thus, an initial rapport is established. Furthermore, this rapport is strengthened as the weekly casual chatting between interpreter and deaf member in the waiting room becomes routine during the course of treatment. As a result, a more informal relationship usually develops between interpreter and deaf member as the sessions continue over a period of time.

In addition, an initial affinity with the interpreter and guardedness with the hearing therapist, when it does occur, is also related to cultural influences. Nash and Nash (1981), in their ethnographic research of the role conceptions that deaf people have with regard to hearing persons, rated deaf persons' perceptions of interpreters as "almost the closest to us," second only to hearing children of deaf parents. Although a sample of deaf persons rated interpreters as "suspicious" and working for both extrinsic and intrinsic rewards, nevertheless, they were also rated as trustworthy. However, the ratings of interpreters were in marked contrast to the sample of deaf persons' ratings of other hearing professionals, such as therapists. Such professionals were rated as "least like us," as working for extrinsic rather than intrinsic rewards, as suspicious, and as untrustworthy. Glickman and Gulati (in press), Sussman and Brauer (1999), and Boyarin et al. (1987) have also addressed the dynamics that commonly occur between a hearing therapist and deaf client.

Consequently, this possible alliance structure between the interpreter and deaf member must be handled carefully. If it is acknowledged and worked through by a therapist who is nondefensive, the interpreter may function not only to introduce two strangers (hearing therapist & deaf family member) to each other, but more importantly may function like a diplomat between two relatively disengaged parties. Stated more precisely, the interpreter may mitigate negative transferential aspects of initial joining between the hearing therapist and deaf family member. The interpreter, in this sense, becomes a buffer. In this regard, MacEachin (1982) described a therapy session consisting of a male therapist, a male client, and a female interpreter. The interpreter was perplexed that the patient appeared so comfortable discussing his sexual preference and homosexual activities. However, the client was experiencing homosexual panic, and merely having another individual in the room reduced the patient's sense of threat of being propositioned by his therapist. In this case, having a female interpreter was also an important factor.

If this initial alliance structure that excludes the hearing therapist is not openly and supportively addressed and worked through, the therapist will not form an alliance with the deaf member. The deaf family member may come to perceive the interpreter as the primary helper, rather than as a bridge to the therapist. Here, the therapist's skill at joining the deaf member, as discussed in chapter 6, becomes crucial. In addition, as is elaborated later in this chapter, the therapist and interpreter must understand and discuss this initial process of bonding with each other and plan together for what would be most therapeutically helpful.

Reactions of the Hearing Family Members

There are many possible reactions of hearing family members to the introduction of an interpreter, depending on the idiosyncratic family dynamics around deafness and the deaf child. From a systemic perspective, one can conceptualize the effect of using an interpreter as providing "news of a difference" (Bateson, 1971). The introduction of an interpreter poignantly serves to demonstrate in vivo the rich, fluid, and effortless linguistic sharing that such families miss on a day to day basis at home. Families are quite often surprised and impressed with how easily they are able to converse with the deaf member during the treatment session in marked contrast to the fairly elementary, concrete, and telegraphic discourse that frequently occurs at home. Thus, it is often the case that hearing family members appreciate the presence of an interpreter because, from their points of view, interpretation "makes it easier to communicate."

For example, one father in treatment was delighted to have a philosophical discussion with his deaf 18-year-old daughter during one session on "the meaning of life, future aspirations, what we're on this earth for, is there life on other planets, etc." It was a sad but therapeutically important moment when he metacommunicated by discussing both his relief of having this "high level kind of discussion" but also of the limited, awkward, and strained discussions that occur at home. The father commented that typically "most of what we talk about involves only 'yes– no' answers." It is one thing to simply resign oneself to accepting that "yes–no" answers are the norm and in fact constitute unchangeable reality; but it is another thing to become aware of the different possibilities. In this father's words, "it doesn't have to be this way!"

In contrast, some hearing family members directly or indirectly react to this "news of a difference," as represented by the interpreter, with extreme anger, defensiveness, and hurt. Families may criticize the interpreter or therapist. Alternately, other families may exhibit overt acquiescence regarding the presence of an interpreter but may simultaneously sabotage, or even terminate the therapeutic process. Consider the example of a family who requested psychological treatment for their 15-year-old prelingually deaf son because of withdrawal and other depressive symptoms. When asked about using an interpreter, the boy immediately smiled and, with animated signs, indicated his approval of the idea. Although both parents overtly acquiesced, their apparent anger was expressed by continually speaking at a pace too rapid for the interpreter. Their behavior persisted in spite of repeated reminders and instructions. In this particular case, as their degree of resistance appeared too formidable and counter therapeutic, I opted to initially use communication Option 4, oral communication without interpretation, as described in chapter 7. After approximately 3 months of treatment, the family began to acknowledge communication difficulties and to connect these difficulties with the presenting problem of withdrawal. At that point, the parents and therapist invited an interpreter to the meetings and the parents began sign language classes.

Most reactions of hearing family members fall in between these two extremes and are characterized by significant ambivalence. One parent reported that "I am grateful to be able to communicate fully with my deaf daughter, but the interpreter shows me that I have a long way to go; I want to be able to say more things to her." In this case, the process of the therapist amplifying and examining this parent's ambivalent reaction characterized much of the therapeutic work.

Reactions of family members when a deaf or hard-of-hearing therapist works with an interpreter has received scant attention in the literature. This chapter also does not address this situation in detail, as my direct clinical experience (my context) is as a hearing therapist. However, it is important to note that, for a deaf–hard-of-hearing therapist, the introduction of an interpreter to the family treatment session is, in some ways, often much easier than for a hearing therapist. The deaf–hard-of-hearing therapist can justify an interpreter to help him or her understand the family discourse, thereby avoiding premature confrontation of the family's possible denial of intrafamilial verbal communication difficulties. This represents a very effective "use of self" in terms of modeling for the family's linguistics and other issues of deafness.

EFFECTS OF AN INTERPRETER ON FAMILY MEMBERS' PERCEPTIONS OF DEAFNESS AS THE FIGURE OR GROUND

Absence of an Interpreter Makes Deafness More Prominent

An interpreter ensures ease of verbal communication during a treatment session and therefore makes it possible to focus more on the content of what the family wishes to discuss. Consider one instance when an intact family, consisting of one hearing and one deaf sibling, initiated treatment to focus on poor grades that the hearing child was obtaining in school. The hearing members of the family did not sign and the deaf member relied on sign language. There was no interpreter during this initial session. The following nine-step sequence occurred:

1. mother described the problem to the therapist;
2. the hearing child glanced over at the deaf child and interrupted;
3. the deaf child began to play with his pencil;
4. father asked him if he understood;
5. the deaf child feigned understanding and nodded;
6. as the conversation resumed, the deaf child then disturbed objects in the room;
7. the hearing child, in turn, began to misbehave;
8. father asked mother how much the deaf child really understood; and
9. mother and father argued.

Although this sequence provided the therapist with vital interactional information, it also significantly detracted the therapist from understanding more about the hearing sibling's academic situation. The nodal points during the session had to do with the family wondering whether the deaf child understood the conversation. Hence, in this example, the absence of an interpreter made deafness issues more prominent.

The Presence of an Interpreter Makes Deafness Less Prominent

During the next course of treatment with the family noted previously, in which an interpreter was included to equalize all family members' linguistic access to information, the hearing and deaf siblings were attentive and did not distract the meeting. Thus, it became possible to ascertain that the hearing sibling had a learning disability that was not being properly addressed within the academic institution. Here, the presence of an interpreter precipitated the children behaving themselves and allowed the concerns of the hearing sibling to be more prominent and deafness issues to be less prominent.

The Presence of an Interpreter Makes Deafness More Prominent

As treatment progressed, the hearing sibling began to share her relief at having an interpreter in the room so "the therapist would know that he [deaf sibling] is not lost during the conversation," and the hearing sibling and parents frequently commented on "how we would like to take the interpreter home with us." The presence of the interpreter also cued the hearing sibling to elaborate on her tendency to sacrifice her own needs in favor of taking care of the deaf sibling and her habit of excessively worrying about the deaf sibling's welfare. It, thus, became clear that the nine-step sequence of behaviors that had occurred without an interpreter had served as an enduring supporting context for the hearing sibling to misbehave and to do poorly in school, perhaps because she felt responsible for her deaf brother feigning understanding during the session (the 5th step in the recursive sequence) or because she resented having to interpret for him.

During this phase of treatment, the hearing sibling's references to these and other effects of deafness on herself and on the family were augmented by the therapist frequently referring to how the interpreter "was signing and helping the deaf child and family" and then by the therapist eliciting the interactional patterns of different family members with respect to the deaf sibling at home. The father stated that he talks loudly to his deaf son; mother reported that she worried about him getting into an accident on his bicycle, and so on. Here, the presence of an interpreter served as a reminder of the deaf sibling to the hearing sibling and family, an effect that was utilized to make deafness more prominent.

The Absence of an Interpreter Makes Deafness Less Prominent

This was illustrated in this family by their description of a typical dinner table discussion. Although at the beginning of most meals, the hearing family members would tend to interpret for the deaf member or explicitly take care to include him in the conversations, as time progressed and as multiple side conversations occurred more frequently, the family and deaf member would give up; and the deaf member, in his words, would "learn to daydream a lot." Thus, the absence of an interpreter kept deafness issues in the background.

It becomes apparent that both the presence or absence of an interpreter can be used as a means to vary the degree of emphasis on deafness issues. As discussed in chapter 7, without an interpreter the therapist can focus on the resulting intrafamilial verbal communication difficulties, or may need to focus on other hearing members, whereas, the deaf member is temporarily linguistically isolated. (The therapist may wish to later comment on the deaf member's passivity, perhaps learned helplessness, which serves as a context for the family ignoring him or her and for the family's denial of verbal communication problems.) With an interpreter, the therapist can properly assume that more intrafamilial linguistic accessibility is occurring and therefore focus, not on deafness issues, but on other issues that the family presents; or he or she can use the interpreter as a stimulus or cue to elicit discussion about deafness issues. In regard to this last possibility, there are a number of different ways that an interpreter makes deafness more prominent. This is the subject of the following section.

THE INTERPRETER AS A CATALYST FOR "NEWS OF A DIFFERENCE" WITH DEAFNESS ISSUES

The presence of an interpreter frequently serves as a symbol of deafness to the family members. Consider the following transcript from a therapy session that included two hearing parents, their deaf daughter (12 years old), an interpreter, and the therapist. This family had been in treatment for approximately 4 months without an interpreter, as the parents had initially been quite resistant. However, 1 month prior to this segment, the parents and daughter had agreed to include an interpreter in the therapy session to "make communication easier."

Mother: [voicing]; [to interpreter] How do you sign school?
Therapist: [voicing with interpreter signing] It is tempting now for the interpreter to step out of her role, huh?
Mother: [laughs] She wouldn't care to teach me, anyway.
Therapist: How come?
Mother: Well, you know, all those people [interpreter and the Deaf community] think that we parents should sign. I sense their anger.
Therapist: Would you tell that to Sue [daughter]? [Mother and daughter discuss this and the daughter soon becomes angry.]
Daughter: You know I can't understand you half of the time!
Mother: [to therapist] I guess I sometimes wish she was hearing ... would be a lot easier. Signing reminds me that she is not [hearing].
Therapist: That's really important. Would you discuss that with Sue?

Subsequent to that dialogue, the mother and daughter were able, for the first time, to discuss their relationship in terms of acceptance and nonacceptance of deafness. The daughter later gave her mother and father their first sign language lesson, which prompted them to get further training elsewhere! It seems clear that the presence of the interpreter had served as a symbol of deafness and of the Deaf Community. This important influence was incorporated systemically into the treatment process, and facilitated the amelioration of the presenting problem.

Another major influence of an interpreter on participants in the session is a consequence of the interpreter often being viewed as symbolic of deafness and of the interpreter's well-defined role: simply to facilitate communication and not to volunteer any opinions or personal information (RID, 1976). From a psychological perspective, the interpreter is a tabula rasa, a blank slate, particularly to family members. Thus, family members (and the therapist) are free to fantasize about the interpreter's thoughts and feelings regarding the sessions or regarding any participant in the sessions.

Specifically, the psychological lack of identity of the interpreter encourages participants to exhibit the ego defense mechanisms of projection and displacement or transference. It is important to note that, other variables being equal, transference and projection are most likely to affect one's perceptions and interactions with another person when the latter's unique personal identity remains vague (Colby, 1951; Nicholi, 1988). This is the sine qua non of interpreting! Moreover, persons tend to increasingly exhibit such ego defense mechanisms as a function of the longevity of the vague relationship; for example, in the case of one interpreter consistently being present during family sessions over months or years.

Psychodynamic theory posits that persons tend to repress or suppress unresolved, anxiety laden issues and emotions having to do with previous or current relationships by acting them out with other relationships (A. Freud, 1966). Furthermore, acting out issues from a previous unresolved relationship via transference or displacement is most likely to occur when the less threatening individual in the present is perceived as similar to the original individual who had precipitated anxiety. Consider the triad of a deaf child–interpreter–parent. Clearly, the original and frequently ongoing trauma for many parents about having a deaf child meets the requirement for unresolved issues with that relationship. Many parents find their feelings of rage, anger, grief, depression, embarrassment, and so on, toward their deaf child to be unacceptable (Harvey, 1998, 2001; Moses, 1976; Stein & Jabaley, 1981; Vernon & Andrews, 1990). Consequently these feelings are suppressed or repressed, depending on the degree of conscious awareness. As stated earlier in this chapter, interpreters are perceived by deaf people as highly similar to themselves (Nash & Nash, 1981), and many parents perceive an intimate connection between Interpreters for the Deaf and deaf persons (see Fig. 8.1). Thus, it

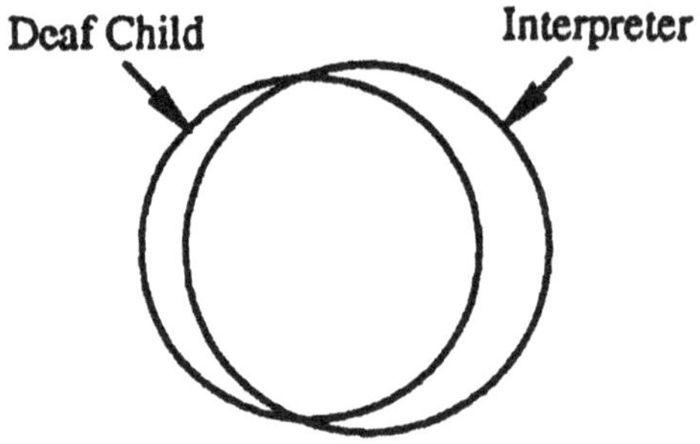

FIG. 8.1 Parents' perceptions of interpreter and deaf child.

becomes clear that many parents may displace, transfer, or project their own unacceptable feelings in reference to their deaf child onto the interpreter; they act out in the presence of the interpreter.

For example, one father manifested extreme anger toward the interpreter while experiencing an altercation with his deaf son who just smashed the family car. The father did not appear angry at his son but was quick to yell at the interpreter for being 2 min late for the session and "for making faces," associated with signing. He also emphatically asked whether the interpreter was "doing a good job translating everything I am saying to him [son]." The father's feelings of anger and perhaps intimidation and helplessness in regards to the interpreter were openly discussed in the presence of the interpreter, who, as prescribed by her role, did not volunteer personal sentiments. It soon became apparent to the father that he harbored identical feelings of anger and helplessness with his son, and that, he had displaced his unacceptable feelings about his deaf son onto the interpreter; the interpreter merely served as a catalyst for these feelings to become conscious.[1]

The father and son were then instructed to discuss this new information without the interpreter interpreting any dialogue between them, in this case so that verbal communication difficulties and deafness issues would become more prominent. As both parties openly acknowledged their hostility, helplessness, and frustration in regard to communicating with each other—which the father had previously displaced onto the interpreter— they began to effectively problem solve. They were then instructed to share other pieces of new information with each other, such as how the father felt about generational "communication breakdowns" with his own father. To facilitate the

[1]Alternately, a case could be made that the interpreter (or therapist) was indeed consciously or unconsciously acting out anger toward the father, and that the father correctly perceived this anger. This is when the qualifications of the interpreter, his or her psychological awareness, and the relationship between interpreter and therapist (described later in this chapter) become particularly critical. In this case, the interpreter and I both assessed that the interpreter was not experiencing anger toward the father and therefore that the father's perceptions represented a displacement reaction.

sharing of this information and to make deafness less prominent, I then asked the interpreter to intermittently interpret their dialogue during this interchange. (As is delineated later in this chapter, this piece of "therapeutic conducting" could not have occurred successfully unless the interpreter and therapist were in sync with each other.)

Similar to the grieving stages of shock, denial, anger, depression, and acceptance that characterize the experience of many parents in reaction to their child being diagnosed as deaf (Moses, 1976; Stein & Jabaley, 1981; Vernon & Andrews, 1990), parents will often experience the same stages when first confronted by the presence of an interpreter during a family therapy session. In light of the previously described transference and displacement reactions by parents with reference to their deaf child and an interpreter, it becomes evident that, in many cases, the presence of an interpreter in treatment is a symbolic recapitulation of their earlier discovery that their infant is deaf. Given that those influences on family interaction have been delineated, it behooves the family therapist to at least privately acknowledge them and/or to more overtly make therapeutic use of them.

For example, if it seems too threatening for the parents to be asked directly about their fears as to what their deaf child may think of them or what they think of their deaf child, the therapist has an option of eliciting the parents' fears about what the interpreter may think of them. Consider one circumstance in which the parents had perceived disdain from the interpreter, that the interpreter viewed them as rejecting. After a period of therapeutic work, they realized that their perception was influenced by their own fear that their deaf child viewed them as rejecting. Finally, the parents were helped to realize that they themselves were experiencing feelings of rejection toward their child, feelings that they had not been able to acknowledge. Once their feelings were brought to a level of awareness, they could be dealt with and resolved by the parents. Through this process, the parents gained control of these feelings, instead of vice versa.

Apart from transferential factors, the mere presence of an interpreter often poignantly demonstrates the linguistic competency of the deaf family member. Some families operate in accordance with a myth that the deaf child is relatively helpless, immature, and generally not too bright because he or she may not communicate in an articulate manner via vocal communication. In marked contrast, the deaf child whose primary language is ASL will frequently demonstrate quite articulate, and in fact eloquent, communication via ASL. As an interpreter voices in English what the child signs in ASL, the family is often quite impressed and realizes their child is not helpless; or, in rehabilitation jargon, that being disabled is not being handicapped.

However, what family members characteristically do not report, and what is clinically relevant, is that they often feel both increasing guilt for not having learned ASL—"the interpreter can communicate with my child but

I cannot"—and anxiety for not accepting deafness. Paradoxically, their feelings of guilt represent the flipside of their feelings of anger or rejection for the use of ASL. In my experience, this ambivalence on the part of the parents typically becomes more pronounced as treatment progresses, because new issues are brought up and old latent issues are reexamined more fully. It is clear that this intervention of introducing an interpreter can catalyze a change in a parental subsystem and help them become more amenable to positive change.

The therapist can also augment the impact of the interpreter to make deafness linguistic issues more prominent, particularly when a deaf member uses ASL. In working with interpreters in families consisting of a deaf member whose primary language is ASL, it is impressive how well a skilled interpreter transforms the vocabulary and syntax of spoken English to that of ASL. Interpreting happens quite quickly and with seemingly great ease. Indeed, hearing family members may take an interpreter for granted; that is, they may well be unaware of how interpretation actually happens. Here the therapist can make accessible to the hearing family members the several complex decisions that the interpreter makes throughout the session to interpret spoken English to ASL. In other words, the therapist, who is fluent in ASL, can voice, or more technically, "gloss," verbatim what the interpreter has signed in ASL from what a person has said in English. The therapist can use exactly the same grammatical sequence inherent in ASL.

Consider the following transcript in which a hearing, nonsigning mother and her deaf daughter, who used ASL, were communicating through an interpreter who was interpreting between ASL and English:

Mother: [voice] Mary, a lot of our experiences haven't been good, just as experiences in life aren't always good. Why should we let you go through the same pain and anguish, frustration, if we can point out a simpler way to do something? You're going to make enough mistakes on your own. You should accept the experiences of others.

Daughter: [signing with interpreter voicing] I listen to you, don't I need to make my own mistakes.

Therapist: [voicing with interpreter signing] This conversation seems easy. Does it go as smoothly at home?

Mother: No, it's much more difficult without an interpreter.

Therapist: [to mother] Do you know how the interpreter is interpreting what you say in order for you to communicate clearly to Mary?

Mother: No.

Therapist: Let me try to voice it for you—voice some of what the interpreter was doing in American Sign Language ... MANY TIME, WE-TWO EXPERIENCE NOT GOOD. PEOPLE THEIR EXPERIENCE SOMETIME GOOD, SOMETIME BAD. OUR EXPERIENCE

> SOMETIME PAIN, SOMETIME ANGUISH, FRUSTRATE. WE WATCH YOU, YOUR EXPERIENCE SAME OURS. PAIN, ANGUISH, FRUSTRATE. WE WANT HELP. FUTURE YOURSELF WILL MAKE MISTAKE, MISTAKE, MISTAKE. OUR EXPERIENCE TEACH YOU. ACCEPT YOU SHOULD.... That is sort of the verbal translation of what the interpreter was saying in ASL—the different grammar, different words. [Mother and Therapist practice verbally "interpreting" a few sentences from English syntax to ASL gloss.]

The mother realized, in her words, "what the interpreter was doing" and subsequently learned to use ASL-like gloss when orally communicating with her daughter. The mother began to use a different word order and explain concepts differently while voicing to her daughter; she approximated some principles of ASL. Although it clearly would have been optimal for the mother to learn to sign ASL, nevertheless the therapeutic intervention of making the process of interpretation accessible to the mother had powerful benefits toward improving verbal communication.

ASSESSING ALLIANCES, BOUNDARIES, AND HIERARCHY VIA AN INTERPRETER

Logistically, it is my common practice to allow family members to negotiate initial physical placement of the interpreter, although I may ask him or her to move later in treatment. Careful observation of how this is negotiated within the family offers valuable diagnostic information about family variables, such as alliances, boundaries, and hierarchies.

Let us consider alliances first. As an example, a family consisting of two hearing parents, a hearing sister, and a deaf brother frequently argued at the beginning of each session about where the interpreter would sit. After several sessions, it became evident that the sister would typically wish the interpreter to sit in a position such that she (the sister) could maintain minimal eye contact with her deaf brother. The sister requested that the interpreter sit in a triangular arrangement with her and her brother so that he would be forced to look at the interpreter when she spoke. It was only when the therapist inquired about the sister's intent that she first began recounting her anger and resentment towards her brother: "... and I don't want to hear again how sad he is." Both during this session and at home, this sibling allied with everyone in the family except the deaf member.

Consider another family that included hearing parents, two hearing siblings, and one deaf daughter. One hearing sibling was consistently the most adamant in asking the interpreter to sit in a position that would maximize visual contact between the deaf daughter and mother. She later explained that "she [deaf daughter] always misses out, and I feel sorry for her." In this manner, the alliance between the hearing and deaf sibling became clear.

Careful observation of how the family positions the interpreter may also indicate boundary patterns. Consider one mother who consistently requested that the interpreter sit next to her and away from her deaf daughter. When asked about this, the mother stated that it would make it easier for her to "tell the interpreter what my daughter really means." The mother alternated between frequently criticizing the adequacy of the interpreter's receptive and expressive skills (which were in fact superb) and whispering to the interpreter intimate information about her daughter to "help the interpreter." (The interpreter, in turn, interpreted mother's whispering.) Consider the following therapy transcript from this five-member, intact family:

Brother: (voicing while interpreter signs; to father) Ya know dad, I get real irked when ...

Mother: (voicing while interpreter signs; to interpreter) That sign you just used is for 'anger,' but it is not that (she demonstrates). What my son meant by 'irked' is sort of on-going kvetching [yiddish word for complaining] (demonstrates different sign). She [deaf daughter] gets very upset at anger. Her psychiatrist told me that she can't handle it ever since she was a kid and was abused by our neighbor. Now will you two [interpreter and brother] be careful!

Therapist: (signing without voice while interpreter voices; to daughter) You have two interpreters! (ha) You are lucky. (voicing while interpreter signs; to brother) Now what *did* you mean?

The enmeshment between mother and daughter was vividly illustrated by the triangle of interpreter–mother–daughter.

In regard to assessing hierarchical factors, it is important to observe who in the family appears to exert the most influence about where the interpreter initially sits. It is one thing to observe that the deaf member assumes, or is given, more authority on where it would be visually best for the interpreter to sit. In terms of assessing the hierarchy, it is another thing for the deaf member to be overruled by another member of the family.

Consider the following transcript of a family consisting of mother, father, and a 13-year-old deaf son. This sequence occurred during the first few minutes of the initial session: father, son, mother, interpreter, and therapist (in that order) entered the office where there were five available chairs. The father was the first to be seated, the son waited for his mother to sit, and then he sat down. Then they moved their seats together in a line and the father pulled an empty seat next to him in the line for the interpreter. The mother tacitly agreed with her husband's nonverbal directive. I sat in the remaining seat, but moved it opposite the family (see Fig. 8.2).

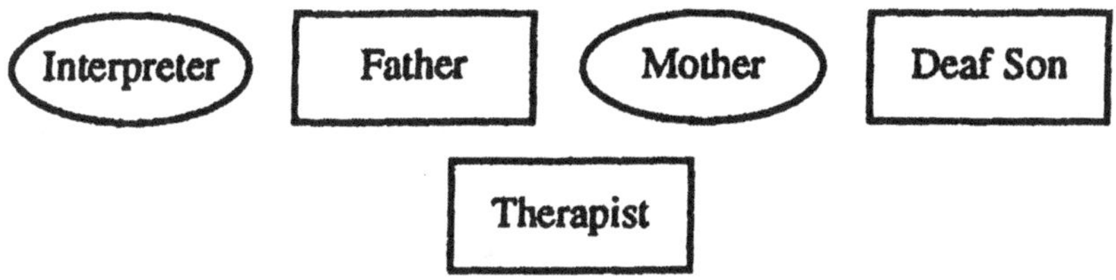

FIG. 8.2 Seating placement.

Therapist: (ASL without voice with the interpreter voicing for him; ha) I feel like I'm lecturing in a class.

Father: (voicing while interpreter signs) We want to tell you what the problem is. (proceeds to explain)

Therapist: (to deaf son) Your neck must be getting tired when you turn to look at the interpreter every time your father, or anyone for that matter, talks. Why don't you ask her [interpreter] to move?

Son: (looks at his father and then to interpreter; signs in ASL while interpreter voices) Could you sit there? (asks the interpreter to sit opposite him)

Father: (to son) You have to learn, you know, not always to have things your own way. Dear [to mother], where do you think it would be best for the interpreter to sit?

Son: (turns his head away in disgust and resignation)

Clearly, these initial moments of the meeting contained important diagnostic information. The parents and son were engaged in an ongoing, symmetrical power struggle that had recently spiraled upwards and gotten out of hand. What was verbally discussed and elaborated with the therapist much later was nonverbally enacted immediately on commencement of our initial meeting in regard to placement of the interpreter.

REGULATION OF ALLIANCES, BOUNDARIES, AND HIERARCHIES VIA AN INTERPRETER

Therapists are not restricted to simply observing where the interpreter is placed by the family for assessment purposes, but can also change the position of the interpreter relative to other family members to begin modifying various dysfunctional structural patterns. Like a symphony conductor who regulates the loudness and rhythm of different instrument sections in the orchestra, the therapist can request that the interpreter physically sit in specific spatial configurations relative to family members to encourage different subsystems to increase or decrease their "loudness."[2]

Varying the physical placement of the interpreter affects the degree and frequency of eye contact between any two persons and thus affects the probability of alliances. As family therapists and interpreters well know, with eye contact comes a host of possibilities for nonverbal, or analogic communication, frequently at an implicit level. Maximizing the frequency of eye contact between two persons increases the probability that more affective exchanges will occur (Minuchin, 1974). Indeed, this is the rationale for interpreters traditionally sitting slightly to the side and in back of the nonsigning, hearing person: so that the deaf person can obtain maximum visual exposure to the hearing person's affect.

Similarly, therapists can vary the position of the interpreter to demarcate boundaries. Much like the standard moves of structural family therapists who may, for example, move people around the room to increase and decrease ease of interaction among other members, here, the position of the interpreter has the same function. For example, in a hearing family in which the mother and son are enmeshed and father and family are disengaged, the mother might sit quite close to her son and to the interpreter while the father sits quite far from the family. The therapist might implement a standard structural move by asking them to switch positions in order to "pull in the father" and strengthen the boundary between son and mother. Alternately, the therapist might ask the interpreter to move away from mother and towards father, which would have the identical structural effect of increasing the degree and frequency of eye contact between the son and the father.

Therapists can also vary the position of the interpreter to further modify hierarchical relationships. After observing the family negotiate placement of the interpreter, the therapist can assign one person (i.e., the deaf member) to place the interpreter. Consider the mother in the previously described family who initially took charge of placing the interpreter next to her. As predicted by Stansfield (1981) and Taff-Watson (1984), the deaf

[2]As with other systemic interventions with interpreters, very important issues are raised here, namely for whom is the interpreter working: the deaf member, therapist, or family? What if the deaf member objects? In this regard, it is important to emphasize that this technique, as with all techniques, is implemented in the context of a mutually respectful relationship and a clear therapy contract with the deaf member as well as his or her family. Thus, the situation of the deaf member objecting to the interpreter moving around the room has never come up in my experiences thus far; the purposes and goals of all interventions are, as much as is clinically possible, clearly understood by all family members. In the presented clinical examples, the deaf member did not feel exploited by, and, in fact, appreciated the purpose of enactment and of modifying the interpreter's behavior. The essential factor is the context and quality of the relationship between the deaf member and the therapist. However, as an alternative factor, I am aware of the "learned helplessness" of many deaf clients: What if the deaf member agreeing to this technique is one example of many instances when he or she maintains a passive stance toward the environment? These issues merit further discussion.

child initially viewed mother and interpreter as comprising a coalition against him, as if the interpreter belonged to mother. As a result, conflict quickly ensued, having to do with power or hierarchical negotiation. When the therapist, exerting his authority, instructed the deaf child to place the interpreter, the mother at first responded angrily but then began recounting her feelings of helplessness and her insecurities in raising a disabled child. The more helpless this mother felt, the more she exerted inappropriate control, and the more dysfunctional the hierarchy.

THE EVOLVING INTERPRETER–THERAPIST RELATIONSHIP

This chapter has alluded to the critical importance to successful treatment of an open, mutually supportive, and respectful relationship between therapist and interpreter. If this relationship is conflictual, it is highly probable that conflict will be inappropriately manifested during the treatment session. If the relationship is disengaged, or distant, much confusion and isolation will occur that will impede progress. These professionals must function as a team.

The quality of any dyadic relationship depends, in part, on the idiosyncratic characteristics and personalities of each individual and on the context in which they find themselves. One of the many ways of describing the context of an interpreter and therapist during a treatment session is to note that there are two "subsystems" (Minuchin, 1974) that are simultaneously operating independently and in connection with each other: the professional–helper subsystem, which consists of therapist and interpreter, and the recipient, helpee, subsystem, which consists of the family (see Fig. 8.3). The interpreter–therapist dyad and family constitute separate subsystems in that, at any given time, both groups may be separated by rigid or fluid boundaries; the members of each group discusses certain information among themselves and elects what to share with the members of the other group. During pre- and postsession meetings (as recommended by Stansfield, 1981; Taff-Watson, 1984) the interpreter and therapist, for example, may discuss theoretical aspects of treatment or linguistic considerations that they may or may not share with the family. Similarly, the family certainly elects to share or withhold certain information from the interpreter–therapist dyad. Each subsystem then affects, and is affected by, the other.

Interpreter = Therapist | **Family**

FIG. 8.3 Two subsystems.

The context of the interpreter–therapist relationship can also be described by the time factor. Does a particular interpreter work with a particular therapist for one time only? Do they work together on an occasional basis with one given family? Do they work together occasionally with several different families? Do they work together with consistent and varied families over a long period of time? These different temporal possibilities suggest markedly different propensities for an evolving relationship between interpreter and therapist. After all, the interpreter and therapist are both physically and therefore affectively present for the gamut of intimate human disclosures that typically characterize the process of therapy. When two people are involved together over a period of time in this kind of intimate process, a bond inevitably develops between them.

Before embarking on a description of the interpreter–therapist relationship, a cautionary note must be mentioned. It is difficult at best, and perhaps impossible, to accurately portray any relationship on paper, as this mode of description is restricted to providing only an artificial dissection and sequential analysis of its component parts. This is a gross distortion of the "gestalt" of a relationship that is more than the sum of its parts. Inevitably, this section, too, artificially divides up and describes only the parts of the interpreter–therapist relationship with the fallacious assumption that it all adds up to form a whole. The reader, however, is urged to imagine all of the described components as blended and molded together to form a gestalt, an entity that becomes unique to itself.

Initial Defensiveness of Therapist

It is one thing for me to select portions of my videotaped clinical work for presentations in front of colleagues. It is quite another thing to work live in the presence of another professional who is privy to both the therapeutic magic moments, as well as to the therapeutic blunders, the latter preferably forgotten. Clients do not have an exclusive monopoly on transference. Therapists exhibit the same phenomenon, only then it is called *countertransference*. As an example, I recall trying to impress an interpreter during the initial sessions of family treatment with clever therapeutic interpretations made to the family, clever reframes and artistically executed interventions. Although it was clearly theoretically necessary to wait for the proper time and situation to implement particular interventions, I nevertheless began to feel somewhat inadequate in front of the interpreter about seemingly "doing nothing." Thus, I attempted to intervene cleverly before it was therapeutically appropriate. This understandably precipitated more resistance from the family, which, in turn, precipitated more defensiveness–anxiety–embarrassment from me.

Analysis of my reactions during my own psychotherapy and clinical supervision confirmed that my fears about how the interpreter viewed me were related to my countertransference issues. Dealing with these issues privately in my own supervision and in individual therapy while continuing to work with the interpreter allowed me to understand the origins of my reactions more fully. In contrast to how our relationship had begun, I soon not only felt quite relaxed during the sessions but also missed the interpreter when she could not attend a meeting. This milestone also made it possible for the two of us to work together in a variety of creative ways, as described in the rest of this section.

Information Sharing

The interpreter has information of therapeutic value to share with the therapist. What was the quality of verbal communication of the deaf family member, of the therapist, of the family? Did the deaf member understand the discourse? Why or why not? What was being communicated subtly, nonverbally, or cross culturally? What communication was the interpreter unable to interpret? Similarly, the therapist has information that the interpreter needs. What was the theoretical basis for certain questions? What was the therapist trying to get at? Did the therapist necessarily expect that all of the family members, including the deaf member, understand completely what he or she was saying to another family member? What help does the therapist need and expect from the interpreter?

The degree of mutual trust, risk taking, and nondefensiveness between the interpreter and therapist will directly influence the quantity and quality of information that they must necessarily share during the pre- and postsessions. For example, the interpreter will be free to admit that he or she might not have been "with it" during a particular session and therefore interpretation was inadequate, possibly influencing the quality of the sessions. This is obviously vital for the therapist to know. Alternately, the therapist can admit to the interpreter feelings of defensiveness in front of him or her during the treatment session. The therapist can admit to the interpreter that he or she was trying to accomplish certain goals during the session and succeeded or failed. These acts of self-disclosure markedly decrease both persons' anxiety and thus would be expected to facilitate optimal functioning and creativity during the session (Jourard, 1971).

Modeling Dyadic Interaction for Families

A comfortable interaction between interpreter and therapist also inevitably "spills over" to positively affect the interaction among all members of the session and vice versa. For example, I once attempted to ask a deaf adolescent a "circular question" (Palazzoli, Boscolo, Cecchin, & Prata, 1980): "If you felt sad, who in your family would be the first to notice?" I signed it twice but noticed that I was not making myself clear. The interpreter let out what seemed to be a mock sigh and said to me "let me do it" while shaking her head. At the same time, she smiled and made eye contact with me in a warmhearted way. I laughed as did the family. I then said to the interpreter in mock indignation "Ok, you try!" After she signed it successfully, the deaf adolescent teasingly said to me "Oh, that's what you meant!" and laughed. I then shrugged my shoulders. The affinity between the interpreter and me made this interchange fun and helpful in that it provided a bit of necessary respite for the whole family during what was otherwise a fairly intense session. However, it is apparent that the above interchange could easily have made an intense session more tense and less productive, had the interpreter and I not enjoyed and respected each other. Moreover, soon after this exchange, other family members began to mimic the observed camaraderie between the interpreter and myself.

Working Through Ego Defensive Reactions by Family Members

A positive relationship is essential toward helping particular family members work through ego defense mechanisms, such as projection and transference, which, as noted earlier in this chapter, are often inadvertently elicited by the mere presence of an interpreter. Let us return to the earlier example of a father becoming angry at an interpreter, as opposed to becoming more directly angry at his deaf son. The father's conscious feelings of anger toward the interpreter (a transference reaction to mask his own unacknowledged anger toward his son) and wondering whether the interpreter was intimidated by him (a projection reaction to mask his own feelings of intimidation in front of his son and the interpreter) were openly discussed and analyzed in the presence of the interpreter who did not volunteer personal sentiments. I maintained intermittent eye contact with the interpreter during this piece of therapeutic work to convey that I was implementing a therapeutic technique that we had previously discussed during pre- and postsessions.

Clearly, it was vital for the interpreter and I to have already discussed the concept of transference and the therapeutic plan, namely, in this case, to utilize the transference reactions of father to therapeutic advantage. In addition, it had to be quite clear to everyone that the interpreter would not be expected to answer the father's queries about "is she angry or intimidated with me?" There had to be sufficient trust between the interpreter and me for her to know that I would not put her on the spot by asking her to reveal personal sentiments.

Therapeutic Enactment

As described earlier with reference to the same example, the father and son were instructed to discuss this new information concerning the transference directly with each other, but unlike previous times, with only intermittent interpretation by the interpreter. Enactment often beneficially "stresses the system" (Minuchin & Fishman, 1981) and creates "news of a difference" (Bateson, 1979); it helps create a new and stressful situation that would spark new interactional patterns. As the purpose of this technique was not known by the particular interpreter, we were sure to discuss this during our pre- and postmeeting sessions. Thus, the interpreter felt on solid ground while helping me to implement this therapeutic technique. This therapeutic conducting via requesting that the interpreter stop and start interpreting during enactment could not have successfully occurred unless the interpreter and I were in sync with each other, and were clear about what each other was doing. Again, it becomes apparent that the interpreter needs to have a clear idea of the therapeutic intent and have trust in the therapist to interpret correctly and ethically.

Fluid Balancing of Roles

As my relationship with the interpreter continued to evolve toward furthering mutual trust, certain linguistic interventions that the interpreter and I had overtly structured became markedly less dependent on my cue and more fluid. As an example, as I continued to implement enactment both with and without interpretation with several different families but with the same interpreter, the interpreter began to interpret and not interpret on her own accord without my conscious cue. She had developed a gut sense about what I was trying to do, became adept at reading my subtle nonverbal body cues, and thus independently initiated regulating the ease of communication and therefore affective intensity within dyads by only intermittently interpreting their interactions. The particular instincts of the interpreter in conjunction with how our relationship had evolved made it possible for the interpreter to participate in a cogent, helpful, and ethical manner and in accordance with our shared therapeutic goals.

Similarly, in regard to the previously described effects of varying the position of the interpreter to effect specific structural and interactional changes, I typically explicitly cue an interpreter to shift positions in the earlier stages of our relationship. However, at a later stage in our evolution, this rule typically becomes more fluid. One relationship with a particular interpreter had evolved into a comfortable, trusting, and fluid dance; at some point the interpreter and I nonverbally orchestrated the therapeutic scenario. I alternately distanced and involved myself in the exchanges among family members while the interpreter herself initiated positional changes. It was a very effective session for the family and was personally satisfying for both the interpreter and myself.

However, an important clarification must be emphasized at this point. As DeMatteo, Veltri, and Lee (1986) rightly emphasized, the interpreter is not a cotherapist. The therapist has ultimate responsibility for the direction of treatment. Thus, in as much as the interpreter and my roles

became more fluid, the interpreter would maintain frequent eye contact with me which we knew, from our long history of pre- and postsession discussions, meant "is this okay?" If I assessed the interpreter's linguistic intervention to be in the best therapeutic interests of the deaf member and hearing members, I would respond with a slight grin or eye contact that the interpreter knew meant "go for it." Alternatively, I would often nonverbally or verbally respond to the interpreter's query by requesting that he or she continue interpreting or shift positions. We would rehash and clarify our nonverbal–verbal communications during the post session meeting.

Spontaneity Between Interpreter and Therapist

Spontaneity, creativity, and flexibility between interpreter and therapist are imperative in order to provide optimal services for families. In my case, although I usually have a more or less specific sense of what needs to happen during a given session and of how linguistic communication will occur, it may not happen as planned. The family may come in with a different and more useful agenda, I spontaneously may think of a new and better direction, or my original plan may not work. I recall explicitly informing one interpreter during the presession that I would sign ASL without voice to the deaf member and asking the interpreter to voice for me. However, when the time came, the plan did not fit, as it seemed important to simultaneously maintain eye contact with the deaf child and his parents. Because the child easily understood Pidgin Sign English, I changed my plan and used simultaneous communication with the deaf family member and only much later code switched to ASL. The particular interpreter, by this time, knew that I could not totally be trusted to predict what would transpire during sessions; for presenting situations often would countermand what was planned. Thus, the interpreter very comfortably "went with the flow" in a different direction. While reviewing the videotape of the session, we both marveled at how smooth and easy it appeared.

This unique dance between the interpreter and myself, our creative balancing of roles was a direct result of much hard work, our compatible makeup, and our qualifications. As with any relationship, it could not have worked with all therapists, nor with all interpreters, nor with all therapist–interpreter dyads.

9

Hearing Children of Deaf Parents

There is a small but growing body of literature describing families in which there are hearing children and deaf parents. Increased recognition of this population is long overdue, as 95% of deaf couples bear hearing children (Moores, 1987). In fact, there is now a national organization of Children of Deaf Adults (CODA), which is comprised of children of deaf parents (CODA, 1983).

Anecdotal accounts of deaf-parent families have been provided by Fant and Schuchmann (1974), Greenberg (1970), Preston (1993), and Walker (1986). Bunde (1979) has surveyed 229 hearing children of deaf parents. Hoffmeister (1985) and Lane, Hoffmeister and Bahan (1996) have presented and functional overview of families with deaf parents focusing not on deficits created by the hearing loss, but instead emphasizing the successful adaptations of the deaf parents within the community. Finally, from a psychotherapeutic perspective, R. Myers, S. Myers, and Marcus (1999) described intrafamilial dynamics of deaf-parent families, including reference to cybernetic theory and ecological congruence.

It has been my experience that dysfunctional families with hearing children and deaf parents who present themselves for treatment often manifest minimal verbal communication (i.e., manual or vocal communication) between both generations.[1] Here, the reverse situation of many families with hearing parents and a deaf child occurs: The deaf parents' primary mode of communication is sign language while the hearing children lack fluency in sign language and communicate orally. In this manner, the dysfunctional interactional pattern, which from this analysis, first began between the deaf child and hearing parents is replicated in the next generation when that deaf child becomes a parent of hearing children. What these deaf parents do not linguistically get from their hearing parents, they may find difficult to give to their hearing children.

However, the reasons for the previously described kind of "linguistic disengagement" between some deaf parents and hearing children in the clinical population are more complex than a skills deficit explanation would suggest. This linguistic barrier is also related to rigid patterns of enmeshment between deaf parents and their hearing parents, as described in chapter 2. Patterns of enmeshment, and often infantilization, are likely to begin when the deaf parents were themselves children and to continue during the stage when the deaf children themselves become parents of hearing children.

Inappropriately porous boundaries between the nuclear family (deaf parents and hearing children) and hearing grandparents may take two forms. First, the hearing grandchildren and hearing grandparents frequently enjoy easy and fluid vocal communication with each other in marked contrast to the verbal communication barriers that separate both the hearing children and hearing grandparents from the deaf parents (Rayson, 1987a, 1987b). Therefore, not only are the deaf parents conversationally isolated from much of the dialogue among their hearing children, but also from dialogues between their children and the children's grandparents. Second, when deaf parents remain enmeshed with their own hearing parents, it is not surprising that the latter often usurp much of the childrearing authority from the deaf parents. Thus, as illustrated in Fig. 9.1, it is clinically prevalent to observe an inverted power hierarchy within the three generational family system, in which the hearing children obey their hearing grandparents whereas essentially ignoring their deaf parents (Rayson, 1987a, 1987b). Consequently, in many cases, effective intervention with troubled hearing children of deaf parents often needs to include three generations: the hearing children, deaf parents, and hearing grandparents.

This chapter presents two clinical cases that illustrate systemic intervention strategies toward ameliorating inappropriately disengaged boundaries between hearing children and their deaf parents. In both cases, the hearing

---

[1]This observation of linguistic disengagement between deaf parents and their hearing children is restricted to informal clinical observation. There have been no systematic studies of the prevalence of this family structure. Furthermore, I am not generalizing this clinical observation to deaf-parent families in the nonclinical population.

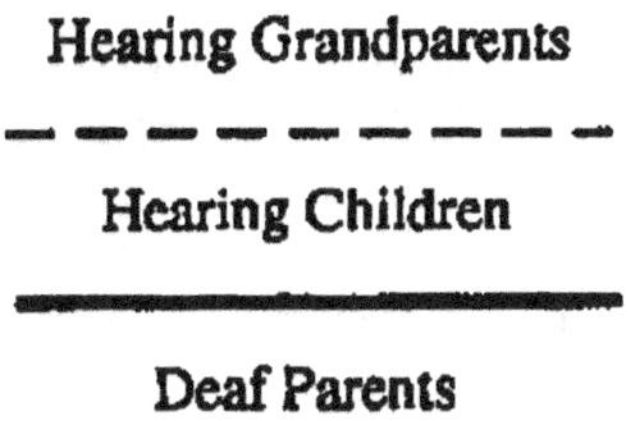

FIG. 9.1 Structural map of an inverted power hierarchy.

children and their deaf parents do not have enough interpersonal access to each other. In the first case, outside-of-family professionals appear to usurp parental authority from the deaf parents. In the second case, presented with verbatim therapy transcripts, the hearing grandparents "parent" both a deaf single mother and her hearing children and support an inverted power hierarchy within the nuclear family.

CASE STUDY 1: MARC

Marc was a 14-year-old hearing child of deaf parents. He was described as a "ruffian, predelinquent" boy by school personnel. Marc frequently disrupted classes, got into fights with other kids, and was often truant. The school, perhaps intimidated by his deaf parents, made only perfunctory attempts to contact them about the worsening situation. After telephoning them a few times but hearing what they described as "weird beeping sounds," they gave up. (The sounds were from the Telecommunication Device for the Deaf, which deaf people use to communicate on the phone.) Instead, they sent an official letter to Marc's home, one that the parents did not understand, as it was written in extremely complex English. Although Marc's parents were quite intelligent and fluent in ASL, they had received inadequate education with English and therefore read at a third-grade level. Marc himself did not inform them of the school situation. In terms of communication within the family, his parents were fluent in sign language and had minimal oral–aural skills. Although Marc demonstrated proficient expressive signing skills, he appeared to have minimal receptive skills. He did not understand, or at least acted as if he did not understand, most of what his parents would attempt to say to him.

To arrive at a useful diagnosis for clinical intervention, I noted a recursive cycle from the reported history that contained the presenting problem of Marc's disruptive and truant behavior. This report also contained my own previous intervention in this system that appeared to have inadvertently helped to maintain the problem. Historically, it became apparent that as Marc had become more truant from school, the guidance counselor and principal had set up a series of meetings in which they reprimanded him.

Marc ignored their reprimands and continued being truant. The cycle then repeated itself in much the same manner, but spatially expanded to incorporate other systems. The school accessed the probationary department to mandate individual therapy with me, thus again reprimanding Marc, but now with a bit more clout. They sent another letter home to his parents but did not receive a reply. I erred by cooperating with the request to meet with Marc for a series of individual meetings; as before, he soon dropped out of treatment and essentially dropped out of school.

The cycle then repeated itself again while continuing to expand to include more systems, this time the family, the legal system, and an Independent Living Center. Marc was charged with stealing a motorcycle. He was arraigned (reprimanded) by the courts, which in turn, mandated the involvement of both his parents to determine the future course of action (reprimands). His mother responded by accessing another system, an Independent Living Center, by requesting training on how to use Boston's transit system, the legal system, and on how to use a courtroom interpreter.

Having finally arrived at a comprehensive and workable systemic hypothesis of the problem (the recursive cycle previously outlined), I again intervened, but this time before the cycle would again repeat itself to include other systems, such as a higher level court system. This intervention occurred at a time when Marc and his parents were each quite anxious (psychological level), and therefore when the established patterns of their family level interactions were unstable. Given that the family had been destabilized, and thus was responsive to therapeutic intervention, it was clear that the intervention should at least include the spatial level of the family. However, should it also include other levels? To assist in making that decision, it was important to note what spatial levels were incorporated in the recursive cycle. Specifically, (a) Marc responded to reprimands by escalating his behavior at school; (b) professionals responded to Marc's escalation by more of the same behavior, namely by continuing to reprimand him via other systems; (c) those other systems (i.e., myself and the probation department) cooperated by too narrowly intervening with only Marc, or in the case of the Independent Living Center, responded by intervening only with the mother; and (d) until the cycle significantly escalated, Marc's deaf parents were neither informed about problems nor involved in problem-solving efforts.

It was, therefore, helpful to include the professional level, as the counselors had previously served an important function in maintaining the presenting problem of Marc's behavior. The Living Independent Skills trainer appeared most appropriate, as she was currently involved in providing training to the mother, was most amenable to change, and was logistically available for intervention.

A meeting was conducted with Marc, his parents, the ILS trainer, and an interpreter. I signed for myself with Marc's parents. As discussed in chapters 8 and 9, the purpose of the interpreter was to facilitate verbal communication between Marc and his parents, and between the deaf ILS trainer and other participants in the session. The meeting began by my asking Marc in detail how he knew what kind of motorcycle to steal, whether it was a good brand, how many horsepower, how he stole it, and so on. Judging from his answers to my questions, it seemed that he had done quite a bit of impressive research. I complemented him on his substantial knowledge and apparent motivation.

Questioning of the ILS trainer and Marc's mother also revealed that the mother had previously discontinued ILS training but resumed it once Marc got in trouble with the law. With this bit of important information, I then again complemented Marc but this time on how he helped his mother; how he, like many hearing children of deaf parents, sacrificed his adolescence to parent his parents. He looked at me askance, but I continued with the reframe and stated that

> Adolescents have many creative ways of motivating their parents to further their own education, to function more effectively in the world. Some kids openly plead with their parents to get their act together, other kids get in trouble with the law, and then the parents have to become proficient at dealing with lawyers, probation officers, courts, etc. You have helped your mother resume independent living skills training. You are a good boy, but you may be too good.

I explained this concept to his parents who responded by insisting that they did not need this kind of help. Marc's affect then changed, as he smirked a bit and nodded his head at me. Subsequently, he volunteered how he constantly worried about his parents. It was, therefore, apparent that my reframe was accepted. Finally, using a familiar strategic therapy technique of reframing and paradoxically prescribing the symptom (Madanes, 1981; Papp, 1983), I requested Marc to continue giving up his childhood as long as his parents indicated that they needed him to parent them. We discussed specific criteria in detail.

The proper systemic diagnosis which outlined at what spatial levels to intervene and when to intervene set the stage of the intervention to succeed; it prompted his mother to continue with ILS training and Marc to go back to school and to generally behave himself. Having observed this fundamental change in the recursive cycle, what Watzlawick, Weakland, and Fisch, (1974) termed *second-order change*, Marc's intrapsychic functioning appeared to have been destabilized. I, therefore, met with Marc several times thereafter for individual treatment. The purpose of these meetings was to help him deal with some of his own feelings about being a hearing child of deaf parents. A 2-year follow-up indicated that no further problems emerged with Marc, that his mother had continued to receive periods of ILS training, and that his father had occasionally attended these meetings.

CASE STUDY 2: THE L FAMILY

Janice was a 30-year-old deaf, divorced mother of two hearing children, Joe (age 8) and Shirley (age 5). Janice had initiated the divorce from the children's biological father, who was hard of hearing, 2 years prior to requesting treatment. She described him as a drug addict and as physically abusive to her, although he reportedly did not abuse the children. Janice requested therapy because her children were exhibiting obstinate behavior. She stated that "they never mind me," and added that they frequently ran away from home, broke windows and walls in the house following a reprimand, and were careless with matches. She felt helpless to enforce limits with them, as "they would destroy my furniture."

During the initial meeting with Janice and both children, the limited linguistic access that they had to each other was striking. The children did not sign at all, and Janice signed fluently but had minimal oral–aural skills. Consequently, the children frequently did not understand their mother and vice versa. This linguistic situation made systemic sense in light of what appeared to be an inverted power hierarchy in the family; Janice's demonstrated helplessness to discipline her children was isomorphic to her helplessness to teach then sign language. In addition, as the interview progressed, it became evident that Janice harbored feelings of inferiority about herself as a deaf person. This was exemplified by her saying that "hearing parents would know what to do with their kids" and by her shame about "having to sign" herself, and by implication, about teaching her kids to sign.

Janice reported that the behavior problems began following the divorce. After elaborating on changes of each family member since the divorce, it became evident that Joe and Shirley were experiencing the postparental divorce struggles, as has been described by Wallerstein and Kelly (1980). Both children tearfully admitted missing "daddy." Janice also described her feeling related to becoming a divorced, single mother; helplessness, loneliness, depression, and so on.

In light of this information, several hypotheses to explain the children's acting out behavior came to mind. The children may have been acting out their rage about the divorce against Janice, whom they perceived as having caused their father to leave. Janice, in turn, perhaps feeling guilty and responsible herself for a failed relationship, may have found it easy to accept what she viewed as punishment, or sentencing, from her children. Alternatively, Janice may have perceived and reacted to her son, Joe, with initial helplessness as she had with her ex-husband. Or she had not yet developed the parenting skills, or wherewithal, to take over the difficult tasks of being a single parent. Or the children were acting out in the hope of luring father back into the family. Although these hypotheses were different from each other, all of them had to do with the father–mother–children triangle.

However, there was another important triangle that included the children's acting out behavior, one that has already been reported as being common with families in which there are deaf parents. Janice, in answer to my question, "what else changed in your family following the divorce?," reported that her hearing parents, who lived a mile away from her house, began to visit much more frequently, and Joe frequently ran away from home to visit Grandma. Janice then complained of her mother and father disciplining her children "wrong ... telling me what to do too much," and infantalizing her. How Janice supported her mother infantalizing her, specifically how it related to her feeling impotent with her children, remained unclear. Nevertheless, it became apparent that dysfunctional interactions within the mother–children–grandparents triangle also functioned to support the presenting problem.

The first diagnostic probes and interventions included individual and family meetings with the nuclear family of Janice, Joe, and Shirley. The meetings with Joe and Shirley, both individually and together as a dyad, provided a means to assess their coping reactions to the loss of their father, who it seemed visited inconsistently and who had moved to another state. During individual sessions with Janice, we discussed parenting strategies and self-concept issues with herself as a deaf person and as a deaf parent. Regular family meetings focused on behavioral management.

Regular individual family meetings for a duration of approximately 9 months produced some improvement, but the inverted power hierarchy remained largely intact. Joe, in particular, remained quite disruptive at home, frequently telling his mother what to do (i.e., "get me ice cream now"). Janice would usually acquiesce to his demands. Given my original assessment of the mother–children–grandparents triangle, it became apparent that the grandparents and grandchildren were covertly coalescing against mother. Thus, to facilitate improvement within the nuclear family, I invited the grandparents, Sally and Herb, to some of the family sessions.

What follows are verbatim therapy segments from five meetings with this three-generation family. These meetings were interspersed over a 9-month period that also included meetings with the nuclear family. The total duration of treatment was approximately 2 years.

The first session consisted of Janice, Joe, Shirley, and the maternal grandparents, Herb and Sally. An interpreter was also present to interpret voice to sign of intrafamily communication among the hearing members and communication between myself and the hearing members, for the benefit of Janice. The interpreter also frequently interpreted sign to voice when Janice simultaneously voiced and signed herself, for the benefit of the hearing family members who often did not understand her. Janice had explicitly requested the interpreter to be present for these reasons. In addition, at Janice's request, I communicated to her directly using simultaneous voice and Pidgin Signed English. The meeting began with a discussion of who has the problem.

Herb:	I don't know what's wrong with him.
Therapist:	With whom?
Herb:	With Joe. I don't know what's wrong with him, what's eating him. I try to be good to him, he don't pay attention; he's good at that.
Therapist:	Janice, do you feel Joe's a bother?
Janice:	Yes.
Sally:	I don't have as big a problem as they do, number one.
Therapist:	Who's they?
Sally:	Well, any of them. (points around the room)
Therapist:	How come?
Herb:	Cuz he frustrates …
Sally:	Cuz he frustrates him [points to Herb] to no end, and her [points to Janice]; he scares her to death with this running away bit.
Therapist:	Let me ask you Sally, who do you think Joe frustrates the most? Out of all of you one, two, three, or four people; from your point of view, who does he frustrate the most?

This question precipitated the family expanding the locus of the problem to include conflicts between Janice and both of her parents with respect to their parenting roles. The grandmother, Sally, in particular, critiqued Janice's mothering skills. Although the content of her advice was well founded (i.e., "consistency is important") it also helped to infantalize Janice and disempower her with respect to her children.

Sally:	They run tight, they run close, (points to Janice & Herb). He gives his mother a hard time cuz I think the biggest word in Janice's life is consistency: she should have consistency. Herb is not home all the time but when he is, Joe is always there and Joe knows he can aggravate him. And of course he will if he can't get his own way with his mother. Then Joe swears at Herb no end, calls him some very unpleasant names and no-one should have to put up with it. He's [Herb] totally frustrated cuz if he goes after Joe, Janice gets mad. But one day when Joe tried to kick our front door out, Herb picked Joe up and gave him a couple of bumps on the behind and put him down and said stay there. And Janice was mad with him for touching Joe. But I told Janice that it was quite natural for her father to do what he did. That wasn't unnatural. Joe's in our home and it's his … Grandpa's house.
Janice:	He screams [points to Herb]! He screams loudly and he has to take it easy. He screams and everything gets worse when he screams too much.

Sally: And Janice don't know what I go through with her. The yelling, screaming, if she can't give me respect how can Joe and Shirley give her respect? If she can't respect me without yelling and screaming and putting all the faults on me how can her children respect her if she's screaming at me and I'm her mother? If they see her being disrespectful to me, they're going to think nothing of being disrespectful to her. I wouldn't dream of being disrespectful to my mother. And it's true, Janice has made me cry many a day.

The next segment included explicit inquiries about verbal communication among members of the three-generational family system. The grandchildren and grandparents, as they are hearing, had no difficulty verbally communicating with each other; but this was in marked contrast to Janice and her parents, and Janice and her children. Consequently, the boundary between Janice and her children was dysfunctional and rigid, whereas the boundary between grandchildren and grandparents was enmeshed. Thus, in addition to the conflict between Janice and her parents, linguistic accessibility between grandchildren and grandparents and relative linguistic inaccessibility between mother and children also served to support mother's continued frustration about discipline.

Janice: Joe, sit up. Be a good boy. Can you understand me?
Joe: Yes.
Therapist: Can you always understand what your mother says, Joe?
Joe: No. She don't talk right.
Janice: You don't know sign. You won't let me teach you. But sometimes you understand me O.K.
Therapist: Let me ask you Janice, are you able to understand your kids always?
Janice: Sometimes yes, sometimes no. Sometimes they talk and they don't face me. Because I'm deaf, if they're not looking at me I can't read their lips. I don't know what they're saying. I have to try and look at their face and they turn their head. When they're looking right at me then I have a chance. That's a problem.
Therapist: So why is it that your kids haven't learned sign language?
Janice: Well, I want them to learn sign language, but they keep thinking ... Daddy talks and he's hard of hearing. I want them to learn sign language but they refuse.
Therapist: Do you understand your parents?
Janice: My Mom, I understand her most of the time, and with my Dad, sometimes I understand him, sometimes not.
Therapist: OK, Sally, how do you understand your daughter?
Sally: I will wait there until the wall freezes to get it right, so I'll understand what she's saying except when she gets mad she raves off to a point

where when she yells I can't understand anything! But I just tell her she's gotta calm down and I will try. She'll have to be just a little patient, just like I will.

Janice alluded to the theme of "to be hearing (or hard of hearing) is to be competent, but to be deaf is to be incompetent" in this transcript and it was pervasive throughout the family sessions. However, at this point, I only privately noted this theme; the first task was to elevate Janice's status with respect to her mother and by proxy to her children. Later, it would be more appropriate to directly address deafness self-concept issues.

The following segment is from a session that took place approximately 1 month later. It more vividly illustrates the inverted power hierarchy within the three-generational system, namely that the grandmother, Sally, held the power to successfully discipline Joe and Shirley. Sally had begun the session by announcing that she was in a bad mood.

Therapist: Why are you in a bad mood?

Sally: Why? We had a little incident before we left home and I wasn't too happy about it. Considering I pushed and pushed and pushed to make the time, and just, you know, I had to eat in a hurry and then Joe wanted to sit in the front seat of the car and his mother [Janice] wanted him to sit in back. And the minute she said no, he took off and ran away. But guess where he sat? He got the front seat. If he was my kid he would have never sat in the front.

Therapist: So Joe, you won?

Sally: No he didn't cuz he lost brownie points with Grandma. [to Joe] You lost points with me.

Therapist: [to Janice] Did you want him to sit in front or back?

Janice: Back.

Therapist: So how did he end up sitting in the front?

Janice: He wouldn't move, he just stayed in the front. He got his way.

Sally: Seeing as how it's my car, Joe, the next time I will make the rules, OK?

Joe: OK.

Sally: And we will sit in the back if Grandma says sit in the back, won't we?

Joe: Yup.

Sally: Because the only time you get to sit in the front is if you've been a good boy, no more running away and no more episodes and then you'll be able to sit in the front. But until such time, if I say back it's back!

Janice: [to therapist] But he [Joe] doesn't mind me. When I try to punish him, he runs over his friend's house. I walk over to the friend's house and tell him to go home and he says no. And the boys look at me and laugh behind my back. I told him to go home and he gets all upset and takes off. I tell him to come back and he splits again and crosses the street by himself. So I walk over and look for him . . . I find him at Grandma's house.

It was clear that Sally parented both Janice and the children, but it would have been premature at this time to separate Sally and Janice and to delegate full parental control to Janice. Janice herself was both unwilling and unsure of herself and therefore bound to fail and to enlist Sally to reestablish her role. Furthermore, Janice's dependency apparently also fulfilled some of Sally's emotional needs. I, therefore, temporarily supported this dyad, but began to reframe it as "a team," I became, in a sense, a coach to improve the efficiency of the team.

I began by asking them to dialogue with each other about one problem with the children. As Janice was watching Sally, not the interpreter, it was unclear whether she understood. This led into a discussion about the linguistic efficiency of the team:

Therapist: I want both of you to talk together as a team.

Sally: [to Janice] I keep telling you that it is important that you follow through with what you say. You don't. And that just adds more for him to keep doing it because he will still get his way because he will wear you down. Well, he wore me down. He wore me down and I know where you're at because we had that horrible episode where he was supposed to go see Dr. Harvey and I had to chase him up a tree.

Janice: [looks at Sally, and nods her head]

Sally: And ...

Therapist: All right, time-out. [to Janice] Was your mother clear about what she was just saying?

Janice: Yes, last Thursday, he was really terrible.

Therapist: Whoa wait; but I'm wondering if you mother was clear with her communication. Also I wonder if you would mind repeating, sort of summarize, what she just told me. The whole thing.

Sally: What did I say?

Janice: I don't know, I'm tired.

Therapist: But see, that's the problem between you two. You two ...

Sally: I'm sorry I thought she was looking at her. [points to interpreter]

Therapist: No, she wasn't. But, but see ...

Sally: If that's the problem than I'll do it slower.

Therapist: But, you two are a very, very potentially effective team; but you two have two different languages.

I asked Sally and Janice to continue the dialogue vis-à-vis the interpreter. Although the verbal communication was adequate, Sally had done all of the talking while Janice was nodding her head. I then began to more directly address the hierarchical issues between them.

Sally: But you should give the reward to him only if he deserves to go to that house. He can't be running away and everything when he's got to behave; and then he can go with Shirley and wait; and then you should start taking Shirley like across to Jeremy or across to …

Therapist: Sally …

Sally: To Gabriel.

Therapist: Sally, you're lecturing, you're not discussing!

Sally: I'm not lecturing!

Therapist: You were lecturing; you're not discussing with your daughter!

Sally: Yes I am. She can tell me back now.

Therapist: She hasn't said a word!

Sally: She will in 2 minutes.

Therapist: You have just talked for 8 minutes!

Sally: I'm just telling her all my thoughts. Now she can …

Therapist: You have just talked for 8 minutes.

Sally: Well she has equal time to talk back.

Therapist: But that's not a discussion; that's a sequential lecture.

Sally: OK, OK, well now, [to Janice] what do you think, and all that, what is your opinion? What do you think you should do?

Janice and Sally then proceeded to have a productive dialogue. In light of this positive change at the "parental level of the system," I began to focus more on modifying the interactions between Janice and Joe.

Therapist: [to Joe] What do they mean? When your grandmother and mom say they need to straighten you out, what do they mean?

Joe: Straighten me out.

Therapist: What do they mean?

Joe: Be a good boy.

Therapist: And what would you do if you were a good boy?

Joe: I dunno.

Therapist: I want you to do something, ask your mother what she means about you being a good boy. Ask her.

Joe: [Looks at his Janice and mouths the question without vocalizing. I cannot lip-read him.]

This was how the children normally talked to Janice at home, by mouthing the words. During the following dialogue between Janice and Joe, Sally began to intercede. I first excluded her from the dyadic interaction and then allowed her to intercede but only on behalf of promoting the dialogue between Janice and Joe. It was still too early for Janice and Joe to function adequately without assistance; and I felt that it was still a bit premature to usurp Sally's power. It was important for me to join her more first.

Joe: [continues to mouth the question to Janice]

Sally: Can I ask a question?

Therapist: Nope.

Sally: OK.
Janice: [does not respond to Joe]
Therapist: [to Joe] Come here. Ask her [Janice], 'suppose I were a good boy, what would I do?' Ask her.
Joe: What do you mean, good boy? [continues to mouth words without vocalizing]
Janice: I don't understand.
Joe: What do you mean? [begins vocalizing now]
Sally: Talk it, Joe, just say it.
Joe: What do you mean good boy? [uses exaggerated mouth movements while voicing]
Janice: I don't understand.
Joe: What do you mean?
Sally: Say it without making your mouth go funny Joe, just say it the way you would to me. [to therapist] Could I ask one question?
Therapist: Sure
Sally: [to Joe] What is a good boy Joe? What is it?

This time, Sally's interceding was not to promote dialogue between Janice and Joe but was to replace Janice. Therefore, I countered her move by redirecting the interaction to Janice and Joe.

Therapist: [to Sally] That's what I want him to tell his Mother.
Sally: Yea. [to Joe] You tell Mummy.
Therapist: [looks at Sally and Janice] Mother needs to tell him.
Sally: [to Janice] Or you tell him what is a good boy. That's all he wants to know!
Therapist: That's right.
Janice: [voices for herself but is unintelligible]

In the following segment, I continue to work at promoting this dialogue, and instructed the interpreter not to interpret, making the linguistic factors more identical to what had been occurring at home and increasing the stress within this dyad. In this case, it was important to assess what happened between them at home and how much stress they could tolerate. I also asked Joe to move from sitting on the couch to sitting on the floor and to look up at Janice who was sitting on a chair. In addition to decreasing the spatial proximity between Joe and Janice, and thus increasing the intensity of their interaction, Joe looking up to his mother served as a spatial metaphor for reestablishing an appropriate hierarchical relationship.

Therapist: [to Joe] Sit down, sit down. On the floor.
Sally: [to Janice] That's what we want you to tell him.
Therapist: [to Joe] On the floor. Look up to your Mom. Look up to your Mom.

Janice: [signs and voices to Joe exactly what she wants him to do as a "good boy"]

Sally had repeatedly requested that I focus more on individual work with the two children, Joe and Shirley; but I had consistently refused "unless things around Joe and Shirley change," namely the relationship between Sally and Janice. This theme was continued in the next segment:

Therapist: I want to talk to both of you. [Janice and Sally] I can help directly by working with Shirley and Joe but I can't be effective with this until one or two more basic things are changed in the family.
Sally: Ok, we're following your every instruction. [smiles playfully; we seem to be enjoying the power struggle between us]
Therapist: That's fine. But I can't be successful until we make one or two more basic changes. [to Janice] Remember a while ago you told me you feel stuck, that it's almost impossible to discipline the kids because they refuse to either go to their room or when they go in the room they run away or yell, and you feel helpless, right? I need both of you [Janice and Sally] to first work out a system to deal with that first. Then, I'll be a lot more successful working directly with the kids.
Sally: Let me ask you one more question. Do you think we should start with just one area first?
Therapist: Absolutely.
Sally: Alright, [to Janice] what do you want to do first? The first thing you want them to learn. What is the first thing you want to work on? You can only work on one thing at a time, not everything, it's overwhelming. What's the first thing you want to stop, the running away? the throwing? the hitting? Which one do you want to do first? [This is the first time Sally delegated the lead to Janice about planning how to manage the children.]
Janice: Running away.
Sally: Running away. OK. Then what do you think you're going to do about it? What do you think? What do you think?
Janice: [shrugs her shoulders]
Sally: You've got to have a talk with him, we both will. He will understand.
Therapist: Joe, you're being called.
Sally: [to Janice] We both will.
Therapist: [to Joe] Why don't you sit down with me and we'll have a three- or four-way discussion. OK?
Joe: OK.

Sally and Janice began acting like an effective team with respect to Joe. Having begun to address and modify the triangle of mother–children–grandparents, it was now an optimal time to focus more on the triangle of mother–children–father. In the next segment, I talked with Joe about his feelings of attachment to his parents and about divorce issues:

Therapist:	We're talking about you running away, and that your Mom is very, very upset when you run away from home. Do you ever wonder if your Mom loves you?
Joe:	She loves me.
Therapist:	How do you know?
Joe:	She always kisses me good night.
Therapist:	That's one way to figure it out. Is that how you know she loves you? Do you think your Father loves you?
Joe:	Um um (Yes) he kisses me good night.
Therapist:	Where's your Father?
Joe:	In State X [different state].
Therapist:	How come?
Joe:	He's not gonna bring my bike.
Therapist:	He's not going to bring your bike?
Joe:	He said he's going to bring my bike.
Therapist:	But he doesn't, does he?
Joe:	And he won't. He's trying, he's trying to get vacation.
Therapist:	Really?
Joe:	So he can bring my bike.
Therapist:	Do you sometimes ...
Joe:	So I can keep it.
Therapist:	Why isn't your father living with your mother?
Joe:	We're gonna move.
Therapist:	Who's gonna move?
Joe:	Us, me. Shirley and Mommy.
Therapist:	Really?
Joe:	Daddy's gonna buy us a new house.
Therapist:	Daddy is going to buy you a new house?
Joe:	Yup.
Therapist:	And you're all going to move in together?
Joe:	Yup. And Daddy's gonna stay with us.
Therapist:	Now when you tell that idea to Mommy what does she say?
Joe:	[looks at Janice]
Janice:	[to Joe] I don't know.
Joe:	[to therapist] She doesn't know.
Janice:	[signs to therapist without voice; Interpreter interprets sign to voice] It's tough. I don't know what will happen.

Having repeatedly discussed this issue with Janice individually, I knew that Janice did not wish to reestablish the relationship with her ex-husband. Given that she signed "I don't know what will happen" without voicing to me whereas she previously had always signed "sim-comm," it was apparent that she had not yet clearly told the children about her plans. Consequently, at this time, it was important to push the issue in order to obtain clarity and to begin a necessary process of grieving for the children. The issue of guilt with Janice was also addressed.

Therapist: [to Janice] But wait a minute. Joe is saying all of you are going to move into this big house?
Janice: (Signs without voice while the interpreter interprets sign to voice) Yeh. He is confused. Ugh …
Therapist: So, wait a minute, so, so you and Goeff [ex-husband] may get back together again?
Janice: No, I'm sorry. But, it's not possible. I can't do it, I'm sorry. But no way!
Therapist: Ok, that's clear. Although hard to say, it's very clear. Your children need to know that.
Sally: Well, she's afraid to say it in front of me. Don't worry about it.
Janice: [to Joe and Shirley in sim-comm] Daddy and I are not moving in together. We are divorced. We are not … [looks down]
Therapist: [to Janice] It's OK, [to Joe and Shirley] OK. What did your Mom just say? Did you understand it?
Joe: Nope. I don't.
Therapist: Then ask her again.
Joe: What'd you say?
Janice: Daddy and I are not married. We are not moving to a new house. He is living in [State X], and we are here. I will never live with daddy again. It's over. No more.
Therapist: [to Joe] What'd mommy just say?
Joe: That she is not going to get back together with Daddy.
Therapist: Do you know why?
Joe: Divorce.
Therapist: That's right, what's divorce mean?
Joe: Means you don't come back together again.
Therapist: Right, you know why?
Joe: Yea.
Therapist: Why?
Joe: They scream at each other.
Therapist: And it's no fun for you, your Mother, or your Father if Mom and Dad scream at each other, right? You look sad, is that sad? You look sad, I would be sad if I were you. Did you know that my own parents were divorced, too? Did I tell you? I was sad when they were divorced, and guess who I was angry at?
Joe: [looks up, eyes dilate] Who?
Therapist: My mother.
Joe: How come?

Therapist: Cause I thought it was her fault.
Joe: Was it Daddy's fault?
Therapist: I thought it was my Daddy's fault for a while, too. You know what I figured out when I was about …
Joe: Seven?
Therapist: No [laughs], several years later.
Joe: What?
Therapist: I figured out it was nobody's fault.
Joe: Did they go back together?
Therapist: Nope. Know what my Mother did?
Joe: What?
Therapist: My Mother married somebody else, my stepfather, whose name is also Joe, like yours. Joe, my stepfather, is a real nice person; he bought me my first electric guitar as a teenager.

In the next segment, the task was to connect the presenting problem, Joe acting out at home, with the divorce triangle. This was accomplished by indirectly addressing Joe through a made up third person, "Tom," a technique of indirect hypnosis (Haley, 1967). It became clear that Joe had attributed the reasons for the divorce to himself and that he attributed to himself the power to get his parents back together again by either acting badly or properly. This dynamic is common in families of divorced parents and is not idiosyncratic to hearing children of deaf parents.

Therapist: [to Joe] You know what some kids do to try to get their Mother to go back with their Father when they're divorced?
Joe: What?
Therapist: Well, I'll tell you a story, OK? I know somebody named Tom. Want to know how old Tom is?
Joe: How old?
Therapist: He's about 7 or 8; and you know about his parents?
Joe: What?
Therapist: His parents are divorced.
Joe: What did he do?
Therapist: Well he ran away a lot from home and also did not mind his Mother. Know why?
Joe: Why?
Therapist: Well, cause Tom figured out that if he does that enough, his mother will be so unhappy, so helpless and so fed up that she'll say "I need my husband back again. I'm going to get back together with Tom's father." That's why Tom decided to run away and not mind mother. What do you think about that?
Joe: Maybe if he don't run away and then …
Therapist: And when what?
Joe: And they'll go back together again.

Therapist:	No. You see, Tom had made a mistake in thinking he could help his parents get back together again, but he can't cause he's only 8.

I then asked Joe for a consult. I role played Tom and asked him to play Dr. Harvey:

Therapist:	(pretending to be Tom) Dr. Harvey, my mom just said a few minutes ago that even if I behave perfectly, she's not going to go back with Daddy! She just said that to me. Dr. Harvey.
Joe:	(pretending to be Dr. Harvey) Then what will you do?
Therapist:	I'll feel sad.
Joe:	And what else?
Therapist:	I'll feel angry.
Joe:	What else?
Therapist:	I'll feel scared.
Joe:	Then what else are you going to do?
Therapist:	I'll probably talk about it to my Mommy.
Joe:	OK.
Therapist:	Want to see me talk to my Mommy?
Joe:	OK, go ahead.
Therapist:	Watch me, Dr. Harvey. (therapist, role playing Tom, talks to Janice) I really feel sad that you're not going to get back with my father.
Janice:	(sighs)
Therapist:	I feel sad that you're not going to get back together with my Dad, Mommy.
Janice:	(sighs)
Therapist:	Should I talk to you about it when I feel sad?
Janice:	(sighs)
Therapist:	Well, Dr. Harvey just said that when I talk to you when I'm sad you might feel guilty and not want to talk about it.

It was quite apparent that Joe understood the role play and got the message from it. It was also clear that Janice, feeling guilty, inadequate, and responsible for the marital breakup, could not give Joe what he needed: opportunities to openly grieve the loss. Therefore, work began with Janice around psychoeducational issues of children needing to grieve and how important and helpful simply talking could be. Janice indicated that she understood and felt comfortable clarifying to the children that the marital relationship with her ex-husband was terminated and also more directly comforting the children.

In the next session, I summarized this piece of work, reclaimed my role as "Dr. Harvey" and talked with Joe. It became clear that Joe understood my use of Erickson's indirect hypnotic technique: namely, that I was referring to him (Joe) by inventing a character named Tom:

Therapist: Well, I'm gonna be Dr. Harvey again for a minute.
Joe: OK, I'll be Tom.
Therapist: [laugher] You certainly will be Tom.
Sally: Yes he will.
Therapist: And now, I think your mother needs to tell you very clearly that there's no way her and your Daddy are going to stay married. And that, Joe, it doesn't depend on you. You don't have any say. Now I know how it feels. It feels lousy, doesn't it?
Joe: Grandma, can we stop for ice cream?

Joe had a familiar way of indicating that he had enough of talking about a topic. His last sentence also illustrated that Grandma was still the boss and that Janice remained regulated to an inferior status.

The following segments occurred during the third meeting with members of the nuclear and extended families. At this point, a stronger therapeutic alliance with Sally was evident; in part, because of not having prematurely excluded her from the dialogue between Joe and Janice. I also liked her tenacity and could feel the torment and pain that had characterized much of her life. During the previous meetings, we had enjoyed a sort of jostling match with each other over control of the session. She had consistently been quite loquacious and hesitant to give up control, but it was time to be more confrontive with her toward helping her give up some of it.

Another major remaining task was to directly address Janice's negative feelings about herself as a deaf person, which in part, were manifested by the verbal communication problems with her children and by Janice allowing herself to be infantilized by her parents.

In the following segment, Sally began the session with a long monologue about Joe's bad behavior:

Sally: [about 10 minutes] … and Joe was kicking it to pieces.
Therapist: Sally, Sally, Sally, you have a terrific load on your shoulders. I know that.
Sally: Naturally.
Therapist: But the heavier the load gets the more you don't listen, and talk, talk, talk! I'm trying to help but you won't let me.
Sally: I'm fine.
Therapist: I would like to …
Sally: I'm very calm and I'm fine. Except when they're all screaming at one time and he's kicking …
Therapist: There's no screaming now.
Sally: Not now, but when they're … When he is screaming at the top of his lungs and kicking and everything all for noise, it just breaks my head right off. And I've had enough, and I go boom.
Therapist: Would you like to help me help you stop it?

Sally: Sure. You can tell both of us what to do. I'm not going to say me, both of us.
Therapist: We're talking the same language then.
Sally: I didn't say just me.
Therapist: Alright. [smiles]

One indication that we had joined was that Sally reframed my statement about "helping you stop ..." to a problem that both she and Janice needed help on. I accommodated to her, saying that "we're talking the same language then." My use of the word language also paved the way for a later discussion about verbal communication—sign language.

Sally: OK. I can hear you. I even know what you're going to say next. Bet I can tell you word for word?
Therapist: [laughter] OK, what is it? Tell me. What will I say?
Sally: You'll say, 'OK Sally, will you please calm down, will you please be quiet so I can tell you exactly what you can do to help both of us.'
Therapist: [laughter] Well, sort of, yea! What's my help going to be?
Sally: I don't know, because I don't know how these two here are going to straighten out. [reference to Joe & Shirley]
Therapist: OK.
Sally: But I do know a few things need to be done. But go ahead; and you know what I'll do? I'll give you a break. I'm going to let you be the doctor for the next 30 minutes, and then I want my say.
Therapist: [much laughter] Well, I'll tell you what. You let me be the doctor for 30 minutes and you can have the last ...
Sally: 10 minutes, 5 minutes.
Therapist: Five minutes.
Sally: I only need 5 minutes at the rate I talk. Fair?
Therapist: [I think to myself that I know when I'm getting a good deal; to Janice] Your mother has allowed me to be the doctor, which is probably difficult and gutsy for her to do.
Sally: Not really.
Therapist: [to Janice] I think it's absolutely a shame that you two ... (Sally checks the clock to time the therapist) [much laughter; to Sally] I love you, I really do! If you were only younger or I was older, or whatever.
Sally: (laughter)
Janice: She [Sally] was real excited because she bought a car. Really proud.
Sally: Eleven years. I didn't even buy it brand new. Oh I'm sorry I'm not supposed to be talking. [winks at therapist]
Therapist: [to Janice] I think it's absolutely a shame that Joe and Shirley cannot understand a lot of the very important things you have to say.

I then asked Janice to place her mother and children on the couch and for her to stand up, and instructed Janice to begin teaching a sign language class. During the class, I instructed Janice to sign without voice, as I did, without the interpreter interpreting. Janice, at first, was quite unsure of herself in this new role.

Therapist: Now you have three sort of willing students. Know that?
Janice: (sighs)
Therapist: So I want you to teach them five new signs. New ones, not old ones, new ones. Go ahead.
Janice: New ones? Like what?
Therapist: You know many signs. Pick one.
Janice: (sighs and begins to sit down)
Therapist: [asks the interpreter to interpret voice to sign while I make a telephone call, saying to my wife "I may not be home until 2 or 3 in the morning, depending on how a class goes.
Don't wait up for me"; looks at Janice]
Janice: (smiles) [begins class and nicely teaches them four new signs]
Therapist: [signs without voice—no interpretation] Good, wonderful! Tell them all good job. The teacher is pleased, right? Now, one more sign.
Janice: [signs without voice—no interpretation] Book. Read book.
Joe: [signs without voice] Read book
Sally: [voices] You don't go this way? This way? I thought it was this way. Oh.

The session ended with a prescription that Janice teach her mother and children five new signs every day and to give them an examination every week. I asked her to bring me three report cards for our next session.

The following segments are from the last session that included Sally and that occurred approximately 1 month later. This time, the grandfather, Herb, decided to attend. He reportedly "had to work" during the other meetings. As Sally appeared to wield a lot of power in the family, he had not been required to attend the meetings.

Janice entered the office while proudly presenting the report cards to me. Joe and Shirley got As; Sally was given a C+. In addition, both children, particularly Joe, were enthusiastically learning sign language and were regularly signing with Janice. In fact, Joe reported wanting to become deaf, a far cry from his previous sentiments about wanting to be with "grandma because she is hearing." However, with progress came a new concern; Joe indicated that he planned to "stick a pencil into my ears to make me deaf like mommy."

This session began with a discussion about power.

Sally: I'm very confident with Joe and Shirley, telling them what to do, and it comes across, because they're not gonna walk all over me!
Therapist: Do you teach Janice to be that confident?
Herb: She tells them [Joe and Shirley], she tells them.
Therapist: The way Sally does?

Herb: Oh, yes, sometimes.

Sally: [to Janice] No, there's got to be a way about this instead of screaming, you've got to look eye to eye and be very sure of yourself. Not physical, [to therapist] but she tells me ...

Janice: [screaming] You're hearing! When you talk to them it's easier. I'm deaf and it's different and it's harder.

Sally: All you need is three or four words; you don't need a big vocabulary.

Janice: (unintelligible)

Sally: No. What you have always told me is that I'm very strong. And I told you, you could be just as strong. You have to just know what you won't take, and it doesn't take a lot of beating or screaming!

Herb: I take it it's kind of hard for her because she's ...

Sally: It's hard, she's deaf.

Herb: She's deaf.

Sally: I could teach her a few words.

Therapist: Bullshit, it's hard! Wait a minute. [to Janice; sim-comm] Before, it was a lot harder, because the communication was lacking between you and Joe. Joe couldn't sign, didn't want to sign; often Joe would say things you didn't understand, often Joe would not understand you, etc. Now Joe signs well. So I think it is becoming an advantage that you're deaf, not a hindrance. It is becoming an advantage. And I think you could become as powerful as your Mom, and more so. Particularly because you're deaf. For God sakes, Joe recently was going to try to become deaf like you. That is a whole other problem, I know, but ...

Sally: I see. Hmmm.

Therapist: [signs without voice; interpreter interprets sign to voice] That's the thing, you know; that your deafness is becoming for you a real point of strength. Do you believe me? Do you see it the same?

Janice: Joe did want to be deaf real bad. He did want to become deaf like me. He really did!

Therapist: Your deafness is your strength. But see, you need to believe that yourself. It may have been growing up in your family when the educational system was lousy, that deafness was a real negative thing. That may have been true. [looks at Sally and signs and voices simultaneously] Now, with the educational systems improved, with your grandchildren beginning to learn sign language, wow! [looks at Janice] Deafness is becoming much better; but you have become so used to growing up in your time, when, for you, deafness was negative. It has become a habit now, and you have thought that deafness makes you inept. It may have been that way before; now, I don't think so. But you need to know that. You need to know that.

I then called Joe into the discussion. He and Shirley were in the other section of the office playing:

Therapist:	Why do you want to be deaf, Joe?
Joe:	I like sign language.
Therapist:	Do you want to be deaf like Mom?
Joe:	Yea!
Therapist:	[to Janice] That's where your strength is.

I continued to work with Janice, Joe, and Shirley and had intermittent telephone contact with Sally. Janice was ready to "fly on her own"; and Sally was ready to give up her role as primary parent. Her husband was grateful because in his words, "my wife is back." As Janice continued to assert herself more as a parent, Joe soon discontinued wanting to puncture his eardrums to become deaf. Janice became more comfortable with herself as a Deaf person and her children as hearing, and vice versa from the perspectives of Joe and Shirley.

The next major segment of work was essentially to duplicate for Shirley the work I did with Joe. Although Shirley was not a "behavior problem," she nevertheless clearly harbored similar issues as Joe, commensurate with her developmental stage.

10

Treatment of the Individual–Family–Vocational Rehabilitation Systems

In this chapter, we turn our attention to clinical interventions for treating a deaf or hard-of-hearing individual's presenting problems when the ecological context of those problems includes a Rehabilitation Counselor for the Deaf (RCD) from the state Vocational Rehabilitation Agency. An RCD's role is to assist the client in becoming gainfully employed, which frequently includes providing supportive counseling and coordinating the provision of a variety of other services, such as advanced technical training, academic course work, or independent living skills training as it pertains to vocational pursuits (Nowell & Marshak, 1994; Wright, 1983). Although the importance of family factors is acknowledged, the primary focus of rehabilitation efforts has been toward the disabled individual.

This bias has important implications both for the outcomes of the RCD's rehabilitation efforts and for the clinician's therapeutic efforts to help a particular deaf or hard-of-hearing individual. In the case of an RCD attempting to assist an adolescent or adult who has not yet individuated from his or her nuclear family, the RCD often forms a strong alliance with the individual and remains relatively disengaged from his or her parents and surrounding context. Alternately, the RCD may unwittingly join with the individual against his or her parents, or join with one parent exclusive of the other, thereby becoming part of a coalitional structure in the family–professionals system, exacerbating conflict, and finding that his or her rehabilitation counseling efforts are thwarted.

In this manner, vocational rehabilitation counselors often make systemic interventions without knowing it. The RCD, as with any helper, both affects and is affected by the context: To be helpful to the individual client, it is often necessary to modify the surrounding ecological context that, from the RCD's perspective, includes family members and other professionals, such as the clinician. In many cases, the RCD failing to carefully take these ecosystemic factors into account creates an unnecessarily high probability that a client's family and other members of the context will prevent, retard, or modify the goals of the RCD and client; or that the combined goals of RCD and client, not formulated in conjunction with parental input and guidance, may likely be inappropriate. In either case, the deaf–hard-of-hearing client makes little or no vocational progress.

This poor outcome has important implications, not only for the RCD, but also for the clinician who also functions within the ecological context of the "identified patient" and who is also trying to be helpful. As described previously, the RCD's move to rehabilitate the individual client may be incorporated within the dysfunctional transactions within the ecology to paradoxically result in thwarted individuation for the client, and can therefore be properly viewed as part of the problem. Thus, in this case, the therapist must modify the dysfunctional transactional patterns around the presenting problem of a deaf–hard-of-hearing adolescent, which includes involvement of the family and the RCD.

It becomes apparent that both the clinician and RCD, to be maximally helpful to a given client, must often modify the surrounding context that includes the other. It would, therefore, make sense that they work together. This chapter presents one such example. It presents verbatim therapy transcripts of a cooperative effort on the part of an RCD and myself, in the capacity of family therapist, to intervene systemically to assist Joan, a deaf 19-year-old. Joan was the middle of three siblings in an intact family, all of whom were hearing. Joan's primary and preferred mode of communication was ASL, and she had minimal oral–aural skills. Her family did not sign. I had been working with the family for about 1 year to help resolve frequent and explosive family conflicts having to do with individuation issues. Joan had dropped out of high school, severely abused alcohol, moved back home with her parents, and become quite depressed. Her parents, Dan and Marge, alternated between resenting Joan's presence and feeling reluctant and frightened to see her go out on her own.

After 1 year of individual and family treatment, I suggested that Joan receive rehabilitation counseling to work toward becoming more self-sufficient by pursuing high school, college, or vocational training. Her parents overtly supported this plan. However, in light of their history of power struggles with Joan, it seemed likely that the mere incorporation of another helper would only provide fuel for the conflict to escalate and for Joan to sabotage progress. In the past, rehabilitation counselors would develop a plan in the office, the Individualized Written Rehabilitation Plan (IWRP). Joan would announce the plan at home, a fight would ensue, Joan would act out in a variety of ways, and would drop out of vocational counseling.

Because all of the previous RCD's efforts had become incorporated in the recursive cycle that supported Joan's symptomatology, I invited the current RCD to attend a family therapy session to (a) formally assess how Joan's family would react to the RCD's interventions; (b) assess how the RCD, in turn, would react to the family's counterinterventions; and (c) intervene in the newly formed family–RCD system to increase the probability that the RCD's interventions would be supported by Joan and her family. The intervention strategy was to provide a context for the family to enact their conflicts about the IWRP in front of both the RCD and myself; to pave the way for the RCD to become a direct participant in the family transactions, as opposed to becoming an external irritant to the family, which would eventually be purged from their system.

In this particular case, from my clinical perspective, the vital initial joining with the RCD had already occurred. The RCD and I had already worked together in a number of different contexts, and clearly respected and trusted each other. As is illustrated in the following transcripts, when working together with Joan and her family, we supported each other as cotherapists in making probes and interventions from our respective orientations and with complementary and compatible views of the problem. Thus, the rehabilitation interventions did not become incorporated as part of the systemic problem but instead became incorporated as effective solutions. The importance of this initial joining cannot be overemphasized. If we had been unable to work together comfortably, many, if not all, of our clinical and rehabilitative interventions would probably have been doomed to failure.

The following transcript is from a presession between the RCD, the interpreter, and myself. The importance of a presession including the interpreter was emphasized in chapter 8. With the RCD, the purpose of this meeting was to clarify goals and the ways we were to work together. By this time, the RCD had already met one time with Joan and her mother.

Therapist: (to RCD) I want us to know together the history of how this family has interfaced, for lack of a better word, with rehab counselors in the past. I suspect that there will be a battle about how much involvement Mother and Father will have with you because that's been the issue during most of Joan's life. So I think you will probably be in the same position. So I'll probably start by saying that we have Neil Glickman here, and I'll say something nice about you and thank you for coming. I will say that it looks like one option is for Neil and Joan to work together, and that I want to explore what each of you [Joan, Mother, and Father] would like to do with Neil, how all of you would like to be involved. And then you can explain how you think you can be helpful. Then Mom and Dad can ask questions of you. Then we can work towards separating our roles. How about that?

RCD: The thing is, I've only had one session with Joan and her Mother. I had the feeling that Joan was dragged to my office and did not want to be involved. And we haven't really had the time yet to set up a plan, much less establish rapport. I think we will establish one relatively quickly though. During the meeting, I didn't have an interpreter, so I had the problem of interpreting Mom and the whole anguish issue with the Mother right there.

I have a sense of her [Joan's] basic situation of being stuck at home, wanting a GED. I'm not sure why she didn't complete high school, something happened, I don't know what it was. She had three months left 'til graduation. She wants a driver's license. But this will be hard if the parents refuse to give her a car to practice with. That's the obstacle to getting a driver's license. She can set up with an agency, AAA or something, but she still needs to practice.

I got a sense from the Mother that they're not going to help Joan. She can go to school, great, but they're not going to give her transportation. They're not going to give her any money.

Therapist: So if that's the stance, Hmm … this is exciting and helpful. I can do some stuff with the Mother and Father, so we can play with that; how they have "helped" [shows the sign for "help" going upward to mean support], and "helped" [shows "help" going downward, to mean suppress or stifle] Joan by doing her laundry for her and by not letting go. So what "help" [shows sign for "help" going upward] Joan needs from parents via the rehab plan and then we'll explore conflicts.

RCD: I'm not sure about Joan's motivation for school, for a job, for a license, for independence; I'm not sure of that. I could be effective in helping her do those things but she needs to want that. At our first meeting, I didn't see an involved person …

The next segment was from the initial moments of the first session. As Joan's primary and preferred mode of communication was ASL, the RCD and

I signed ASL to Joan (therefore without voice) while the interpreter interpreted sign to voice for the benefit of the hearing family members. We used spoken English with the hearing members, whereas the interpreter interpreted voice to sign for Joan. Finally, the interpreter interpreted intrafamily communication; she voiced when Joan signed, and signed when the family spoke. These communication logistics were described in chapters 7 and 8.

The mother (Marge, age 45) and father (Dan, age 46) entered, followed by Joan (age 19), and Joan's younger sister Karen (age 18). The interpreter, RCD, and therapist then seated themselves. It is important to note that Karen had received vocational rehabilitation services, beginning 1 year ago, in light of a psychiatric disability of severe depression. She was allied with Joan in that both shared the role of identified patient.

The first task was to facilitate the RCD's entry into the family system by introducing him in a complementary manner. Subsequently, the discussion focused on this family's history with other vocational rehabilitation counselors to assess their current expectations of the RCD and to predict their reactions to possible thwarted expectations.

THE FIRST THERAPIST–RCD–FAMILY MEETING

Therapist: [to parents] Well, as I told you, I invited Neil in for this session. This is the first time Neil and I have worked together in this way. We have worked together in a variety of other ways and in fact the article he wrote on Cross Cultural Counseling is required reading in one of the courses I teach. So quite frankly I am happy he is here, as a part of this group. And I guess I'd like to know from all of you what past experiences you have had with rehab counselors: what you have liked, what you have not liked, etc.

Marge: This is really the first rehab counselor we've ever dealt with.

Therapist: You said a few weeks ago that you had …

Dan: Well, we interfaced with [X].

Marge: With who?

Dan: With VR services over some of Karen's earlier problems.

Marge: That has nothing to do with Joan!

I noted what had been a common pattern of parental bickering, which would characterize their discussions of the children.

Therapist: Okay, but what was your experience?

Marge: I saw the lady for five minutes one day, that's all. She told me "Karen is of age and I no longer want to see you." So I said sayonara.

Therapist: So you saw her for five minutes and you were told …

Marge: All they wanted to know was how much money we made and they shipped me out.

Therapist: I guess that would translate into, "I've had at least one bad experience with a rehab counselor." (laughs)

Dan: We were never able to gain knowledge about what went on when we asked the kids when they came home. We were never really able to get much information. The kids were kind of like a filter.

Marge: The only way I feel about that is as long as they live in my home and I'm supporting them, I don't think it's fair that we can't know their business.

Therapist: That's why we're meeting together, so we can sort all of this out.

Dan: I think this is a spin-off from the Privacy Act or whatever. But as parents, we're trying to help out. And before it was very frustrating (Looks at RCD).

In the sequence just presented, the parents bickered with each other until they agreed on wanting more information about their children's activities with, for example, vocational rehabilitation services. I wondered if this sequence was isomorphic to a previous outside-of-the-session sequence, in which the parents bickered with each other until they joined in anger against Karen's VR counselor who withheld information. In both cases, it appeared that the children and professionals withholding information from the parents served to stabilize their marriage. It was unclear, however, whether Joan would take Karen's place in this triangle when Karen's behavior would no longer be viewed as a problem.

It became immediately apparent that the issue of boundaries was a central focal point. Although I was careful not to explicitly condone the parents for their desires for what seemed to be enmeshed relationships with their children, I joined them by stating that the purpose of the meeting was "to sort this out."

Therapist: You [to Joan] had a rehab counselor in [State Y] when you left school, right? How long was this for?

Joan: From about March and it stopped in July, or maybe it was longer than that.

Therapist: How many times did you meet?

Joan: Maybe six times.

Marge: It was not that long.

Dan: Maybe three or four times tops!

Therapist: Wait a minute. [to Joan] I hear some opposition from your parents. Anyway, you said you met about six times. Were your parents involved?

Joan: No. I met with someone, hmmm, I forget his name.

Dan: She's talking about Stuart.

Marge: Stuart [X]. She missed most of the appointments that he made with her. She would fail to show up for any help he was trying to give her. [Argument begins between the parents and Joan about how many times she met with Stuart.]

Therapist: Okay, stop. Question: [to parents] How do you know this information about the number of times that she met with Stuart? I'm just trying to figure that out.
Marge: An interpreter in [State Y] informed me of that.

Marge's last statement is a good example of how professionals are enlisted by family members to become part of the dysfunctional interactions that support the problem. Here, the parents had formed an alliance with Joan's interpreter to give them information about Joan's activities, thus weakening the alliance between Joan and the interpreter and strengthening the enmeshment between the parents and Joan. It was an enigma how the interpreter had justified this, given the RID Code of Ethics, whether or not the interpreter was certified; and more important, from a systemic perspective, how Joan might have acted out, perhaps creating a danger to herself or others, that necessitated the interpreter informing Joan's parents. The latter question would be investigated later in treatment.

At this time, with this history acknowledged in the presence of the RCD, parental boundary expectations in regard to Joan and the RCD were ascertained.

Therapist: [to parents] With Stuart, in some ways you were involved only in the fact that you knew what was going on, right?
Dan: Right.
Therapist: You would have liked to have been involved more and therefore I suspect, as parents, you would like to be involved on some level with Joan and Neil as they work together?
Marge: I don't want to sit in on all of the meetings like that, but I think that we should be kept informed on any decisions that are made. It involves our lives, too, when she lives in our house.
Therapist: Yes.
Marge: So I think it's important that we know some of these things.
Therapist: Okay.
Dan: Depending on the situation and how things are going, they act as pretty good filters, depending on what they want you to hear and what they don't want you to hear.

At this time, it was important to cue the RCD to become more directly involved as a participant, specifically in regard to the issue of boundaries. Here, the importance of our presessions and shared view of the problem and solution became important in that we agreed that rigid boundaries around the RCD and client with respect to parents would have been inappropriate. Thus, the RCD introduced a third option for parental involvement other than total involvement in the rehabilitation process (enmeshment) or no involvement (disengagement), namely the option of "balancing confidentiality."

Therapist: [to RCD] Well, just to summarize for them some discussions that you and I have had over some lunches about how many therapists and rehab counselors only work with the individual and ignore, if you will, the family, and how that doesn't make sense. But we need to have a clear sense of what you expect from the family and what the family expects from you.

RCD: [to parents] I hear you both saying that you want to help Joan, and at the same time you want to have a sense of what's going on, especially in terms of making decisions. That makes sense. That has to be balanced with confidentiality. The fact is that, in almost all sessions between rehab counselor and client in the office (i.e., between me and Joan) I am not allowed to discuss what goes on in the session without Joan's permission. What I try to do, and in practice almost always works out, is to get her permission to discuss certain parts of our session with another person, such as parents. This is especially important when we're at the point of deciding on license, school, job, and how we're going to go about that, especially when there are money issues involved, as there sometimes are. If Joan chooses not to give me permission to talk to you, I'm stuck.

Marge: I would say you are! Because at that point, I mean, every appointment she's ever going to have involves our lives. The two of us have to take off work, I mean that's a direct involvement in our lives. So what is she going to come to me and say, "you have to take me to your office but I'm not going to tell you what for!?"

Dan: Well, we can't leap to that conclusion, Mother.

Marge: Well, starting off with the doctor appointments, we're going to have to transport her, and that's an involvement. (Appears angry at Dan).

RCD: That's right.

To facilitate the establishing of more appropriate boundaries within the therapist–RCD–family system, I asked the RCD to change his seat so he would sit next to Joan and could more easily talk directly to her.

Therapist: Can I ask you to switch places with me, Neil, and talk to Joan about what she would like from you, and, in part, how she would like to establish boundaries between you two and her parents?

RCD: [changes seat. to Joan] Hi. We just met about two weeks ago, and we hadn't really talked in depth about what we planned to do. I'm wondering how you feel I can help you?

Joan: Well, I need a job so I can be able to support myself. I need to have money so I can pay for an apartment, a car, food, and be able to move out of my parents' home. I want to go back to school, and get a license so I can get back and forth to a job.

RCD: What I was also wondering is how can we get your parents involved? How do you want them to be involved?

Joan: I have no idea.

RCD: There is a rule about confidentiality, so I need to have your permission to talk with them. Do you want your parents involved? Do you not want your parents involved, or what?

Joan: I don't know; it depends.

RCD: Yeh, I agree. It sounds like we need to develop a plan that involves school, work, and getting a driver's license. These are all important decisions. Your parents need to know some of what's going on with that, if you're going to ask them maybe for some help. Do you think it's possible that maybe we could ask them to join us for a meeting and share your plans with them?

Joan: Sometimes. Not all the time.

RCD: Oh, I agree, not all the time. We're not talking about all the time. Most of our meetings will be one-to-one and confidential. But if you have specific plans for school, or job, or your license ... you think it's important for your parents to be involved?

Joan: All right. That's fine.

Thus, Joan agreed with the RCD's suggestion to "balance confidentiality." The question naturally comes up of what would have happened had Joan not agreed with his suggestion? However, it is more fruitful to ask how did it happen that Joan agreed to the RCD's suggestion? Joan's affirmative response was not random good luck; it was a function of the RCD and therapist having already joined with her during previous individual and family sessions.

Joan subsequently began to argue with her father about prioritizing her goals, and both parents responded by attempting to enlist the RCD to be on their side against Joan.

Joan: [to Dan] You're always telling me that I need to get a job right now and school maybe later. But I need a car license and want to go to school. I need to think about my future.

Dan: [to Joan] That's good; we understand that. Remember what we discussed previously about the money involved? And I pointed out to her [looks at RCD] the other day, if she gets a job for four or five dollars an hour, whatever, and if she pays three to four dollars an hour on the average for upkeep of a car, then there's not a lot of good that can come from that.

Joan: Don't worry about it!

Marge: [to RCD] The important issue is to get her some day to understand that her priorities have to be placed in the proper position and fully realized, as far as I'm concerned, that her first priority should be to get a job, earn money and save it. Then get a driver's license and a car. The driver's license, anyone can get one of those; [to Joan] what are you going to do with it?

Both parents were actively attempting to form alliances with the RCD, and to collude with him against Joan. As stated earlier in this chapter, this process occurs quite frequently among parents, VR counselors, and clients. The critical, difference here was that this process was occurring in the office in the presence of both the RCD and therapist. It, therefore, could more easily be assessed and modified, as illustrated by the following segment:

Therapist: [to Marge] Well, instead of talking to Neil, why don't you talk to Joan? Let the two of us [RCD and therapist] watch the dialogue, because I have not seen this particular dialogue. You've had it at home. So say that to Joan now, and let us see how that goes.

Marge: [to Joan] I think you should get a job and start saving money for a change. That is the priority. For the car and the driver's license, and whatever you want to fit school into that, that's another thing. But the first priority I see being listed from you to Neil is, "I want a driver's license," and I'm murmuring, "What are you going to do with it?" and furthermore ...

Therapist: Okay, Joan's turn to talk.

Joan: But I need a license!

Therapist: Wait a minute. Can we switch here? [Therapist asks the interpreter to change her seating to next to Mother to maximize eye contact between Joan and her Mother.]

As predicted in chapter 8, the interpreter changing her seating so that there was more direct contact between Joan and her mother also increased the level of affective exchange between them in that their conflict dramatically escalated. It was a conflict that they had become quite used to and that has functioned, in part, to impede the effectiveness of rehabilitation services that had been provided for Joan.

The following transcript occurred after a discussion about Joan's ability to manage her own funds. In reaction to the RCD inquiring about the feasibility of Joan managing her own checking account, the parents enacted what had become a stable pattern of disagreement about Joan's readiness for more independent functioning.

Dan: [to RCD] It's more convenient for us to write checks and let Joan mail them out to the various businesses.

RCD: Why doesn't Joan have her own checking account?

Marge: She doesn't know how to manage one in the first place ...

Dan: [interrupts Marge] We're trying to help her; to show her how to manage her money. What I've done is establish a little book, and she gives me money and I put it in my bank; this book is just like a checkbook, and if she writes $5 or $10 to go out, then I put that in there.

That way, she can see how her money is being spent, depreciating if you will. And we show her how she spends each and every dollar of the money she receives.

RCD: [to Dan] At what point would you feel comfortable letting her have control of the money, to have her own account?

Dan: We did this initially because it was convenient and she wanted to get the bills paid right away. And as soon as I see signs that she can control her money, well then that's fine. There's no problem; she can have a checking account.

RCD: [to Marge] Do you agree?

Marge: The only reason I see a problem is because the thing she's going through right now like, "I want a new TV for my own room," and she's still in debt! And I can't see her going out and going in debt more to buy a television. Her values are all screwed up!

Dan: But, you know, she can write a check any time she wants to. If she had the mind to, she can go out and sign the check and buy that.

Marge: And that's exactly what she'd do, go out and buy a color TV. You don't see this; I do. I'm home with her more.

Dan: But she has a check herself, she can go do it if she want to. I'm just saying she has the option to go out and buy one.

Marge: Well, you've always been an optimist.

Therapist: Time out. [to RCD] So this is how you get involved in family disagreements. You are now being presented, and you will continue to be presented, with both Joan's ideas about what she wants to do with her life right now, as well as her parents' ideas. Her parents have ideas about how they want to guide her life. They may agree, they may disagree; we don't know. But I think that's how you and I and the family can be involved and work through this complicated internal family negotiation process.

RCD: I can see this is why it's difficult to be absolute about confidentiality. I mean, she has to come up with a plan; and I think it's obvious that she and I would have to share that plan with her family. If you [parents] disagreed with the plan, we would have a problem. [To therapist] It makes sense to bring it back here.

Throughout these transcripts, it is tempting for clinicians and VR counselors to assert that Joan is of age, that her parents have no right to impose their values about what she should do with her life, and that the proper interventions should have been to encourage Joan to get out on her own despite her parents' resistance. However, it is important to remember that Joan herself participated in maintaining this enmeshed relationship. She was not developmentally ready to "leave the nest," as evidenced by many instances when she had moved out by herself, gotten in serious trouble with the law for intoxication, been evicted from numerous apartments, and so on. At this time, left to her own resources, Joan would have only confirmed her parents' opinion of her as inept.

After this first session with the parents and RCD that supplemented the information that had been obtained from previous family therapy sessions, a tentative systemic diagnosis was hypothesized: an eight-step recursive sequence containing the presenting problem of Joan's acting out and immaturity.

1. Mother and father argue about Joan's readiness for independence;
2. their conflict expands to include shifting coalitions among mother, father, and daughter;
3. Joan elicits the aid of a VR counselor and excludes her parents from that relationship, now colluding with the RCD against her parents;
4. The VR counselor complies and establishes a one to one, confidential relationship with Joan;
5. the parents stop fighting with each other and collude against the VR counselor by subverting VR goals;
6. Joan gets intoxicated, gets in trouble with the law, quits VR counseling, or leaves home;
7. the parents enlist other professionals to monitor Joan and find that she is unable to cope independently; and
8. Joan reestablishes this enmeshed, dependent relationship with her parents.

Eventually, her parents again argue between themselves about Joan's readiness for independence, and the cycle repeats itself.

In light of having delineated the recursive cycle that contained the symptom, the task was to attempt to disrupt the cycle so that it could no longer provide an enduring context for the symptom. Therapeutic efforts had already begun toward disrupting the third step of this cycle: Joan and an RCD establishing a relationship that excludes the parents. During the following 2 months as family sessions continued, Joan met twice with the RCD, and they developed a tentative IWRP. They were preparing to present it to Joan's parents during the next family meeting.

Improvement had been noteworthy; Joan no longer prematurely left home and refrained from getting into trouble so as to reestablish the enmeshment with her parents. However, she still appeared depressed, spent most of her time at home watching television, and avoided active participation in working toward achieving her vocational rehabilitation goals.

THE SECOND THERAPIST–RCD–FAMILY MEETING

The following segment illustrates that Joan was not an innocent victim of her parents' over protectiveness, but was also an active participant (Step 8 of the recursive cycle). Prior to this meeting, the RCD had asked Joan to be sure to bring the IWRP to the session.

RCD: Do you have the paper we wrote down? Do you have that with you?
Joan: I left it at home ... I left it at home.
RCD: Well, I have it.
Joan: (Laughs)

The power struggles and shifting coalitions between Joan and her parents in regards to individuation issues (Step 2 of the recursive cycle) is illustrated by the following segment in which Joan began to read the IWRP. As the first plan was to be a simple appropriation of funds for new hearing aids for Joan, both the RCD and I naively assumed that the discussion would be relatively simple and clear cut. However, the process of this seemingly innocuous content issue quickly mushroomed to include other isomorphic issues of control.

Joan: [reads from the IWRP] First I want to talk about a hearing aid. I need a new hearing aid. My molds are too small and it squeaks and gives me a headache.
RCD: So here is the plan that we're proposing. The first item on the list of goals is the hearing aid. The hearing aid is no problem. We will purchase the equipment.
Marge: What would we do?
RCD: You have to pick it up, and you're responsible for the repair and upkeep of it.
Marge: When will I be notified to go pick this up?
RCD: The hearing aid dealer will notify you. I haven't spoken to them yet, but they will probably send a letter to Joan.
Marge: [appears perturbed] You say the letter hasn't been sent yet?
RCD: No, because there was a question of which dealer we would use.
Marge: [leans forward in her chair toward RCD] Well, the reason I would like to buy the hearing aid from Dealer X is that I've used him before with Joan and ...
Dan: [to RCD] I didn't realize about the delay. I thought you already got a copy of all the tests and everything. I thought it had already gone through.
RCD: The hearing aid dealer hasn't received any paperwork yet. He won't begin work until he gets the authorization from us. And I wanted to clarify ... Joan had some questions about whether or not you wanted to use this dealer.
Dan: Oh, really?
Marge: [to Joan] I guess I just would like to know what problems there are. First of all, when you have a hearing aid you have to wear it! As far as I'm concerned, there's a lot more involved in it than just jumping in

the car and running out to classes and changing appointments. [to RCD and therapist] During conversations we've been having with Joan, she informed us that she doesn't have to see Mike if we're the ones having problems, that we forced her into having therapy, and that there's nothing wrong with her head.

Joan: You didn't understand me; you got it all wrong. I was talking about money; you showed me the bill from Mike, and I said I can't afford to pay for this.

Dan: That started it. I told you [Joan] it was difficult to come here and you told me that you didn't have to come.

Marge: The bill that we got from Mike started it because father showed her the bill, she blew her stack and said I'm not paying it, I don't need to go to it, it's you who has to see Mike. Then she said that her head is not fucked up. That's the exact terminology she used. She said we are the ones that need the therapy from Mike.

Dan: [to Marge] You don't have to get so excited, you know.

The essence of the power struggle between the parents and the VR counselor, (Step 5 of the recursive cycle) was succinctly exemplified by Marge when she referred to a recent discussion she had with the RCD, following a family fight.

Marge: [to therapist] Neil and I had quite a talk the other day after that because I was really furious. I was not trying to, you know. [to RCD] I know you were trying to help her, but I happen to know her priorities better than she does!

During this second family meeting with the RCD, four goals of the IWRP were eventually negotiated, albeit interspersed with much conflict as illustrated above: namely, purchasing new hearing aids, attending a GED preparatory program, attending driver's education classes, and investigating part time employment. Joan's parents agreed to transport her to school because it was quite far and not accessible by public transportation. They also agreed to driver's education classes on the condition that Joan procure some form of employment.

It was approximately 4 months until the next combined meeting with the family and RCD. Joan was well on her way to obtaining a GED and was beginning to take driver's education. However, her progression towards achieving more independence dramatically affected her parents' marital relationship; marital estrangement and conflict that had been only implicit and had been deflected onto Joan rapidly became more explicit and localized between them.

Just as Marge had pushed to clarify Joan's priorities in life, she acutely realized that she needed to clarify her own needs and desires, particularly in relation to Dan. She decided to separate from Dan to "think about my own priorities for a change." For 2 weeks, she spent most of her time alone in a hotel room "stewing about how soft Dan is, how he gives in all of the time to the children, and how I always end up being the bad guy, how we always have children in our house!"

At each person's request, three individual meetings with Marge and two individual meetings with Dan were scheduled during their 2-week separation. The purpose of these meetings was to support them through the dramatic systemic changes. After 2 weeks, assessing that both Marge and Dan had done ample soul searching and therefore, would benefit from renewed contact with each other and negotiation about how things would be different, a conjoint meeting was set up with Marge and Dan. During that meeting, Marge gave Dan an ultimatum of "me or the children." (Only 1 out of 3 children had left home.) She eloquently explained that it was about time that they help the children grow up, leave home, and "get their act together." It was important to support Marge for her gumption on making the first forward move, and to emphasize that indeed all of their previous attempted solutions toward helping Joan grow up had backfired. This precipitated a productive dialogue between Marge and Dan. Dan, for the first time, openly admitted his helplessness and despair, and he agreed to follow Marge's lead.

THE THIRD THERAPIST ... RCD ... FAMILY MEETING

The following segments are from the third and final meeting with the RCD and the family and occurred 4 months after the preceding transcripts. We began by reviewing progress. First, Joan's sister, Karen, had recently moved out of the house on her own and was receiving some moral and financial support from Dan and Marge. Second, Joan announced that she planned to move approximately 60 miles away from her parents' home, got a job, and get an apartment.

At first glance, Joan moving out appeared to be a positive move; Joan at this time seemed more psychologically equipped to individuate from her family and, in turn, her family seemed more flexible and would allow it. However, a characteristic response from Joan, and one that had been embedded in the recursive cycle, was to move out on her own prematurely before she was equipped to do so. Consequently, a familiar strategic technique of anticipating that a person's symptoms may reoccur and then predicting the recurrence of those symptoms was employed at this juncture. The judicious use of this technique, as described by Madanes (1981) and Papp (1983), has the effect of challenging a family to act differently, in this case, of challenging Joan and her family to act differently around possible consequences of Joan's moving out.

Therapist: [to Joan] Okay, you plan to move into your own apartment. You are telling me that you plan to keep in touch with Neil and work on what you have planned with your job? That takes guts and you must have thought about it a lot. No w I want to see what your parents predict will happen once you move into your apartment. [to parents] Well?

Marge: We've been through this before.

So far this indeed was only a reenactment of the cycle. However, Joan now began to change her part in it.

Joan: [to therapist] They don't believe me; I'll prove it!

Therapist: [to Marge] What will happen if what Dan fears becomes true: namely, that Joan does what she did in State X—play, play, party, party, party; what then?

Dan: I don't know. That's the reason we originally went to [State X] and brought her back, because she was going down the tubes. That is some of my reluctance to initiate another operation like this. It may not get off the ground. She hasn't got a dime.

Therapist: And that indeed may happen. Joan may get her own apartment, and may decide to have a good time partying and she'll invite everyone in the country; so what then?

Marge: So we're back at square one.

Joan: I'll learn.

Dan: You'll learn all right!

Therapist: What then; what are you going to do?

Dan: We may have to start from square one all over again.

While inquiring as to the parents' behavior should Joan's symptomatology re-occur, I also explicitly labeled and emphasized Step 1 of the recursive cycle, which had previously been implicit: namely that Dan and Marge's marital–parental disagreements and estrangement had made it difficult for Joan to leave home.

Therapist: [to Dan and Marge] Let me ask you specifically, and this is serious, so let's get the cards on the table. What do you think would happen between you two if Joan continues partying and not getting her act together? What will happen?

Marge: It depends on what he [Dan] means, "back to square one."

Therapist: What is your fear?

Marge: As hard as we have worked with Joan, and then for us to have drive all the way every weekend to State X and see her end up in the situation she's in today is another experience. And I don't care to go through that again. Should we have to give her another chance if she screws this one up?

Therapist: I'm not suggesting that you do; I'm asking you.

Marge: This is the position at this point; I really don't know what I would do.

Therapist: What do you think; what would happen? What kind of dialogue would happen between you two? (looks at Dan and Marge) You've been together several years, right? What do you think would happen?

Marge: I'll tell you one thing, that I would fight; that she would never come back to my house again.

Therapist: And what does your husband say?

Marge: I kind of think that he would agree with me at this point.

Therapist: Really? Is that a change?

Marge: Yes, that is a change.

Therapist: How is that a change?

Marge: Because he's never ever agreed with me in the past on who should be in the house and who shouldn't, about her [Joan] and this other daughter [Karen]. He always has made it easy for them to come back home, bailing them out at the first sign of trouble, giving them money without my knowledge, convincing them to come home. Now, I don't see him [Dan] as so insistent about having them live at home.

Therapist: [to Marge] I'm curious because something very profound has changed between you two parents, ever since you moved out of the house. Could you say just what that is so I understand? And I'd like to ask Dan what has changed, also.

Marge: I think, if one thing doesn't work, I think there has to be something else to try. And that was never permitted to happen before.

Therapist: I don't know what that means.

Marge: Well, he thought as a father he was trying to be a good father, which I never ever degraded him for. But, by trying to be that good father, we end up with two kids who, in technical terms, are screwing us royally! And that didn't work.

Therapist: But what did he do as a good father which, from your point of view, was in disagreement with you?

Marge: Letting them in the home every time they fell down once; to help them all financially, supplying them with the necessities of life.

Therapist: So what has shifted between the two of you now [Dan and Marge]? From your point of view?

Marge: Well, because there's been one change of Karen not living at the house any more, and I refuse to let her come back. However, I am still working with her on the outside of the household.

Therapist: So that's what changed in respect to you and Karen?

Marge: And it keeps me in a better state of mind because I don't have to tolerate that extra problem at home. I can therefore work better with her on the outside.

Therapist: And how has that changed things between you and Dan?

Marge: Because I'm not the bitch I was before. I can still be one because I still have a problem at home.

Therapist: (laughs) Okay, you're less bitchy. But what has happened between you and your husband?

Marge: We have a better relationship between us because we now talk about the problems that happen or any decisions that have to be made for either her or Karen. It just seems different. We can talk about them now and not have to have that hatred feeling in the back of our minds towards one another's attitudes.

Therapist: So you're more of a team?

Marge: Yes, I feel.

Therapist: So you think Dan feels that too?

Marge: I think so because I'm not doing something I'm not discussing with him at some point, because I see him along the way.

Therapist: [to Dan] Well?

Dan: I want to see what they can do on their own, to see where they're going. I saw before she [Joan] never left because we weren't getting anywhere. I really don't see at the moment that there is a viable alternative; and what she's [Marge] suggesting is worth a shot, certainly. We're not going anywhere the way we're going. So ...

At this point, although clear change was evident, the authenticity of Dan's overt acquiescence to Marge's plan remained in question. I therefore probed a bit.

Therapist: So you're willing to take the lead from Marge at this point?

Dan: I don't know it's taking the lead. We agreed between us that this is an experiment and we're going to try. As I said, I'm reluctantly going with it. I hope that they do fine and I'm really concerned like what comes next. But there's a limit as to what I will give. I am scared though about Joan. I can see her going down the tubes and I don't want that.

Marge: You do agree that we have to get them out of the house in order for them to even attempt to be on their own? I'm not saying they don't need support from us; they do! But there's a limit to what our support is. These changes can not take place as long as they stay in the household. If anyone has a better suggestion, I'd like to hear it. But I don't see a better suggestion. Help them get out on their own; give them the opportunity to make or break themselves.

Dan: Unless Joan comes into some kind of windfall, I don't see it working to get an apartment, to get herself settled, then exactly the same thing that happened all over again.

It is important to note the parents' clarification that they would appropriately help Joan get started, like they had recently done with Karen. They would not err by kicking Joan out of the house without appropriate support.

Dan appeared to be overtly expressing mother's covert doubts and fears. At this point, to strategically challenge the family to act differently (Madanes, 1981; Papp, 1983), I predicted the reoccurrence of the recursive cycle to the family by addressing myself to the RCD, parents, and Joan, in that order.

Therapist: [to RCD] We can all bet money on what will happen. I think what will happen is that Joan will go into the apartment, Joan will say that she will visit you [RCD], work with you on developing a plan which includes continuing with the GED and a new job and whatever else. I think Joan will have good intentions, but I wonder if things will come up that will make it difficult for her to visit you. And I think she may become depressed and discouraged and party a lot, and spend a lot of money and collect a lot of bills, at which point her parents will start to fight with each other; at which point Marge will say, "let her sit there for a while," and Dan will say, "NO," having a soft heart himself. Then Mom and Dad will fight some more; Joan will get in more trouble, at which point Joan will then be back home with her parents. And that's how it will be!

Marge: I don't intend to handle her situation the same way as before. Obviously, we can't just throw these kids out of the household without a dime in their pockets. With Karen, we offered to pay her first month's rent, which will help Karen if she gets a job.
We need to give them a start. I'm not saying that we would have to never give them anything else again. But I will never tolerate the situation Joan was in before in State X where we pay for everything!

Therapist: But you might just get dragged back into paying everything again.

Marge: I won't do it!

Therapist: Your husband might.

Marge: No, he won't.

Dan: I'm glad you said "we," Mother, because it is "we."

Marge: We did, we spent a fortune. We spent thousands trying to keep that kid going. We will not do it again. The more we gave her, the more she spent. We never fought about that, we were both willing to do that, but we both learned. We both learned the hard way.

Therapist: [to Joan] Suppose you move out to an apartment yourself, try to take care of yourself, and you fail. You have a lot of bills, you owe everybody money, things really get worse for you. Suppose it happens. Which of your parents, your father or your mother, do you think will tend to help you more? Give you money?

Joan: My father.

Therapist: Your father. Right, I agree. Father always. He's soft.

Joan: Yeah, but my Mother will say no, I know that.

Therapist: So then that will cause problems between your parents?

Joan: Yeah, it will.

Therapist: What do you think will happen?
Joan: I don't know. Maybe my mother will leave home.
Marge: Now that's an interesting observation.

It is amazing how astute children are about their parents' marital relationship.

During the following several months, regular individual and family sessions were conducted. Joan indeed moved out in an apartment of her own, approximately 60 miles from her parents' house. This distance made it difficult to meet with the RC, and she declined the offer of a transfer to another RCD. However, she obtained a GED and a job. A 3 month and a 1 year follow-up revealed that she has not been involved in any legal or psychiatric difficulties. According to Joan and her mother, "things are generally doing well."

CONCLUSION

In the case of Joan, as with all presenting problems of deaf and hard-of-hearing persons, it was necessary to constantly focus both on factors specific to hearing loss and on more general interactional patterns in the ecology to formulate a systemic diagnosis of the presenting problem. Throughout treatment, tracking the changing patterns of relationships between the presenting problem and the biopsychosocial systems levels, and then assessing which spatial levels were amenable to change at a particular time, provided a useful map from which to understand the systemic problems and to formulate cogent interventions. A variety of clinical modalities could then be used to target changes at specific levels at specific times.

The process of providing psychotherapy with deaf and hard-of-hearing persons is far from simple and straightforward, but rather is extremely complex. However, I hope that this book provides a point of departure for recognizing and addressing these complex epistemological and treatment issues; that it serves as one step in a recursive cycle amongst service providers to stimulate an ongoing dialogue. If the goal is realized, this shift at the professional level of the ecology should co-evolve with shifts at other systems levels to result in more effective treatment.

ACKNOWLEDGMENT

I thank Neil Glickman, who was the rehabilitation counselor of the deaf in this case.

11

Coping With Ordinary Evil

It wasn't like Joe to lock himself in his room. He was a happy-go-lucky kid, typically dashing out of the school bus to grab whatever junk food he could find, ride his bike, play basketball, hang out at the pizza shop—do anything but stay home. Although his mainstream school experiences had their share of challenges—as they would for any deaf student—he had always done well, both academically and socially. He was bright and a gifted athlete, now in the ninth grade. Moreover, his teachers were committed to giving him any extra services he needed.

I first met Joe's parents at a family learning workshop. Steve and Linda impressed me as warm and savvy people, dedicated to learning as much as possible about deafness. Both had taken the time to learn ASL, Joe's primary and preferred mode of communication; they regularly attended Deaf community events; had worked hard with the high school staff to ensure his continued academic and emotional development; and even hired interpreters for large family holiday events so that Joe would feel included. I remember thinking that there should be more parents like them.

One morning, I received a call from Linda to request a family therapy appointment as soon as possible. Her voice sounded anxious. I was happy to squeeze them in later that afternoon, frankly anticipating a welcome break from some difficult families in my practice. I scheduled them between two appointments with deaf-member families—one who didn't sign at all and the other who would make only token attempts to sign; both families very much denied the implications of deafness and all too frequently subtly or not-so-subtly badgered their deaf children to act hearing, even bordering on emotional abuse. The art of scheduling appointments is a delicate balance between taking care of client needs and oneself.

The three of them arrived on time. Although Steve and Linda juggled two demanding careers (advertising executive and attorney, respectively), Joe, their only child, had always been their top priority. Other things could wait. It was Steve who began the meeting with a well organized chronicle of the background information: Joe entered a mainstream elementary school program, and he and Linda had to go through adversarial due process hearings to ensure adequate support services. Linda added that they had moved to a more progressive town about 4 years ago and received more cooperation from special education. Both Steve and Linda signed everything clearly in Pidgin Sign English (PSE) intermixed with ASL. Per their family policy, they didn't vocalize, as they had been taught that the quality of their signing would suffer. We would communicate in sign language for all of our sessions.

Linda finished by proclaiming how proud she was that Joe had recently won a spelling competition. By all counts, everything had been smooth sailing, albeit with much hard work on their parts. They seemed to have a step-by-step plan for raising Joe, with contingency plans to meet the challenges of any obstacle which blocked his optimal development. As I marveled at their advanced fluency in sign language, I found myself remembering my initial positive impressions of them. At the same time, however, I couldn't help but wonder whether they operated by an unstated, implicit motto: "If we do everything right, our son will never suffer." Was I looking for dysfunction where there was none, or was I perhaps projecting my own parenting anxiety?

The reason for Linda's apparent urgency on the phone wasn't yet clear—everything had gone so well! I turned to Joe, who had been sitting patiently and politely, taking it all in. Until moments ago, I had seen him only from a distance at various Deaf community functions, most recently when he had starred in a signed version of "Death of a Salesman." He impressed me as a low-key, happy, bright, socially adept young man. After some initial pleasantries, I asked him in ASL if he knew why he and his parents were here.

"I beat up my ex-friend and got suspended," he signed back. A short, to-the-point reply. It caught me off-guard. So much for the veracity of impressions made at-a-distance.

"Oh!" I signed. "Would you say more?"

"He pissed me off! He's an asshole!" Joe scowled. His ASL revealed much of his anger that had been hidden behind his persona of calm patience: clenched fingers, tight jaw, and prominent, bold signs. However, then, as he perhaps sensed that I was truly interested, he shared more of his pain: "He was my best friend before. It didn't matter that he was hearing. Mark wanted to learn sign and I taught him; he even took sign classes with my parents; we were on the same basketball and soccer teams; we always went camping together ..." A long list of intimacies ensued, clearly leading up to a rift.

Indeed, as the story unfolded, I learned that Joe and Mark had been inseparable since first grade. Frequently, they would share each other's clothes, sometimes leaving them over at each other's houses for weeks. Linda had even decorated the guest bedroom with Mark's sports idols because he slept over so often. Having had an hysterectomy soon after Joe's birth, Mark became an unofficial adopted sibling of the family—both a brother to Joe as well as a trusted ally to help him to navigate the social and linguistic challenges of the mainstream hearing school. During recess and other unstructured school times, Mark would frequently function as an interpreter between Joe and his peers.

The Rift. Enter Gloria, a ninth-grade, hearing cheerleader. Joe had confided to his trusted ally–adopted brother that "She's the most beautiful girl in the entire universe!" Day and night, he couldn't stop thinking about her, whether he was playing sports, watching TV or "instant messaging" his friends. He fervently hoped that maybe someday, somewhere, somehow Gloria would bestow even an ounce of her attention on him.

Sure enough, one day after school, Joe's wish came true. He and Mark were hanging out in the playground and Gloria actually approached them! She looked at Joe and finger-spelled her name! In Joe's own words, "My heart almost exploded out of my body" and he instantly became overwhelmed with rapture! Thank God, however, he recovered enough to sign some well-rehearsed conversation openers to her, with Mark voicing (she did not know sign language). He asked her what classes she was taking; how she liked the cafeteria food; and even what music she liked. (He wanted to impress her with his knowledge of hearing culture.) She responded, while Mark interpreted voice to sign. Ten minutes later the school buses came and it was time to go home.

During the course of subsequent triadic conversations, with Mark assuming his usual role as interpreter, Gloria's initial comfort with Joe diminished. Instead of addressing Joe directly, she asked Mark, "Can he talk? Can he lip-read?" Gradually, she gravitated more toward Mark, even applauding him with "My, you sign so well!" At first, he dutifully interpreted everything to Joe, even once giving Gloria a 2-minute speech on how to use an interpreter—"You should look directly at him ... Don't speak in the third person," etc. However, Mark's missionary zeal backfired. It served to thwart Joe's opportunity to be the one to educate Gloria on the "ins and outs" of deafness and to flirt directly with her. (Or perhaps that was Mark's intent, Joe later surmised.)

As days went on, when Gloria approached the two of them, it was only to converse with Mark. Joe recalled that one time Gloria "said many sentences" to Mark who only signed "She's just talking about Western Civilization." They were smiling and looking intently at each other. Then Mark stopped signing all together and "both of them were giggling and making eyes at each other." Joe added that he then asked Mark to sign, but for reasons unknown, he responded only with grunting noises, apparently in mockery of deaf speech. Then Gloria burst into hysterics, obviously joining Mark in his ridicule and defamation.

"He was being an asshole," Joe sighed. Undoubtedly, a short-hand metaphor for his devastation. Poor Joe. Adolescents, and adults for that matter, can be so cruel, I thought.

"So then what happened?" I asked.

"They went to study hall together and I had to go to Math class. But I couldn't concentrate. Some kids kept giving me weird looks and whispering something, but I couldn't understand them." Joe then turned his head toward the window, psychologically leaving the room to whereabouts unknown. His final words were "But it's no big deal." The "low-key, happy, bright, socially adept young man" that I remembered from "Death of a Salesman" had briefly exposed his private pain, only to quickly retreat to a protective persona of nonchalance.

A familiar saga: On the surface, Joe was engaging in a normal flirting ritual with "the most beautiful girl in the entire universe." We all have been there. However, his exchanges were markedly different from the norm in that all his communications with Gloria were interpreted by a third party: namely, Mark. The communication was therefore subject to, not just linguistic misunderstandings but also common deaf-hearing cross cultural dynamics, described as follows.

In mainstream environments, it is often the hearing peer who befriends the Deaf peer—not the other way around (Hoffmeister & Harvey, 1998). For a variety of reasons, a hearing peer(s) may be interested in learning sign language and become more fluent than most of the other students; and often that is the primary determinant as to whether a Deaf student wishes to befriend a particular hearing student. As Joe put it, "It didn't matter that Mark was hearing. He wanted to learn sign and I taught him ASL."

The relationships may be relatively stable until a third, nonsigning, person expands the dyad to become a triad. Often the hearing friend volunteers or is asked by the Deaf person to interpret communication with this new member. The hearing friend is then in a position to control the language and the information exchange, and thereby is in a power-based role as a linguistic "gate-keeper" to the Deaf person's world. Technically speaking, that role is potentially oppressive, or to use Harlan Lane's phrase, may be enacted with a "mask of benevolence" (Lane, 1992) that may not be consciously realized.

Perhaps Joe could have forgiven Mark for what may be termed unconscious oppression. However, how could he reconcile his "ex-friend's" very much conscious malice? Indeed, he couldn't even make sense out of Mark's abrupt about-face. Why did he purposely truncate his interpretation of Gloria's "many sentences;" then abruptly stop signing all together; then mock his speech by making grunting noises; and finally join Gloria by laughing at him? Joe was left with wounds filled with a volatile mixture of bewilderment and rage. In addition, to add insult to injury, he returned to his classroom, only to feel emotionally victimized by his hearing classmates as they "kept giving me weird looks and whispering something."

The events in the classroom seemed easier to understand. Perhaps Joe's perception of his classmates' behavior was his own projected shame or, at best, his overinterpretation. Alternatively, his perception may have been reality based: deaf students are often the objects of ridicule in mainstream environments. However, I too, could not understand the reasons for Mark's abrupt shift from what had been such a close, intimate relationship. Certainly, I have my own memories of how the entry of a third party—particularly of the opposite gender—has the power to destabilize a heretofore intimate dyad. However, it is never that simple. The relational change between "brothers" merited further exploration.

"Joe, help me understand what happened between you and Mark. You had been inseparable! Why do you think he turned on you like that?"

"I don't know."

"Speculate." (I fingerspelled this and mouthed it. Joe understood).

"He started picking on me for no reason and—"

"I'm sure he was trying to impress that girl," Linda interrupted. "I don't know why boys do that, but—"

"Let Joe finish, dear," Steve said, now leaning forward in his seat. Linda sat back.

"Yeah," Joe addressed his mother. "He probably wanted to impress Gloria but it was at my expense! Don't you get that?" Joe gave her an irritated look and then made bold, "screaming" signs. "It wasn't fair! It was mean! It was evil! I couldn't take it anymore, because he kept doing it, any chance he could get."

"I'm sure he didn't mean to—" Linda persisted, trying to get her son to calm down.

"Fuck him and fuck you!" Joe now exploded! "Don't tell me he didn't fucking mean to do it. He fucking well did mean to do it. I'm glad I beat the shit out of him."

"What did you do?" I asked.

"I pinned him against the brick wall, behind the school," Joe screamed. "I pounded my fist against his rib cage until I knew he would never forget it. I kept hitting him as hard as I could. He's an asshole and I'm gonna—"

"You don't have to swear like that," his mother said, now half-scolding. "I know you're upset but—"

"For God sake, Linda, let him talk!" Steve jumped in, raising his voice at his wife. "Don't you understand that—"

Now I interrupted, trying to cap their escalation, and said to Linda, "Let's see if I can help you and Steve negotiate a swearing policy." Then, looking at Steve, I asked, "As his dad, do you think he should swear like that?"

"He has a right to be angry. I sure as hell would be."

"Do you think it's all right for him to swear like that?" came my persistent question.

"Yes, of course it is. He deserves to let it out. This competitive bullshit happens all the time, but it's rough stuff! But we can't protect him from that! [he gave Linda a pleading and scornful look]. I wish it wasn't that way, I mean, I wish there wasn't evil in the world. We've been lucky so far, but kids can be mean; many adults can be mean; the whole damn, fucking world can be mean!"

I privately noted Steve's provocative use of various swear words, but opted to focus on facilitating both parents reacting to Joe in a congruent manner and without conflict between them. It seemed to me that Joe was feeling compelled by his mother to put a lid on his anger and rage, whereas feeling compelled by his father to fully express it. Mixed messages. Now facing Linda, I asked, "Then can you two [Steve and Linda] agree on a swearing policy for at least just this discussion? We can establish a Permissible Swear Zone—PSZ for short." After a brief "policy" discussion with her husband, Linda reluctantly agreed to give Joe free rein.

"Please continue," I looked at Joe. However, by this time his anger had subsided and he sat there stupefied and in obvious pain. Silence enveloped the room. "It's tough to know why he did this to you?" I finally muttered.

"Yeah," came his only reply. Again he stared out the window.

From a distance everything looks so smooth. I had idealized this family; I had perceived them sans conflict, even though I rationally knew that conflict is part of the fabric of all relationships. However, now, at close range, these people became more three-dimensional, more human, less smooth. A tentative recursive cycle: Joe expresses his anger; Mom discourages it; Father encourages it. Tension threatens to erupt between Mom and Dad. Joe squelches his anger. The cycle repeats itself.

Their ambiguity about naming Mark's behavior was noteworthy and perhaps served to escalate the tension. Was he being an asshole, as Joe put it? Did Mark suffer from a variant of diminished capacity—"He didn't mean to do it"—as Linda seemed to imply? Or, as Steve observed, was Mark echoing a kind of archetypal malice—"competitive bullshit"—for the affections of a third party, analogous to the biblical story of Cain murdering Abel for God's "affections?" I have come to view such behaviors as constituting ordinary evil.

Ordinary Evil

Is evil too strong a word? Certainly, Joe didn't think so. Recall his pained outburst: "[Mark's behavior] wasn't fair! It was mean! It was evil!" Joe's attribution of evil to Mark's actions is consistent with Baumeister's (1999) operational definition of evil as "when someone intentionally harms another person." Acts of intentionally inflicted harm to others—physical or psychological—are, in the words of M. Scott Peck (1983), "quite common and usually appear quite ordinary to the superficial observer." In the language of family therapy, evil is an important contextual variable within the biopsychosocial hierarchy which must be understood, particularly when treating deaf or hard-of-hearing persons.

I told the captive audience in my office about an informal, pilot survey on ordinary evil I had conducted. The following query was sent to 30 people, between the ages of 14 and 70:

> List maybe five or so examples of what may be called 'ordinary evil' that particularly affect you. It may happen to you or you may witness it or hear about it. Ordinary evil is defined as 'evil' that is not evil enough to make CNN, but that is ordinary enough to happen all the time.

Their responses were immediate and impassioned, and could be categorized as personal experiences of Disrespect, Abuse of Power, Deceit, and Prejudice (Harvey, 2001).

I asked Linda and Steve if this concept resonated with them and if they could volunteer any personal examples. An affirmative answer was a safe bet as they had been nodding their heads during my short speech. Steve recalled when "someone deliberately bumped into me in a line and didn't even bother to say they're sorry. It was no big deal—it happens all the time," he noted. "But it got under my skin."

"As an attorney," Linda added, "I see ordinary evil all the time. In my office, for example, I think the deliberate nastiness of one employee to another is ordinary evil, like not giving a civil answer to a question; or instead of handing a document to a person, throwing it on the other person's desk without saying anything."

Both of them gave several more examples of common, ordinary acts which felt evil to them, which "got under their skin" for several days or even weeks. The concept of ordinary evil clearly resonated with Steve and Linda, even prior to their son's schism with Mark. However, Joe was conspicuously quiet, reminiscent of when he had patiently and politely sat through his parents' chronicle of the history during our initial visit. I asked him for his thoughts. "It's nothing new to me," he noted. "Ordinary evil happens to deaf people all the time. Sometimes I get used to it; and other times it boils up inside of me."

Joe echoed an important truth. Although of lesser intensity than extraordinary, "news-worthy" evil, the cumulative effects of ordinary evil causes significant, long-term harm before (or if) it is discovered and discontinued. The Columbine High School massacre, for example, was a result of a culmination of repetitive, ingrained acts of ordinary prejudice and disrespect that were barely recognizable. Moreover, ordinary evil—oppression of various forms and degrees—is more prevalent for Deaf people (Pollard, 1998). Glickman & Gulati (in press) listed several examples, including insensitive management of Deaf schools by hearing people; a prohibition on the use of of sign language in schools; an obsessive focus upon speech and speech reading to the exclusion of other academic subjects; the imposition of hearing aids on students who do not want them; forced surgical procedures for deaf children; forced isolation of deaf children using the rationale of mainstreaming; paternalism, pity, or contempt; and the exclusion of the Deaf Community from decision making on key matters. As mentioned in chapter 1, Lane (1984) referred to these and other oppressive actions as reflective of "audism": bigotry against deaf persons within the cultural level of the ecology.

The following vignette, entitled "A Boy Learns to be Deaf," was circulated on the Web by a group of Deaf people. In reading it, I thought of Joe:

> A young hearing boy goes into the kitchen where his mother is baking. He puts his hands in the flour, mixes it with water to make it become dough and fills his ear with it. He looks at his mother and says, "Look momma ... I'm a deaf boy." His mama slaps him hard on the face and says, "Boy, go show your daddy."
>
> The boy goes into the living room and says, "Look Daddy, I'm a deaf boy." His daddy also slaps him on the face and says, "Boy, go show your grandma."
>
> So the boy goes to see his grandma and says, "Look Granny, I'm a deaf boy." She slaps him on the face and sends him back to his mother.
>
> His mother says, "Well, did you learn something from all of this?" The boy shakes his head and says, "I sure did. I've only been a deaf boy for 5 minutes and I already hate you hearing people."

Manifestations of ordinary evil are omnipresent in the lives of other oppressed minorities and must be dealt with in an adaptive manner.[1] As Gates and West (1996) noted with respect to the Black culture, one must endure "ontological wounds, psychic scars, and existential bruises;" and one must "constantly fend off insanity and self-annihilation." Their analysis of two common effects of ordinary evil is particularly relevant to Joe and many other Deaf persons: "The two major

[1]There is one important distinction, however. Other minorities, such as Black families, pass on the lore of such ordinary evil to their offspring, as part of vertical enculturation. It adds to the child's developing resilience in the face of ordinary evil. Since the deaf sociocutlural experience is typically "horizontally passed," (as most deaf children have hearing parents) hearing parents cannot share in the lore and cannot pass the resilience to the young generation in the same manner (Pollard, 2002).

choices in black culture (or any culture) facing those who succumb to the temptation of hate are a self-hatred that leads to self-destruction or a hatred of others ... that leads to vengeance of some sort" (p. 128).

Joe most clearly demonstrated the vengeance option. I assumed he was also experiencing self-hatred, but exploration of that would have to wait until later. The ripple effects of Joe's vengeance were more resonant: It caused his school suspension; it fueled a conflict between his parents, as his violence was endorsed by his father and opposed by his mother; and it threatened to result in retaliation by Mark. Ontological wounds, psychic scars, and existential bruises from ordinary evil are not limited to affecting only an individual, but reverberate throughout one's family and larger networks.

In response to Joe admitting that sometimes the remnants of ordinary evil "boils up inside of me," Linda slumped in her seat and appeared sad, almost in despair, seemingly sinking under the weight of her son's pain. In contrast, Steve's reaction was one of outrage, as though the label finally gave him permission to release his own pent up rage. He pounded his fist on his knee and screamed, "Joe damn well gave him what he deserved!" in reference to his son's act of retribution toward Mark. Perhaps surprised at his own outburst, he then became rigid and speechless; but his continued clenched fist said it all. We fell silent.

Linda then shared her thoughts: "Ordinary evil may be everywhere in this world—like discrimination and people saying 'deaf and dumb'—but Joe shouldn't have to be victimized by it. He already has enough on his plate. He's gotta ignore it and not let it ruin his life! He should look the other way—not let people like Mark get to him so much!" She began to cry. Probably the worst way to hurt a parent is to hurt their child. I still remember when my daughter was stung by a bee more than 10 years ago. I swear it hurt me more than her.

On one level, Linda's sentiments and advice seemed reasonable. Certainly, ignoring certain things—"picking your battles"—is one hallmark of maturity. In addition, given the plethora of challenges that Joe faced as a deaf person, why should he also have to deal with peer ridicule and cruelty? Her point was well taken: in her words, "Just because there's ordinary evil in the world doesn't mean it has to come all down on Joe, for God's sake!" she lamented. However, all three of them had already affirmed that, like it or not, ordinary evil is part of the Deaf experience. In my judgment, it is essential for parents to validate a deaf child's experiences of incurring ordinary evil that unfortunately is so prevalent. It is via such validation that a child's feelings are contained and that allows for the learning of healthy, assertive ways of dealing with evil. Perhaps a parenting motto for a deaf-member family should be a slight but important modification of what I had imagined Joe's parents' motto to have been: "If we do everything right, our deaf child will never suffer alone."

The next task was to help this family deal with the psychological fallout of feeling victimized. Joe needed to debride his psychological wounds, which were left by Mark (and others); and in turn, so did his parents, having been vicariously wounded (Harvey, 2001). I would begin by helping Steve and Linda validate their son's pain. I asked Joe who he thinks understands most how he feels toward Mark. He quickly responded with, "My dad gets it; but my mom's in outer space somewhere."

"Let's see if we can get her down," I responded.

"She's never been in a fight in her life. She has no idea of—"

"Neither have you till now," Linda interrupted, somewhat defensively.

"It doesn't fucking matter. He fucking well deserved it. He ..." Joe gave an essentially same version of his pained outrage that he had given before, but also seemingly milking his earlier PSZ (Permissible Swear Zone) victory. I needed to redirect him to what he needed from his mother and father.

"Excuse me, Joe. But I'm still wondering—and I think your mother is, too—what it would look like if, as you say, she comes down from 'outer space.' What do you need from her?"

"She doesn't get it! She never will get it!"

"By 'get it' do you mean agree with you? Agree with you about being violent toward Mark?" I asked.

"She doesn't agree with me!"

"And maybe she never will. But that begs the question: what then do you need from her."

Steve then interjected, "Dr. Harvey, this may be a guy's thing, you know, because—" A defeated and disempowered Linda shrugged her shoulders.

"C'mon," I responded to Steve with annoyance. "Your son needs something very important from both of you—both genders—that has nothing to do with a 'guy thing.' Both of you can give Joe very different kinds of essential support that he desperately needs." Admittedly, I reacted with a bit too much annoyance, probably triggered by Steve's obvious attempt to collude with me against Linda, even for the first time, referring to me as "Dr. Harvey." On reflection, I was also probably reacting negatively to him supporting Joe's violence. It scares me. Acknowledging one's countertransference is a humbling experience.

No one spoke for several minutes, perhaps as a result of my mild outburst. Finally, I again looked at Joe and said, "Even though she may never agree with you, how would it be for you if she understood your feelings?"

"My Dad gets it; she doesn't."

"Your Dad agrees more with you; your Dad, as a guy, may have had similar experiences. Steve, have you?" I asked, now attempting to repair a possible rift. He nodded his head. Returning to Joe, I then said, "But you as a soon-to-be-man need both this female [Linda] and this male [Steve] to understand and talk about how you feel. Silence is poison. The germs inside of you will multiple and explode; it's not good for you."

The three of them then had a productive discussion where both parents told childhood stories to their son of feeling enraged at a neighborhood bully and wanting to "beat the shit outa them." Linda even swore a couple of times, which prompted Joe to give her a thumbs up. In addition to providing humorous respite, this was a very important juncture. Both parents were on board.

It was now time to give Joe some interpersonal, conflict resolution strategies to use in the service of understanding and repairing what went wrong with Mark. Perhaps he had earlier offended Mark? It never ceases to amaze me how the relational positions of victim and victimizer frequently shift as a function of context. It was my hope that he and Mark would gain an empathic understanding of each other's perspective and vulnerabilities around their recent schism. Joe, amidst his anger, admitted to feeling deeply saddened about the loss of a dear friend and said that he would consider "talking to him." However, it was unclear how ready he was for a productive dialogue, as opposed to fueling a reescalation of their conflict.

I would start with eliciting advice from his parents. "If you were in Joe's shoes, what would you say to Mark?" I asked Linda.

"I would tell him how I feel; that I'm hurt and angry because of what he did," his mother advised. Steve nodded his head and added, "And you should demand an apology."

It is easy to remain entrenched in a victimized position that precludes honest, exploratory dialogue with the supposed victimizer. Although Joe certainly had a legitimate reason to feel victimized—which, in my view, merited the label of ordinary evil being applied to Mark's behaviors—his perception seemed too one-sided; half the story, too simple, too lineal.

"I agree that an apology is in order," I countered. "But could you start from the position of curiosity? Questions to ask might be 'What happened?' 'Help me understand why you did so and so,' 'It would mean a lot to me if you can explain your motives for ...,' etc." I wanted to promote a dialogue between Joe and Mark that would lead to a more systemic understanding for the shift in their relationship. After a few minutes of cajoling, Joe and his parents gave their tentative agreement.

For the remainder of the session, we role played several prospective exchanges between Joe and Mark with all of them taking turns playing the respective roles. Joe looked increasingly confident and seemed like he was enjoying the role playing. Accordingly, I gave him homework to have a frank discussion with his "ex-friend," when he feels ready, again emphasizing that he should begin by asking questions, not by demanding reparation. We bid Joe good luck and arranged an appointment for the following week.

I anticipated our next meeting with some trepidation. I wondered whether I was being too idealistic, perhaps setting Joe up for further exploitation. Wednesday afternoon at 3:00 came quickly, however. However, they arrived a ½ hr late—not a good sign, I thought. Reportedly, Joe was delayed getting out of school. Immediately after everyone took their seats, I had to ask Joe the obvious question: "Well, did you?" My eagerness got the better of me.

Joe nodded his head, but reluctantly. His parents looked frustrated. Clearly the meeting had not gone well. "I started by asking Mark why he acted like such an asshole," Joe reported. "And I said that I was really pissed off at him because of what he did," Joe began. "Mark yelled something but didn't sign. I told him to sign and then he signed 'Fuck you!' I told him 'Fuck you, too!' and then he took a punch at me. I hit him back."

"Not exactly the scenarios we role played last week," I sighed.

"I'm glad I beat up that mother fucker," Joe chimed.

By this time, Linda was squirming in her seat. "Don't you understand that violence toward Mark is just going to make it worse?" she yelled, glancing at Steve, raising her voice and making pronounced signing movements. Then she turned off her voice, code-switched to ASL and addressed her son: "He'll beat you up; then you'll beat him up again; he'll get some of his cronies against you; you'll do the same. Where does this end? He did a wrong thing; I don't know why he did it but he did. Let it go! Talk to him; tell him how you feel; and try to forgive him."

An eloquent oration, I thought—one that was also once given by Martin Luther King:

> The ultimate weakness of violence is that it is a descending spiral, begetting the very thing it seeks to destroy. Instead of diminishing evil, it multiplies it. Through violence you may murder the liar, but you cannot murder the lie, nor establish the truth. Through violence you may murder the hater, but you do not murder hate. In fact, violence merely increases hate. So it goes. Returning the violence for violence multiplies violence, adding deeper darkness to a night already devoid of stars. Darkness cannot drive out darkness: only light can do that. Hate cannot drive out hate: only love can do that.

I privately sided with Linda (and Martin Luther King). However, our time was up; it was a short meeting because of their late arrival. We agreed to continue our discussion next week.

A haunting juxtaposition, one that surpassed my worst nightmare. The content of our consecutive sessions could not have been scripted more surrealistically. Our next meeting would be on September 14, 2001—*three days afterwards*.

I greeted the three of them in the waiting room as before; we took the same seats as before; and I waited for one of them to begin the session, also as before. However, how could anything ever be the same? I had been at the then-deserted Logan airport the previous evening, (where two of the ill-fated planes had originated), until after midnight, as a member of a critical incident debriefing team for American Airlines flight attendants, pilots, mechanics and other ground crew. Later in my sleep and the during the next day, I kept replaying in my head the words of one flight attendant who had asked her friend to cover for her on Flight 11; and the story of another employee who recounted the "oh my God, oh my God" last words of his coworker on board as she noticed the plane heading down toward "big buildings" in New York City. I was in shock, very tired and very scared.

We began with somber silence. There was too much to say and not enough words. It was Joe who finally began. "We gotta kill that bastard!"

"Kill who?" I asked. It was a reflex question to ensure specificity, but I knew who he meant.

"This guy, Osama bin Laden. The president's right. We gotta get him, dead or alive." I noticed that Steve and Linda were both nodding their heads. Admittedly so was I.

We spent the next several moments acknowledging the trauma that transformed our lives and took the lives of several thousand others; and the recognition that more deaths would follow. We shared our muted irritation at the television networks for continually replaying the World Trade Center explosion, but admitted that our eyes were glued to the TV. On one level, it seemed ludicrous that we could have focused so much on *ordinary* evil only days before September 11th. All of our concerns seemed so petty.

Nevertheless, we half-heartedly shifted our discussion to the seemingly mundane, petty focus of our family therapy meetings: Joe's conflictual relationship with his hearing friend, Mark. Isn't that why were we meeting? However, we couldn't prevent the larger cultural context from intruding, and perhaps, I thought, we shouldn't even try. In marked contrast to the family's initial ponderings about whether Mark's behavior was indicative of ordinary evil, they were quite adamant that Osama bin Laden was the personification of extraordinary evil. An easy call. Only a fool would equate Mark's teasing, inadequate signed–voice interpretation, etc., with the mind-numbing carnage that we had just witnessed.

"We gotta kill the bastard," Joe repeated. I wondered why: for revenge or some larger goal? Essentially the same question was being asked with respect to Mark: Does he need a good pounding for revenge of is there an instructional purpose?

"Why do you think bin Laden, or any of the terrorists, did it?" I asked. A deja vu to our first session. My question was isomorphic, similar in form, to my much earlier question to Joe with respect to Mark—essentially a version of "Why do you think he turned on you like that?" (For the time being, I matched Joe's use of bin Laden as an individual icon to represent the collective but indistinguishable network of terrorists.) Like it or not, we had an uninvited golden opportunity for an important intervention; to explore the systemic nature of both ordinary and extraordinary evil: namely, that evil does not reside in a person, but is contextual. I would also attempt to use the present context of terrorism to set the stage for repairing the broken bond between Joe and Mark.

"He did it because he's evil!" came Joe's quick response.

"Not that simple," I shot back. "He may be evil. Hell, no! He is evil!" I exclaimed. So much for my systemic thinking. Although all of them were enthusiastically nodding in agreement, I had a vague, disquieting memory of standing on my earlier pedagogical "soapbox" about "evil describing behavior, not a person." Admittedly, my own despair side-tracked me from my systemic inquiry. Just as Joe and his parents attributed evil as residing in Mark—not to his behavior in context—I, too, found myself attributing evil as residing in the bin Laden–terrorist network. Indeed, it isn't that simple.

With that thought "book marked" in my head for later reference, I continued to contextualize the terrorists' evil behavior: "My hunch is that bin Laden doesn't think of himself as evil. I suspect that, like many evil people, he views himself quite differently: perhaps as a victim, as righting an earlier wrong, as fighting a holy war in the name of his God. We're victims of terrorism, but terrorists may view themselves as victims of us."

My systemic formulation was more than a hunch and wasn't original. Evil (and beauty) exists primarily in the eye of the beholder, especially in the eye of the victim; most people who perpetrate evil frequently do not see what they are doing as evil (Baumeister, 1999; Beck, 1999; Fromm, 1973). In Baumeister's words, "Many perpetrators regard themselves as victims ... as people who have been unjustly treated and hence deserve sympathy, support and extra tolerance for any wrongs they have committed ... Hypersensitive people who often think their pride is being assaulted are potentially dangerous." (Baumeister, 1999). Again, Colombine comes to mind in that the murderers apparently judged the reason for their behavior as righting earlier wrongs.

Unlike before regarding Mark, now Steve was on my wave length: "America has committed evil in the world, too." In addition, like all of us in the room and undoubtedly in our country, he let out his disgust: "But it made me wanna puke when I saw the video of bin Laden saying that any terrorism against America would be in his self-defense—when he said that 'If avenging the killing of our people is terrorism, let history be a witness that we are terrorists.'" He was referring the October 7th, 2001 videotape of bin Laden saying that 80 years prior to the attack on America, "Islam has suffered in humiliation and disgrace"—apparently in reference to when, in 1918, the Ottoman sultanate, the last of the great Muslim empires, was finally defeated and colonized. (Lewis, 2001).

"What may be our unfair foreign policy doesn't justify killing thousands of people, destroying buildings, ruining peoples' lives!" Linda cried out. Joe also nodded in agreement.

"Amen," I replied. It was now time to return to the presenting problem—the schism between Joe and Mark, an event that I would come to call "pre-9/11 events either happened before and after. "But like with Mark, we have the challenge of understanding the dynamics behind the act. We absolutely don't have to condone it. Let's put bin Laden over here for a minute (I spatialized a position to our right). Mark was wrong to hit Joe; Joe was wrong to hit Mark. But there's still a lot about what happened between you two [now looking at Joe] that we need to figure out. And it's shame—particularly in these awful, terrifying times—that you lost your brother."

Joe nodded his head and remained quiet for the rest of the session.

September 28th. Two weeks later. Something immediately seemed different as they entered my office, perhaps somewhat euphoric. Terrorism hadn't ended; in fact, it was just beginning. I would wait for an answer. After some initial pleasantries and discussion of something called "Anthrax," it was Joe who began. Apparently, sometime after our last visit, he gathered his courage and again approached Mark to resurrect, as he put it, "a cherished pre-9/11 friendship." Joe recounted what had happened:

> As I walked over to Mark, he looked like he was going to walk away so I remembered what we talked about here—you know, to be curious and find out what was going on in his head. So I told him that I missed him, that he means a lot to me; I asked him nicely if he would please explain why he acted so mean and that I really wanted to understand where he was coming from. And then he didn't look so hostile anymore. He only said that he before was pissed off with me, too.

"Isn't that interesting! Pissed off at you for what?" I asked.

"Well, he didn't really tell me at first. He was kind of vague. He kept saying that I was being stuck up, like a snob, like I was too good for him or something like that. But I kept asking for specifics; you know, what I did that was stuck up. I tried not to get angry or defensive.

I told him I really wanna know. Then he told me something like 'You look down on hearing people.' I said 'What?' And he repeated it. And finally it came out; that he was jealous because I've been making more friends with Deaf people and haven't been inviting him. That's why he was so mean to me."

"Your gain was his loss," Steve commented. "You made more Deaf friends and Mark lost his job as your interpreter; almost like you outgrew him. It sounds to me like he felt insecure about his own identity, where he fit."

Steve's assessment was probably quite correct—in fact, I couldn't have said it better (not bad for an advertising executive, I thought)—but I felt there was still more information for Joe to share. "Did he tell you anything else?" I asked Joe.

"Yeah," he replied. After a bit of hesitation, he reluctantly made a final disclosure: "He told me that he was pissed off at me because I made fun of his signing."

"You made fun of his signing?" Linda asked in anger and bewilderment.

"Yeah," he confessed. Now Joe turned away from his mother. Whereas he once loudly proclaimed his victimization and outrage, now—as he was pressured to also proclaim his status as a victimize—he became taciturn, resorting to sighs and one-word responses. I had a fantasy that he would soon plead the fifth.

"Why did you do that?" his perplexed father asked.

"I dunno."

"Please speculate," came my knee-jerk response. Possibly an error, as I did not want to add to the deposition-like atmosphere in the room, but it felt critically important, just as were our earlier efforts to figure out the etiology of Mark's behavior. Now the focus was on Joe.

"He made weird signs like a hearing person."

"So that gives you the right to tease him about it?" Steve scolded him.

"Sometimes I felt more comfortable with my deaf friends" Joe retorted, now a bit indignant, as he countered his father. However, it was apparent that Joe felt ashamed. He finally said, "I know I shouldn't have made fun of him. It wasn't funny teasing; it was mean. I'm sorry." He looked down toward the floor.

"Hey, Joe," I said, trying to be supportive. "I'm really not trying to put you on the stand. I'm only trying to help you and your parents make sense out of your behavior, just as we tried to make sense out of Mark's behavior. Ordinary evil is something all of us humans engage in, often unknowingly. It sounds to me like you two kind of activated each other's insecurities in a cycle that went round and round; you distanced yourself from Mark by mocking his signing ability, and Mark boosted his self-esteem by his selective interpreting and making fun of you, etc." This was my attempt to clarify the sequence of shifting loyalties and to sound more like a therapist—not a cross examining attorney.

"I guess so," Joe responded. A tentative maybe, I thought.

"But whatever Joe did doesn't excuse Mark's behavior," Linda again reminded us, now defending her son. As a mother–attorney, she was not about to exonerate a guilty party.

"No, it absolutely doesn't," I agreed. "But we can now better understand the dynamics behind Mark's ridicule of Joe; just as we're finally beginning to understand the dynamics behind Joe's ridicule of Mark. Which came first is anyone's guess. We're all saints and sinners, as Woody Allen once said; no one is immune to committing ordinary evil. But again, you're absolutely right; it doesn't mean we should condone that evil, whether committed by others or by ourselves. Ultimately both Mark and Joe must be held responsible." Linda and Steve seemed to relax.

"So how did you and Mark leave it?" I asked Joe.

"We're going to get together this weekend and talk." Joe smiled as did his parents. We enjoyed a moment of silence as I imagined a weight being taken off of Joe's shoulders. This time Steve broke the silence: "I'm a great fan of Woody Allen, but he, too, has made his share of mistakes." An indirect affirmation of his son.

"He does make good movies, though," I responded.

Joe shrugged his shoulders and said, "I'd rather see Harry Potter." We bid goodbye and agreed to meet in a month.

Our next appointment was a celebration of sorts. Reportedly, Mark and Joe were among the hundred or so people in line to see the Saturday night midnight, premier showing of "Harry Potter and Sorcerer's Stone." In the weeks to come, they got together more. Joe told us that first they kept it light: they hung out at the mall or shot a few hoops. But soon both boys took the next step of resurrecting their relationship. Although Joe still harbored residual anger and hurt from the ordinary evil in which Mark engaged—as it resonated with many other experiences of being in the often callous "hearing world"—he didn't view himself solely as a victim; he was beginning to learn that "there are always two sides." Joe recounted how the two of them began to establish some explicit rules for discussing what they had euphemistically come to call "our fight"; "we would not argue about who was right and wrong, but instead try to understand how each of us feels and show mutual respect." I remember thinking, somewhat cynically, that this was a bit idealistic perhaps—certainly never to last. However, again, it is important to understand this change of behavior in context. For Joe, and for many others, friendships seemed more important post September 11th; bitterness and hatred seemed more dangerous. In addition, speaking of context, perhaps not so coincidentally, rumor had it that "Gloria dumped Mark."

It became clear that Joe no longer armed himself with hurt and rage, nor with well-rehearsed justifications for his own actions. Instead, he sought to be as clear as possible to his best friend–brother about his own views and also to move out of himself and into Mark's experience, to enter Mark's thoughts and feelings, and to truly see the world as he experienced it. Such experiences of empathy are what many adults continually strive to achieve.

Part of what Joe saw in Mark was himself, including his own dark sides. He, too, had mocked Mark's hearing mannerisms; he, too, had "rubbed it in Mark's face" that he could never be accepted into the Deaf community; he, too, committed ordinary evil. Joe learned an important truth: that to understand the multiple intrapsychic and systemic layers of others who are defined as evi—whether of ordinary or extraordinary proportions—is to better understand those multiple dark layers of ourselves. In the words of Alexander Solzhenitsyn:

> If only it were all so simple! If only there were evil people somewhere insidiously committing evil deeds, and it were necessary only to separate them from the rest of us and destroy

them. But the line dividing good and evil cuts through the heart of every human being. And who is willing to destroy a piece of his own heart? (Zweig & Abrams, 1991, p. 161)

Joe no longer needed to "separate and destroy" Mark, but was finally ready to have honest dialogues with the young man who had been his best friend since first grade. He had never read that Solzhenitsyn quotation, but declared its wisdom in his own words: "When I listened to how Mark felt, I no longer saw him as a monster. I could forgive him. Mark screwed up, but so did I."

We had met for eight visits, originally sandwiched between what I had thought would be two more challenging appointments. So much for predictions. I often marvel how, at one time or another, all four of us struggled with victimization: Joe in reaction to Mark's ordinary "crime" and all of us in reaction to the terrorists' extraordinary crimes. Our shared struggles resulted in affirming an important axiom that is familiar to family therapists but frequently not to lay persons: one's victimization is not caused by an external event(s), but rather is *catalyzed* by it. It was this family's construction of *lineal causality* (victimizer victimizes victim) that had, in fact, caused them to believe that they suffered because of Mark: they judged him as guilty and Joe as an innocent casualty. I, too—more often than I care to admit—still fall into the trap of viewing, at this writing, the current-day terrorism in this manner.

CONCLUSION

We now return to some basic concepts introduced in chapter 1. The lineal causation model of reality offers false clarity and sharp focus, because it saves us from having to struggle with mutual causation and culpability. The etiology of a problem is viewed as residing in one's psyche, and the proposed solution, depending on the circumstance, may be to punish or execute the guilty party; beat him up after school, as in the case of Joe and Mark; or, in a mental health context, provide individual treatment toward modifying intrapsychic pathogenic structures. There are many possibilities. In any case, however, the prescribed solution is a direct outgrowth of cause and effect, lineal thinking; it is aimed at changing something about a particular individual. In the case of my work with Joe's family, one of us either wanted to assault Mark, execute bin Laden (a.k.a. targeted assassination), or—in Joe's case—to do both.

In contrast, a systemic construction of reality does not offer even the appearance of clarity and sharp focus. Instead, as I have attempted to elucidate in this book, it offers complexity; it offers important opportunities to become curious. Cause and effect are reciprocal and not readily apparent; X causes Y; Y causes X; the positions of victimizer and victim continually shift. Initially, it was all so (lineally) clear! Mark ridiculed Joe—end of story. However, then we learned that Joe had ridiculed Mark earlier. Indeed, Mark, who seemed so insensitive at the beginning, then appeared to simultaneously be a victim of ordinary evil; and Joe, who seemed so justified in his righteous rage, then struggled with simultaneously being a victimizer. We find ourselves increasingly curious about how each of them interpreted various preceding communications and events and how the barrage of sequential interpretations—constructions of reality—contributed to the final straw.

Taking this line of reasoning a step further, we can post that a systemic framework is needed to understand *all* behavior, including the extraordinary evil of Bin Laden. A contextual perspective of the World Trade Center–Pentagon bombings was provided by columnist Michael Ventura (2001):

> Most psychotherapists would agree that fanaticism is an extreme form of panic—acted-out panic. September 11 was ... an act of transference in the most literal sense: they transferred their panic onto us. They were seeking not only to destroy us but to make us feel what they feel. They succeeded ... You and I didn't commit the sins of genocide and slavery that helped make America strong. It is not fair that we are held responsible for the sins of our cultural (if not biological) ancestors. Yet, we are their inheritors. We make free use of what they won for us. So, while we are not responsible, it is natural (though not fair) for others to hold us responsible. All of which is to say: The very prosperity that is the ground of our lives is the horror of theirs. If we were living on less than $2 a day; as two-thirds of the world lives, we, too, might rejoice in the streets when the privileged suffered. (p. 31)

Maybe this line of reasoning—my theoretical ponderings—are irrelevant, at best, or even foolish. Admittedly, at first glance, it is a stretch to apply the systemic model to Bin Laden. On the contrary, he provides a more compelling argument for the *un*systemic view that evil is embodied in bad people. I, too, have trouble viewing the terrorists, who perpetrated thousands of deaths and wanton destruction, as exemplifying anything but pure evil which, in turn, directly causes our suffering and therefore warrants us, in President Bush's words, to "get him dead or alive." In addition, although I intuitively agree with Solzhenitsyn that "evil cuts through the heart of every human being," it cuts deeper through some peoples' hearts than others. Evil exists on a continuum. I may tell a lie that "the check's in the mail" or that "it's nice to see you, too" but I wouldn't bomb the World Trade Center; and, I assume—perhaps naively (but I don't think so)—that neither would my family or friends. Moreover, although there are social and historical reasons that help provide a context for bad people doing bad things, these contextual factors don't come close to satisfying our need to understand what presents as "pure evil." We know that the "sins of genocide and slavery" exist, but we also know that people vary in their response to it. In this century we have had Mahatma Gandhi and Martin Luther King who provide profound examples of nonviolent responses to violence that ultimately prevailed.

More critique, this time as I think about my work with Joe and his parents. Did Joe really come to appreciate the systemic nature of his behavior by appreciating Bin Laden in context? Did he really make this connection, or did I, as a systemic therapist, forge a contrived connection to Bin Laden more than the family actually did?

I am *not* making the case that our examination of present day extraordinary evil caused any breakthrough with the present-day ordinary evil. I am only noting that these events happened around the same time. I continually come back to the haunting juxtaposition, the temporal contiguity, of September 11th with our hard-earned success at understanding the systemic nature of ordinary evil in Joe's immediate world. I note that it was when I challenged Joe's wish to "kill the evil [Bin Laden] bastard" that he finally began to appreciate the contextual nature of his behavior with Mark and to break the logjam between them. Stated differently, our shared curiosity about the systemic nature of that extraordinary evil helped us to become curious about the systemic nature of the cruelty—the ordinary evil—that had transpired between brothers.

Perhaps the success of the family interventions was amplified in the post September 11th world—a phenomenon that was introduced in chapter 1: namely, that for an intervention to be successful, it may need to be implemented simultaneously with a shift in another spatial level of the ecology (in this case, from the cultural level of the ecology). I wonder how much my phrase "particularly in these awful, terrifying times, it's a shame that you lost your brother" resonated with Joe. I will never forget how I—as well as many people—wanted to hug my family soon after 9:30 am that morning. Maybe it is human nature that we honor our loved ones more when their existence is threatened.

I think of Steve's reflection that "America has committed evil in the world, too," as he attempted to widen the context to include more mutual culpability. Perhaps it is more comforting to believe that, to the extent that we help set the stage of outbreaks of evil to occur, we have some control over its reoccurrence. In the words of Rabbi Arthur Waskow:

> If I treat my neighbor's pain and grief as foreign, I will end up suffering when my neighbor's pain and grief curdle into rage. But if I realize that in simple fact the walls between us are full of holes, I can reach through them in compassion and connection ... America must open its heart and mind to the pain and grief of those ... who feel excluded, denied, unheard, disempowered, defeated. This does not mean ignoring or forgiving whoever wrought such bloodiness. Their violence must be halted, their rage must be calmed-and the pain behind them must be heard and addressed. (Waskow, 2001)

But we are off the point. The goal of this chapter is not to present a theoretical treatise on the nature of evil; and moreover, that was not part of the treatment plan with this family. However, like it or not, evil broke into our consciousness as an unwelcome, unexpected intruder and pervaded the context of our work together. Perhaps when this second edition of *Psycho-*

therapy With Deaf and Hard-of-Hearing Persons: A Systemic Model is published, that Osama bin Laden "bastard," as Joe put it, will be captured or executed. I certainly hope so. However, that will not solve the problem. Joe would give anything to move back time and prevent Mark from ruining his chances with Gloria; and we would give anything to move back time and prevent the shattering of our impermeability to terrorism. However, we're stuck with the evil that has happened—both ordinary and extraordinary—and we assuredly will bear witness to evil again, whether it be at the hands of others or ourselves. Our task is figure out what lessons it offers.

As discussed in chapter 1, a systemic approach offers one important lesson. Just as there is no fixed psychology of deafness per se, there is no fixed psychology of evil. Instead, as I have attempted to illustrate throughout this book, one's mode of being is inextricably related to context, to overlapping recursive cycles or "completed circuits," which encompass space and time. This also applies to acts of evil, including those that impinge on deaf persons. Like many deaf persons, Joe had the task of distinguishing between the pervasive cultural-based evil from the apparent evil actions of his friend, Mark, and then had the task of acknowledging his own role in the reciprocal escalation of conflict within what we have termed the informal network level of his ecology. A mouthful I admit, but the lesson is clear. To truly empower deaf and hard-of-hearing persons who seek our assistance—whether we attempt to intervene within a level of the ecology that appears to "contain" evil or within any level of the biopsychosocial hierarchy—we must understand those complex and often elusive layers of systemic influences that affect their lives as well as ours.

REFERENCES

Allen, J. C., & Allen, M. C. (1979). Discovering and accepting hearing impairment: Initial reactions of parents. In A. T. Murphy (Ed.), The families of hearing-impaired children. *Volta Review, 81*(5), 279–285.

Allport, G. W. (1961). *Pattern and growth in personality.* New York: Holt, Rinehart & Winston.

American Psychiatric Association. (1994). *Diagnostic and statistical manual of mental disorders* (4th ed.). Washington, DC: Author.

Anderson, G. B., & Rosten, E. (1985). In G. B. Anderson & D. Watson (Eds.), *Counseling deaf people: Research and practice.* Little Rock, AK: Arkansas Rehabilitation Research and Training Center on Deafness and Hearing Impairment.

Armstong, K. (1993). *A history of God.* New York: Ballantine.

Ashley, J. (1985). A personal account. In H. Orlans (Ed.), *Adjustment to adult hearing loss.* San Diego: College-Hill Press.

Ashley, P. K. (1985). Deafness in the family. In H. Orlans (Ed.), *Adjustment to adult hearing loss.* San Diego: College-Hill Press.

Attneave, C. (1984). Tasty hors d'oeuvres—and a promise of a banquet to come. *Family Process, 23*(2), 198–199.

Bahan, B. (1976, May). A chat with a 'hard-a-hearie'. *Deaf Community News,* p. 6.

Baker, C., & Battison, R. (Eds.). (1980). *Sign language and the deaf community.* Silver Spring, MD: National Association of the Deaf.

Baker, C., & Cokely, D. (1980). *American Sign Language: A teacher's resource test on grammar and culture.* Silver Spring, MD: T. J.

Bandler, R., & Grinder, J. (1975). *Patterns of the hypnotic techniques of Milton H. Erickson, M.D.* (Vol. I). Palo Alto, CA: Science and Behavior.

Bateson, G. (1971). A systems approach. *International Journal of Psychiatry, 9,* 242–244.

Bateson, G. (1972). *Steps to an ecology of mind.* San Francisco: Chandler.

Bateson, G. (1979). *Mind and nature: A necessary unity.* New York: Dutton.
Baumeister, R. F. (1999). *Evil: Inside human violence and cruelty.* New York: W. H. Freeman.
Beck, A. T. (1976). *Cognitive therapy and the emotional disorders.* New York: New American Library.
Beck, A. T. (1999). *Prisoners of hate: The cognitive basis of anger, hostility, and violence.* New York: Harper Collins.
Benderly, B. (1980). *Dancing without music: Deafness in America.* New York: Anchor.
Bloch, D. A. (1985). Epistemology and the impaired physician. *Family Systems Medicine, 3*(4), 378–380.
Bodner-Johnson, B. (1986). The family in perspective. In D. M. Luterman (Ed.), *Deafness in perspective.* San Diego: College-Hill Press.
Boyarin, F., Burke, F., Evans, J. W., & Lee, M. (1987). Assessment from the perspective of the hearing therapist. In H. Elliott, L. Glass, & J. W. Evans (Eds.), *Mental health assessment of deaf clients.* Boston: Little Brown.
Boyd, R. D., & Young, N. B. (1981). Hearing disorders. In J. E. Lindemann (Ed.), *Psychological and behavioral aspects of physical disability.* New York: Plenum.
Bronfenbrenner, U. (1979). *The ecology of human development.* Cambridge, MA: Harvard University Press.
Bunde, L. T. (1979). *Deaf parent—hearing children.* Washington, DC: RID.
Burke, F., Elliott, H., & Lee, M. (1987). The initial contact. In H. Elliott, L. Glass, & J. W. Evans (Eds.), *Mental health assessment of deaf clients.* Boston: Little Brown.
Carl, D., & Jurkovic, G. J. (1983). Agency triangles: Problems in agency-family relationships. *Family Process, 22*(4), 441–452.
Carmen, R. E. (2001, March). Hearing loss and depression in adults. *The Hearing Review,* pp. 74–78.
Cecchin, G. (1987). Hypothesizing, circularity, and neutrality revised: An invitation to curiosity. *Family Process, 26*(4), 405–414.
Chess, S., & Fernandez, P. (1980). Do deaf children have a typical personality? *Journal of the American Academy of Child Psychiatry, 19,* 654–664.
Children of Deaf Adults: CODA. (November, 1983). Post Office Box 30715, Santa Barbara, CA. 93130.
Chough, S. K. (1983). The trust vs. mistrust phenomenon among deaf persons. In D. Watson, K. Steitlen, P. Peterson, & W. K. Fulton (Eds.), *Mental health, substance abuse and deafness.* Silver Spring, MD: American Deafness and Rehabilitation Association.
Christensen, K. (2000). *Deaf plus: A multicultural perspective.* San Diego: Dawnsign.
Christie-Seely. (Ed.). (1984). *Working with the family in primary care: A systems approach to health and illness.* New York: Praeger.
Christiansen, J. B., & Leigh, I. W. (2002). *Cochlear implants in children: ethics and choices.* Washington, DC.: Gallaudet University Press.
Clark, M. D. (1998). A hitchhiker's guide to holes and dark spots: some missing perspectives in the psychology of deafness. In M. Marschark & M. D. Clark (Eds.), *Psychological persepctives on deafness, Vol. 2.* Mahwah, NJ: Lawrence Erlbaum Associates, Inc.
Colby, K. M. (1951). *A primer for psychotherapists.* New York: Ronald.
Coles, R. (1991). *The spiritual life of children.* New York: Houghton Mifflin.
Combrinck-Graham, L., & Higley, L. W. (1984). Working with families of schoolaged handicapped children. In J. L. Hansen & E. I. Coppersmith (Eds.), *Families with handicapped members.* Rockville, MD: Aspen.
Coppersmith, E. I. (1982). Family therapy in a public school system. In A. S. Gurman (Ed.), *Questions and answers in the practice of family therapy* (Vol. 2, pp. 268–271). New York: Brunner/Mazel.

Crosby, J. F., & Jose, N. C. (1983). Death: Family adjustment to loss. In C. R. Figley & H. I. McCubbin (Eds.), *Stress and the family.* New York: Brunner/Mazel.

Czikszentmihalyi, M., & Larson, R. (1984). *Being adolescent.* New York: Basic.

Dean, R. K., & Pollard, R. Q. (2001). The application of demand-control theory to sign language interpreting: Implications for stress and interpreter training. *Journal of Deaf Studies and Deaf Education,* 6(1), 1–14.

DeMatteo, A. J., Veltri, D., & Lee, S. M. (1986). The role of a sign language interpreter in psychotherapy. In M. L. McIntire (Ed.), *Interpreting: The art of cross-cultural mediation.* Silver Spring, MD: RID.

Dickens, D. L. (1983). *Problems encountered by clinicians in providing services to deaf psychiatric patients.* Paper presented at the IX World Congress of the World Federation of the Deaf, Palermo, Sicily, Italy.

Dickens, D. L. (1985). Problems encountered by clinicians in providing services to deaf psychiatric patients. In G. B. Anderson & D. Watson (Eds.), *Counseling with deaf people.* Little Rock, AK: Arkansas Rehabilitation Research and Training Center on Deafness and Hearing Impairment.

Diedrichsen, R. (1987). Towards the acquisition of basic rights and services for persons who are hard of hearing. *SHHH,* March–April, 3–4.

Dobson, K. S. (1988). *Handbook of cognitive-behavioral therapies.* New York: Guilford.

Dym, B. (1985). Eating disorders and the family: A model for intervention. In S. W. Emmett (Ed.), *Theory and treatment of anorexia nervosa and bulimia: Biomedical, sociocultural and psychological perspectives.* New York: Brunner/Mazel.

Dym, B. (1987). The cybernetics of physical illness. *Family Process, 26*(1), 35–45.

Dym, B., & Berman, S. (1986). The primary health care team: Family physician and family therapist in joint practice. *Family Systems Medicine, 94*(1), 9–21.

Elliot, H. (1978). *Acquired deafness: Shifting gears.* Speech delivered at workshop for deafened adults, San Francisco.

Elliott, H. (1986). Acquired hearing loss—shifting gears. *SHHH,* November–December, 23–25.

Elliott, H., Bell, B., Langholtz, D., Nguyan, M., & Peters, L. (1987). Assessment from the perspective of the deaf therapist. In H. Elliott, L. Glass, & J. W. Evan, (Eds.), *Mental health assessment of deaf clients.* Boston: Little Brown.

Engel, G. L. (1977). The need for a new medical model: A challenge for biomedicine. *Science, 196,* 129–136.

Erickson, G. D. (1984). A framework and themes for social network interventions. *Family Process, 23*(2), 187–197.

Erikson, E. H. (1968). *Identity, youth and crisis.* New York: Norton.

Evans, J. W. (1987). Mental health treatment of hearing impaired adolescents and adults. In B. Heller, L. Flohr, & L. S. Zegans (Eds.), *Psychosocial interventions with sensorially disabled persons.* New York: Grune & Stratton.

Falberg, R. M. (1985). Maintaining confidentiality when counseling deaf adults in rehabilitation facilities. In G. B. Anderson & D. Watson (Eds.), *Counseling deaf people.* Little Rock, AK: Arkansas Rehabilitation, Research and Training Center on Deafness and Hearing Impairment.

Fant, L., & Schuchmann, J. (1974). Experiences of two hearing children of deaf parents. In P. Fine (Ed.), *Deafness in infancy and early childhood.* New York: Medcom.

Featherstone, H. (1980). *A difference in the family.* New York: Basic.

Fellendorf, G. W., & Harrow, I. (1970). Parent counselling 1961–1968. *Volta Review, 72,* 51–57.

Ford, F. (1983). Rules: The invisible family. *Family Process, 22*(2), 135–146.

Freeman, R. D. (1977). Psychiatric aspects of sensory disorders and intervention. In P. Graham (Ed.), *Epidemiological approaches in child psychiatry.* New York: Academic.
Freeman, R. D., Carbin, C. F., & Boese, R. J. (1981). *Can't your child hear? A guide for those who care about deaf children.* Baltimore: University Park Press.
Freud, A. (1966). *The ego and the mechanisms of deafness.* New York: International University Press.
Gannon, J. (1980). *Deaf heritage.* Silver Spring, MD: National Association of the Deaf.
Gates, H. L., & West, C. (1996). *The Future of the Race.* New York: Vintage.
Gilligan, C. (1982). *In a different voice: Psychological theory and women's development.* Cambridge, MA: Harvard University Press.
Glass, L. E. (1985). Psychosocial aspects of hearing loss in adulthood. In H. Orlans (Ed.), *Adjustment to adult hearing loss.* San Diego: College-Hill Press.
Glickman, N. (1983). A cross-cultural view of counseling with deaf clients. *Journal of Rehabilitation of the Deaf, 16*(3), 4–14.
Glickman, N. (1986). Cultural identity, deafness, and mental health. *Journal of Rehabilitation of the Deaf, 20*(2), 1–10.
Glickman, N. S., & Harvey, M. A. (Eds.). (1996). *Culturally affirmative psychotherapy with deaf persons.* Mahwah, NJ: Lawrence Erlbaum Associates, Inc.
Glickman, N. S. (in press). Affirmative Mental Health Treatment for Deaf Persons: What it Looks Like and Why it is Essential. In N. S. Glickman & S. Gulati (Eds.). *Mental Health Care of Deaf People: The Culturally Affirmative Perspective.* Mahwah, NJ: Lawrence Erlbaum Associates, Inc.
Glickman, N. S., & Gulati, S. (in press). *Mental Health Care of Deaf People: The Culturally Affirmative Perspective.* Mahwah, NJ: Lawrence Erlbaum Associates, Inc.
Greenberg, J. (1970). *In this sign.* New York: Holt, Rinehart & Winston.
Greenberg, M. T. (1983). Family stress and child competence: The effects of early intervention for families with deaf infants. *American Annals of the Deaf,* 407–417.
Gregory, S. (1976). *The deaf child and his family.* Halstead, NY: Allen & Unwin.
Grinder, J., & Bandler, R. (1976). *Structure of magic II.* Palo Alta, CA: Science and Behavior.
Grube, G. M. A. (Trans.). (1974). *Plato: The republic.* Indianapolis, IN: Hockett.
Haley, J. (Ed.). (1967). *Advanced techniques of hypnosis and therapy: Selected papers of Milton H. Erickson, M.D.* (Vol. 1). Palo Alto, CA: Science and Behavior.
Haley, J. (1980). *Leaving home: The therapy of disturbed young people.* New York: McGraw-Hill.
Happ, D. A., & Altmaier, E. M. (1982). Counseling the hearing impaired: Issues and recommendations. *Personal and Guidance Journal, 21,* 556–559.
Harris, R. (1978). Impulse control in deaf children. In L. Liben (Ed.), *Deaf children: Developmental perspectives.* New York: Academic.
Harvey, M. A. (1982). The influence and utilization of an interpreter for deaf persons in family therapy. *American Annals of the Deaf, 127*(7), 821–827.
Harvey, M. A. (1984a). Family therapy with deaf persons: The systemic utilization of an interpreter. *Family Process, 23,* 205–213.
Harvey, M. A. (1984b). Rejoinder to Scott, *Family Process, 23,* 216–221.
Harvey, M. A. (1985a). Toward a dialogue between the paradigms of family therapy and deafness. *American Annals of the Deaf, 130*(4), 305–314.
Harvey, M. A. (1985b). Between two worlds: One psychologist's view of the hard of hearing person's experience. *SHHH, 6*(4), 4–5.
Harvey, M. A. (1986). The magnifying mirror: Family therapy for deaf persons. *Family Systems Medicine, 4*(4), 408–420.
Harvey, M. A. (1994). Systemic Rehabilitation. In R. C. Nowell & L. E. Marshak (Eds.), *Understanding deafness and the rehabilitation process.* Needham, MA: Allyn and Bacon.

Harvey, M. A. (1996). Utilization of traumatic transference by a hearing therapist. In N. S.
Harvey, M. A. (1998). *Odyssey of hearing loss: tales of triumph.* San Diego: Dawnsign.
Harvey, M. A. (2001a). *Listen with the heart: relationships and hearing loss.* San Diego: Dawnsign.
Harvey, M. A. (2001). Vicarious Emotional Trauma of Interpreters for the Deaf. *Journal of Interpretation,* Registry of Interpreters for the Deaf.
Harvey, M. A. (2001b). "What's On Your Mind?" *Hearing Loss,* November.
Harvey, M. A. (2002). *What's on your mind? Journal of Hearing Loss, 1*(2).
Harvey, M. A., & Dym, B. (1987). An ecological view of deafness. *Family Systems Medicine,* 5(1), 52–64.
Harvey, M. A., & Dym, B. (1988). An ecological perspective on deafness. *Journal of Rehabilitation of the Deaf, 21*(3), 12–20.
Harvey, M. A. (1989). *Psychotherapy with deaf and hard of hearing persons: a systemic model.* Mahwah, NJ: Lawrence Erlbaum Associates, Inc.
Higgins, P. C. (1980). *Outsiders in a hearing world: A sociology of deafness.* Beverly Hills, CA: Sage.
Hoffman, L. (1981). *Foundations of family therapy.* New York: Basic.
Hoffmeister, R. J., & Harvey, M. A. (1998). Is there a psychology of the hearing? In N. S. Glickman & M. A. Harvey (Eds.), *Culturally affirmative psychotherapy with Deaf persons.* Mahwah, NJ: Lawrence Erlbaum Associates, Inc.
Hoffmeister, R. J. (1985). Families with deaf parents: A functional perspective. In K. Thurman (Ed.), *Handicapped families: Functional perspectives.* New York: Academic.
Hofstadter, D. R. (1979). *Gödal, Escher, Bach: Eternal golden braid.* New York: Basic.
Holt, M. F., Siegelman, E. Y., & Schlesinger, H. D. (1981). Special issues regarding psychotherapy with the deaf. *American Journal of Psychiatry, 138*(6), 807–811.
Humphrey, C., Gilhoma-Herbst, K., & Faurqi, S. (1981). Some characteristics of the hearing-impaired elderly who do not present themselves for rehabilitation. *British Journal of Audiology, 15,* 25–30.
Imber-Black, E. (1986). Families, larger systems and the wider social context. *Journal of Strategic and Systems Therapies,* 5(4), 29–35.
Imber-Black, E. (1987). The mentally handicapped in context. *Family Systems Medicine,* 5(4), 428–445.
Imber-Coppersmith, E. (1983). The family and public sector systems: Interviewing and interventions. *Journal of Strategic and Systemic Therapies,* 2(3), 38–47.
Jackson, D. D. (1965). The study of the family. *Family Process,* 4(1), 1–20.
Jacobs, L. M. (1974). *A deaf adult speaks out.* Washington, DC: Gallaudet College Press.
Jourard, S. M. (1971). *The transparent self.* New York: D. Von Nostrand.
Kannapell, B. (1983). The trust-mistrust phenomenon. In D. Watson, K. Steitler, P. Peterson, & W. K. Fulton (Eds.), *Mental health substance abuse and deafness.* Silver Spring, MD: American Deafness and Rehabilitation Association.
Katz, J. (1984). *The silent world of doctor and patient.* New York: Free.
Keeny, B. P. (1983). *Aesthetics of change.* New York: Guilford.
Kushner, H. S. (1981). *When bad things happen to good people.* New York: Avon.
Kyle, J. G., & Wood, P. (1983). Social vocational aspects of acquired hearing loss: Final report to M.S.C., School of Education, Bristol, England.
Kyle, J. G., Jones, L. G., & Wood, P. C. (1985). Adjustment to acquired hearing loss: A working model. In H. Orlans (Ed.), *Adjustment to adult hearing loss.* San Diego: College-Hill Press.
Lane, H. (1984). *When the mind hears: A history of the deaf.* New York: Random House.
Lane, H. (1980). A chronology of oppression of sign language in France and the United States. In H. Lane & F. Grosjean (Eds.), *Recent perspectives on American Sign Language.* Hillsdale, NJ: Lawrence Erlbaum Associates, Inc.

Lane, H. (1984). *When the mind hears: A history of the deaf.* New York: Random House.
Lane, H. (1987, July). *Is there a "psychology of the deaf"?* Paper presented at the O. S. E. P. Conference of Research Project Directors, Boston.
Lane, H. (1992). *The mask of benevolence.* New York: Alfred A. Knopf.
Lane, H., Hoffmeister, R., & Bahan, B. (1996). *A Journey into the Deaf-World.* San Diego: Dawnsign.
Langholtz, D., & Heller, B. (1988). Effective psychotherapy with deaf persons: Therapists' perspectives. In D. Watson, G. Long, M. Taff-Watson, & M. Harvey (Eds.), *Two decades of excellence: A foundation for the future.* Little Rock, AK: American Deafness and Rehabilitation Association.
Larew, S. J., Saura, K. M., & Watson, D. (Eds.). (1992). *Facing deafness.* Proceedings of ALDACON III, The Association for Late-Deafened Adults: DeKalb, IL: Northern Illinois University.
Lederberg, A. R., & Prezbindowski, A. K. (2000). Impact of child deafness on mother-toddler interaction: Strengths and weaknesses. In P. E. Spencer, C. J. Erting, & M. Marschark (Eds.), *The deaf child in the family and at school.* Mahwah, NJ: Lawrence Earbaum Associates, Inc.
Leigh, I. W. (1999). *Psychotherapy with deaf clients from diverse groups.* Washington, DC: Gallaudet University Press.
Leigh, I. W., & Lewis, J. W. (1999). Deaf therapists and the deaf community: How the Twain meet. In I. W. Leigh. *Psychotherapy with deaf clients from diverse groups.* Washington, DC: Gallaudet University Press.
Levin, F. M. (1981). Insight-oriented psychotherapy with the deaf. In L. S. Stein, E. D. Mindel, & M. A. Jabaley (Eds.), *Deafness and mental health.* New York: Grune & Stratton.
Levine, E. S. (1960). *The psychology of deafness.* New York: Columbia University Press.
Levine, E. S. (1981). *The ecology of early deafness: Guides to fashioning environments and psychological assessments.* New York: Columbia University Press.
Lewis, B. (2001 November 19). The Revolt of Islam. *The New Yorker,* pp. 50–63.
Liben, L. S. (1978). *Deaf children: Developmental perspectives.* New York: Academic.
Luey, H. S., & Glass, L. G. (1995). Hard-of-hearing or deaf: Issues of ears, language, culture and identity. *Social Work, 40*(2), 177–182.
Luey, H. S. (1980). Between worlds: The problems of deafened adults. *Social Work in Health Care, 5*(3), 253–265.
Luey, H. S. (1987). Hearing loss: Personal and social considerations. *SHHH,* March–April, 8–11.
Luey, H. S., & Per-Lee, M. S. (1983). *What should I do now? Problems and adaptation of the deafened adult.* Washington, DC: The National Academy of Gallaudet College.
Luterman, D. (1979). *Counseling parents of hearing-impaired children.* Boston: Little Brown.
MacEachin, A. (1982, Spring). Issues of psychiatric interpreting. *The Reflector,* 1–3.
Madanes, C. (1981). *Strategic family therapy.* San Francisco: Jossey-bass.
Malmquist, C. P. (1978). *Handbook of adolescence.* New York: Jason Aronson.
Marcos, L. R. (1979). Effects of interpreters on the evaluation of psychopathology in non-English speaking patients. *American Journal of Psychiatry, 136,* 58–67.
Marmor, G., & Petitto, L. (1979). Simultaneous communication in the classroom: How well is English grammar represented? *Sign Language Studies, 23,* 99–136.
Marschark, M., & Clark, M. D. (Eds.). (1998). *Psychological perspectives on deafness, Vol. 2.* Mahwah, NJ: Lawrence Erlbaum Associates, Inc.
Marschark, M. (1997). *Raising and educating deaf children.* New York: Oxford University Press.
Mayberry, R., & Wodlinger-Cohen, R. (1987). After the revolution: Educational practice and the deaf child's communication skills. In E. D. Mindel & M. Vernon (Eds.), *They grow in silence (2nd ed.).* Boston: Little Brown.

Meadow, K. P. (1968). Parental responses to the medical ambiguities of deafness. *Journal on Health and Social Behavior, 9*(4), 299–309.

Meadow, K. P. (1980). *Deafness and child development.* Berkeley, CA: University of California Press.

Meadow-Orlans, K. P. (1985). Social and psychological effects of hearing loss in adulthood: A literature review. In H. Orlans (Ed.), *Adjustment to adult hearing loss.* San Diego: College-Hill Press.

Meichenbaum, D. (1994). *A clinical handbook/practical therapist manual for assessing and treating adults with post-traumatic stress disorder (PTSD).* Waterloo, Canada: Institute.

Mendelsohn, M., & Rozek, F. (1983). Denying disability: The case of deafness. *Family Systems Medicine 1*, 37–47.

Mertons, D. M., Sass-Lehrer, S., & Scott-Olson, K. (2000). Sensitivity in family–professional relationships: potential experiences of families with young deaf and hard of hearing children. In P. T. Spencer, C. J. Erting, & M. Marschark (Eds.), *The deaf child in the family at school.* Mahwah, NJ: Lawrence Erlbaum Associates, Inc.

Mindel, E. D., & Feldman, V. (1987). The impact of deaf children on their families. In E. D. Mindel & M. Vernon (Eds.), *They grow in silence.* Boston: Little Brown.

Mindel, E. D., & Vernon, M. (Eds.). (1971). *They grow in silence.* Silver Spring, MD: National Association of the Deaf.

Mindel, E. D., & Vernon, M. (Eds.). (1987a). *They grow in silence (2nd ed.).* Boston: Little Brown.

Minuchin, S. (1974). *Structural family therapy: Families and family therapy.* Cambridge, MA: Harvard University Press.

Minuchin, S., & Fishman, H. C. (1981). *Family therapy techniques.* Cambridge, MA: Harvard University Press.

Minuchin, S., Rosman, B. C., & Baker, C. (1978). *Psychosomatic families: Anorexia nervosa in context.* Cambridge, MA: Harvard University Press.

Montalvo, B. (1976). Observations of two natural amnesias. *Family Process, 15*, 333–342.

Moores, D. F. (1987). *Educating the deaf: Psychology, principles and practices (3rd ed.).* Boston: Houghton Mifflin.

Moses, K. (1976). On loss, grieving, coping, facilitating, and intervening. Evanston, IL: *Resource Networks.*

Moses, K. (1986 June). *Counseling: A critical point of our practice.* Paper presented at an American Speech-Language-Hearing Association teleconference, Rockville, MD.

Mulholland, A. M. (Ed.). (1981). The philosophical bases of oral education. *Oral education today and tomorrow.* Washington, DC: Alexander Graham Bell.

Murphy, A. T. (Ed.). (1979). Members of the family: Sisters and brothers of handicapped children. The families of hearing-impaired children. *Volta Review, 81*(5), 352–362.

Myers, D. G. (2000). *A quiet world: living with hearing loss.* New Haven, CT: Yale University Press.

Myers, S. S., Myers, R. R., & Marcus, A. E. (1999). Hearing children of deaf parents: Issues and interventions within a bicultural context. In I. W. Leigh (Eds.), *Psychotherapy with deaf clients from diverse groups.* Washington, DC: Gallaudet University Press.

Nash, J. E., & Nash, A. (1981). *Deafness in society.* Lexington, MA: Lexington.

Nicholi, A. M. (Ed.). (1988). *The new Harvard guide to psychiatry.* Cambridge, MA: Harvard University Press.

Nowell, R. C., & Marshak, L. E. (Eds). (1994). *Understanding deafness and the rehabilitation process.* Needham, MA: Allyn & Bacon.

O'Hanlon, B. (1984). Framing interventions in therapy: Framing and deframing. *Journal of Strategic and Systemic Therapies, 3*(2), 1–4.

Orlans, H. (1985). Reflections on adult hearing loss. In H. Orlans (Ed.), *Adjustment to adult hearing loss.* San Diego: College-Hill Press.
Padden, C. (1980). The Deaf community and the culture of Deaf people. *Sign language and the deaf community.* Silver Spring, MD: National Association of the Deaf.
Palazzoli, M. S. (1985). The problem of the sibling as the referring person. *Journal of Marital and Family Therapy, 11*(1), 21–34.
Palazzoli, M. S., Boscalo, L., Cecchin, G., & Prata, G. (1980). The problem of the referring person. *Journal of Marital and Family Therapy,* 3–9.
Palazzoli, M. S., Boscolo, L., Cecchin, G. F., & Prata, G. (1980). Hypothesizing, circularity, neutrality: Three guidelines for the conduction of the session. *Family Process, 19,* 3–12.
Papp, P. (1983). *The process of change.* New York: Guilford.
Peck, M. S. (1983). *People of the lie.* New York: Simon & Schuster.
Perrotta, P. (1986). Leaving home: Later stages in treatment. *Family Process, 25*(3), 461–474.
Perry, A. L., & Silverman, S. R. (1978). Speech-reading. In H. Davis & S. R. Silverman (Eds.), *Hearing and deafness* (4th ed.). New York: Holt, Rinehart & Winston.
Pimental, A. T. (1981). SSI, SSDI and deaf people. *Deaf American,* 33(6), 3.
Pollard, R. Q., (2002). Ethical conduct in research involving deaf people. In V. A. Gutman (Ed.), *Ethics in mental health and deafness* (pp. 162–178). Washington, DC: Gallaudet University Press.
Pollard, R. Q., (1998). *Mental health interpreting: A mentored curriculum.* Rochester, NY: University of Rochester Press.
Pollard, R. Q., (1998a). Psychopathology. In M. Marschark & D. Clark (Eds.), *Psychological perspectives on deafness, Vol. 2* (pp. 171–197). Mahwah, NJ: Lawrence Erlbaum Associates, Inc.
Pollard, R. Q., Miner, I. D., & Cioffi, J. (2000). Hearing and vision loss. In T. R. Elliott & R. J. Frank (Eds.), *Handbook of rehabilitation psychology* (pp. 205–234). Washington, DC: American Psychological Association.
Pollard, R. Q., & Rendon, M. E. (1999). Mixed deaf-hearing families: Maximizing benefits and minimizing risks. *Journal of Deaf Studies and Deaf Education,* 4(2), 156–161.
Pollard, R. Q., & Rinker, N. C. (2001). The misfit: A deaf adolescent struggles for meaning. In S. H. McDaniel, D. D. Lusterman, & C. Philpot (Eds.), *Casebook for integrating family therapy* (pp. 191–204). Washington, DC: American Psychological Association.
Pollard, R. Q. (2000). Personal communication.
Power, P. W., & Dell Orto, A. E. (Eds.). (1980). General impact of adult disability/illness on the family. *Role of the family in the rehabilitation of the physically disabled.* Baltimore: University Park Press.
Preston, P. O. (1993). *Mother father deaf.* Cambridge, MA: Harvard University Press.
Quigley, S. P., & Paul, P. V. (1986). In D. M. Luterman (Ed.), *Deafness in perspective.* San Diego: College Hill Press.
Rainer, J. D., Altshuler, K. A., & Kallman, F. Z. (1963). Psychotherapy for the deaf. In J. D. Rainer, K. Z. Altshuler, & F. Z. Kallman (Eds.), *Family and mental health problems in a deaf population.* New York: New York State Psychiatric Institute.
Ramsdell, D. A. (1978). The psychology of the hard-of-hearing and deafened adult. In H. Davis & S. R. Silverman (Eds.), *Hearing and deafness (4th ed.).* New York: Holt, Rinehart & Winston.
Rawlings, B. (1971). *Characteristics of hearing-impaired students by hearing status, United States: 1970–1971.* Series D., No. 10, Office of Demographic Studies, Gallaudet College.
Rayson, B. (1987a). Emotional illness and the deaf. In E. D. Mindel & M. Vernon (Eds.), *They grow in silence* (2nd ed.). Boston: Little Brown.

Rayson, B. (1987b). Deaf parents of hearing children. In E. D. Mindel & M. Vernon (Eds.), *They grow in silence* (2nd ed.). Boston: Little Brown.

Registry of Interpreters for the Deaf, Inc. (1976). *Code of ethics*. Silver Spring, MD: Author.

Roach, A. (1979). *The hearing therapist and deaf client: Perception of process*. Paper presented at the American Psychological Association National Convention, New York, August.

Roberts, J. (1984). Families with infants and young children who have special needs. In J. C. Hansen & E. I. Coppersmith (Eds.), *Families with handicapped members*. Rockville, MD: Aspen.

Robinson, L. D., & Weathers, O. D. (1974). Family therapy of deaf parents and hearing children: A new dimension in psychotherapeutic intervention. *American Annals of the Deaf, 119*(3), 325–330.

Rosen, R. (1986). Deafness: A social perspective. In D.M. Luterman (Ed.), *Deafness in perspective.* San Diego: College-Hill Press.

Ross, M., Brackett, D., & Maxon, A. B. (1991). *Assessment and management of mainstreamed hearing-unoaured children: Principles and practices.* Austin, TX: Pro-Ed.

Rossi, E. (1982). Erickson's creativity. *Family Therapy Network, 6*(1), 5.

Rousey, C. L. (1970, May). *Psychological reactions to hearing loss.* Paper presented at the Spring Regional Convention of the National Hearing Aid Society, Glenwood Manor, Overland Park, KS.

Schein, J. D., & Delk, M. T. (1974). *The deaf population of the United States.* Silver Spring, MD: National Association of the Deaf.

Schein, J. D., & Stone, H. E. (1986, November–December). Research and service priorities for self help for hard of hearing people), *SHHH*, 12–14.

Schirmer, B. R. (2001). *Psychological, social, and educational dimensions of deafness.* Needham, MA: Allyn & Bacon.

Schlesinger, H. S. (1972). Diagnostic crisis and its participants. *Deafness Annal,* (Vol. 2), Silver Spring, MD: Professional Rehabilitation Worker With the Adult Deaf.

Schlesinger, H. S. (1985). The psychology of hearing loss. In H. Orlans (Ed.), *Adjustment to adult hearing loss.* San Diego: College-Hill Press.

Schlesinger, H. S. (1986). Total communication in perspective. In D. M. Luterman (Ed.), *Deafness in perspective.* San Diego: College-Hill Press.

Schlesinger, H., & Meadow, K. (1972). *Sound and sign: Childhood deafness and mental health.* Berkeley, CA: University of California Press.

Scott, S., & Dooley, D. (1985). A structural family therapy approach for treatment of deaf children. In G. B. Anderson & D. Watson (Eds.), *Counseling deaf people: Research & practice.* Little Rock, AK: Arkansas Rehabilitation Research & Training Center on Deafness and Hearing Impairment.

Seligman, M. W. (1975). *Helplessness.* San Francisco: W. H. Freeman.

Sgroi, S. M. (1982). *Handbook of clinical intervention in child sexual abuse.* Lexington, MA: Lexington.

Shapiro, R. J., & Harris, R. (1976). Family therapy in treatment of the deaf: A case report. *Family Process, 15,* 83–97.

Shaver, K. A. (1987, November). *Medical and psychological implications of maternal rubella and other syndromes.* Paper presented at the Controversies in Mental Health and Deafness Conference, Falmouth, MA.

Sluzki, C. (1984). The patient–provider–translator triad: A note for providers. *Family Systems Medicine, 2*(4), 397–400.

Sonnenschein, M. A. (1987). How does my hearing loss affect my spouse? *SHHH*, September–October, 27–28.

Speck, R. V., & Speck, J. L. (1979). On networks: Network therapy, network intervention, and networking. *International Journal of Family Therapy, 1*(4), 333–337.

Spencer, P. E., Erting, C. J., & Marschark, M. (Eds.). (2000). The deaf child in the family and at school. Mahwah, NJ: Lawrence Erlbaum Associates, Inc.

Stansfield, M. (1981). Psychological issues in mental health interpreting. *R.I.D. Interpreting Journal, 1*, 18–32.

Stein, L. K., & Jabaley, T. (1981). Early identification and parent counseling. In L. K. Stein, E. D. Mindel, & T. Jabaley (Eds.), *Deafness and mental health*. New York: Grune & Stratton.

Stewart, L. G. (1981). Counseling the deaf client. In L. K. Stein, E. D. Mindel, & T. Jabaley (Eds.), *Deafness and mental health.* New York: Grune & Stratton.

Stokoe. (1998). A very long perspective. In M. Marschark & M. D. Clark (Eds.), *Psychological persepctives on deafness, Vol. 2*. Mahwah, NJ: Lawrence Erlbaum Associates, Inc.

Stone, H. E. (1985). Developing SHHH, A self-help organization. In H. Orlans (Ed.), *Adjustment to adult hearing loss*. San Diego: College-Hill Press.

Stuckless, E., & Birch, J. (1966). The influence of early manual communication on the linguistic development of deaf children. *American Annals of the Deaf, 111*, 452–460, 499–504.

Sue, D. W. (1981). *Counseling the culturally different*. New York: Wiley.

Sue, S., & Zane, N. (1987). The role of culture and cultural techniques in psychotherapy: A critique and reformulation. *American Psychologist, 42*(1), 37–45.

Sullivan, H. S. (1953). *The interpersonal theory of psychiatry*. New York: Norton.

Sussman, A. E. (1976). Attitudes towards deafness: Psychology's role—past, present, and potential. In F. B. Crammette & A. B. Crammette (Eds.), *VII world congress of the World Federation of the Deaf.* Washington, DC: National Association of the Deaf.

Sussman, A. E. (1988). Approaches in counseling and psychotherapy revisited. In D. Watson, G. Long, M. Taff-Watson, & M. Harvey (Eds.), *The decades of excellence: A foundation for the future*. Little Rock, AK: American Deafness and Rehabilitation Association.

Sussman, A. E., & Brauer, B. A. (1999). On being a psychotherapist with deaf clients. In I. W. Leigh, *Psychotherapy with deaf clients from diverse groups*. Washington, DC: Gallaudet University Press.

Sussman, A., & Stewart, L. (Eds.). (1971). *Counseling with deaf people*. New York: Deafness Research & Training Center, New York University.

Taff-Watson, M. (1984). Interpreters in mental health settings. In *Proceedings of the Fourth Mental Health and Deafness Conference*. Toronto, Canada: Ontario Institute for Studies in Education.

Thompson, R. E., Thompson, A., & Murphy, A. T. (1979). Sounds of sorrow, sounds of joy: The hearing-impaired parents of hearing-impaired children. In A. T. Murphy (Ed.), The families of hearing impaired children. *Volta Review, 81*(5), 337–351.

Trychin, S. (1991). *Manual for mental health professionals, Part II: Psycho-social challenges faced by hard of hearing people*. Washington, DC: Gallaudet University Press.

Tye, L. (1997, November 4). Spirituality makes rounds. *Boston Globe*, p. 1.

Umberger, C. C. (1983). *Structural family therapy*. New York: Grune & Stratton.

Ventura, M. (2001 November–December). To Speak of the Unspeakable in a World of Shared Danger: What can Therapists Offer Their Clients? *Psychotherapy Networker*, 30–33.

Vernon, M., & Andrews, J. J. (1990). *The psychology of deafness*. New York: Longman.

Vernon, M. (1969). *Multiply handicapped deaf children: Medical, educational, and psychological considerations*. C.E.C. Research Monograph. Washington, DC: Council for Exceptional Children.

Vernon, M. (1974). Effects of parents' deafness on hearing children. In P. Fine (Ed.), *Deafness in infancy and early childhood*. New York: Medcom.

Vernon, M., & Makowsky, B. (1969). Deafness and minority group dynamics. *Deaf American, 21*(11), 3–6.

Vernon, M., Grieve, M., & Shaver, K. (1980, November). Handicapping conditions associated with the congenital rubella syndrome. *American Annals of the Deaf,* 993–997.

Visher, E. B., & Visher, J. S. (1979). *Step-families: A guide to working with stepparents and stepchildren.* New York: Bruner/Mazel.

Walker, B. (1983). The pact: The caretaker–parent–ill-child coalition in families with chronic illness. *Family Systems Medicine, 1*(4), 6–29.

Walker, L. (1986). *A loss for words.* New York: Harper & Row.

Wallerstein, J. S., & Kelly, J. B. (1980). *Surviving the breakup: How parents and children cope with divorce.* New York: Basic Books.

Walsh, F. (1983). The timing of symptoms and critical events in the family life cycle. In J. C. Hansen & H. A. Liddle (Eds.), *Clinical implications of the family life cycle.* Rockville, MD: Aspen.

Waskow, A. (2001). Sermon posted on the Internet.

Watzlawick, P. (1976). *How real is real? Confusion, disinformation, communications.* New York: Random House.

Watzlawick, P., Weakland, J. H., & Fisch, R. (1974). *Change: Principles of problem formation and problem resolution.* New York: W. W. Norton.

Wax, T., & DePietro, L. J. (1984). *Managing hearing loss in later life.* Gallaudet College/National Information Center on Deafness. Washington, DC: Gallaudet University Press.

Woodward, J. (1982). *How you gonna get to heaven if you can't talk with Jesus: On depathologizing deafness.* Silver Spring, MD: T. J.

Wright, B. A. (1983). *Physical disability: A psychosocial approach, 3rd ed.* New York: Addison Wesley.

Author Index

T

U

V

W

Y

Z

Subject Index

T

U

FSC
www.fsc.org
MIX
Papier | Fördert
gute Waldnutzung
FSC® C083411

Kolibri 360 GmbH
Ferdinand-Jühlke-Straße 7
99095 Erfurt, Deutschland
produktsicherheit@kolibri360.de

Impressum

Bibliografische Information der Deutschen Nationalbibliothek
Die Deutsche Nationalbibliothek verzeichnet diese Publikation in der Deutschen Nationalbibliografie; detaillierte bibliografische Daten sind im Internet über http://dnb.d-nb. de abrufbar.

Titelgestaltung: Peter Hörndl, Nashornstudio

www.mauke-verlag.de
ISBN 978-3-948259-16-7

Der Autor

Peter Gertenbach, gebürtiger Regensburger, in Nürnberg aufgewachsen, war nach Studium und journalistischer Ausbildung/Tätigkeit in der Noris und München 25 Jahre lang als Pressesprecher für die zentrale Presse- und Öffentlichkeitsarbeit der Stadt Erlangen verantwortlich. Zuletzt leitete er an der dortigen Volkshochschule den Programmbereich Gesellschaft.